NEIGHBOURS FROM HELL

STEVEN SUTTIE

NEIGHBOURS FROM HELL

Thanks...

I'd like to start with a right massive thank you to all of the people who have read my stuff so far. When you spend a big chunk of your free time writing, like I do –it's great to know that people are reading it.
Cheers. I really mean that.

I've thanked Kaye Moon for helping me to write my first novel, at the beginning of my first two publications. Here is the hat-trick of thank you's Kaye. Seriously, thanks so much for all those hours of work and positive words of encouragement that you gave me, and continue to do so.

Thanks to Lizzie for the proof reading. I hope you didn't miss nothing!

NEIGHBOURS FROM HELL

WARNING

CONTAINS SWEARING

and POOR PEOPLE

Prologue

"Welcome to North West Tonight" said the newsreader, "I'm Roger Thompson. Our top story this evening… a row has erupted in Bury, where the developers of an exclusive new housing development are avoiding bankruptcy, by renting out half of the expensive properties to the council, who plan to use the homes as social housing for homeless families. The announcement this morning was met with anger from the home-owners on the up-market development. Denise Braithwaite is there, and she has this report."

The television screen changed from the news presenter's face to a wide angled shot of a stunning new housing estate with four and five bed-roomed detached properties. Outside the homes, small children were playing happily in the sunshine. All of the homes on the report had expensive new cars parked on the drives. It looked like a scene from an ideal homes magazine.

"Imagine that you'd just bought the house behind me. You'd paid between three hundred thousand, to half a million pounds for one of these luxurious properties, only to find out that your neighbours will soon be homeless people, moving in next door as part of a deal that the council have done with the property developers. Well, it might sound like a nightmare, but this is not a bad dream for the home-owners here at Haughton Park, who woke up to the news this morning."

"It's absolutely ridiculous. It's a scandal!" said one angry resident to the television cameras. The image switched to another home-owner. "I thought it was an April Fools joke, I had to check the date. I soon found out, this is no joke."

"This is Britain today! Punish those people who go out and work, and reward those that stay at home, smoking and watching television. I'd like to say it's unbelievable, but sadly, it's not. I'm absolutely appalled. I really am." Said one, angry older man who looked and sounded like a retired school teacher, as he wagged his finger at the camera while he offered his views.

The reporter, Denise Braithwaite returned to the screen. "Since these homes were built, the mortgage lending industry has crashed. As a result, the developers, Bright New Homes have struggled to sell almost half of the houses. Rather than go bankrupt, and jeopardize the future of its customers, the company has signed a deal with Bury council, a deal which they thought would suit all parties. But from the reaction that we've heard today, that's not quite how it has worked out. We spoke to the Managing Director, Bill Heston from Bright New Homes."

The screen switched again, this time, a smart looking man in his early fifties appeared, looking very sympathetic and sincere. "We want people to settle down, and trust us with this. All that we have done is what any successful business would do in difficult circumstances, and that it is that we have adapted our core business principle in order to utilize the sustainable stock at our disposal."

Bill Heston's face stayed on screen, with a fluffy microphone near his mouth as the reporter asked a question.

"But that doesn't make any sense, it just sounds like politician talk, which many people would describe as gobble-de-gook, Mr Heston."

"Well, I'm sorry, I don't agree. But if you wish to speak in lay man's terms – I think that what people are concerned about here, is a misguided belief that we are dealing with people who will spit at you when you walk past them. We are not. It's simply not the case. This hysterical over-reaction is shocking, and it is as though we have announced that we are handing over half of our homes to the very worst people in society – which is quite frankly a disgraceful suggestion and could not be further from the truth."

"So, what would you say to your customers who are understandably, very concerned about this? Some of them are saying they are scared of what's going to happen."

"We are committed to ensuring that our customers, and our new residents will live side by side in harmony. Any suggestion that we are simply dumping people here to satisfy our own financial concerns is just plain wrong. The media are the ones who are whipping this up, yourselves included I'm ashamed to say, and I am appealing to you all to settle down, and keep a sense of balance in your reports. It's the first rule of journalism, and well you know it."

"But surely you can see why this is a concern for the people who have paid up to half a million pounds for their property?" Denise Braithwaite wasn't letting the managing director off the hook so easily.

"Look, I've tried being polite. Let me ask you a question. If a couple from a council estate won the lottery, and decided to buy a house here – would your news crew be up here, whipping up hatred?" Bill Heston smiled as Denise Braithwaite paused for a split-second to think of a response.

"Sir, with respect, that is not what is happening. You are handing half of your properties over to homeless families. It's a recipe for disaster, people are describing it as a desperate, selfish move on your part – which will lose the home-owners many tens of thousands of pounds in their investments, if not more. How can you be so blasé about it Mr Heston?"

"As I have said. This is a temporary arrangement. We have set up a cast-iron agreement that all of the social housing users will be strictly vetted, and extreme consequences will exist to tackle any anti-social behaviour. Our priority concern is our customers being happy with their new home. If anything happens that makes this arrangement unsatisfactory for them - it will be dealt with in the most serious manner. This is very important, and Bury Council understand one hundred and twenty per cent that the temporary tenants will be on a behaviour bond - and if any incident occurs on Haughton Park that they are unhappy with, I hope that they will let me and my staff know in the first instance, where it will be dealt with swiftly and effectively. Now, instead of coming up here and creating hostility, I would appreciate it if you could try and see what a positive, and exciting opportunity this is for everybody involved. Good day." Bill Heston walked off the pavement and out of view. One home-owner could be heard shouting "You're a fucking wanker Heston!" as he made his way.

"So as you have heard," continued Denise, "we're at

the heart of a very emotive situation tonight at Haughton Park. We'll have more on this story later in the programme. But for now, back to you in the studio."

"Thank you Denise, and good luck to everybody who will be affected by this decision. In other news now, and…"

PART ONE

Chapter One

MAY 18th

Moving In Day

"God, you weren't lying! How smart is this estate? You jammy bastards!" Johnny, the van driver hadn't been up here before, and he was shocked by just how exclusive the new development was, as he drove his van onto Haughton Park. "I'm jealous!"

"Don't be daft Johnny," laughed Rachel Birdsworth, as she sat with her partner Mick Crossley in the cab of the bright orange Ford Transit, smiling at their friend's reaction. "It's only a temporary move. They'll have us out of here as soon as a flat comes up."

"Yeah, it's a bit like at the end of Bullseye, come and have a look at what you could have won!" said Mick. "This is our speed boat." All three laughed. It was a bit of a weird feeling, being upgraded from the static caravan site, to a mansion, knowing they'd be back on the council estate as soon as a property became available.

"Look, they've even got pillars around the doors." Johnny was stunned by the attention to detail. "It looks like the kind of place you see on telly. I can see a footballer living somewhere like this. Posh and Becks living next door! You lucky fuckers!"

"Right, here, this is it, number sixteen Fir Trees Grove - next to the one with the white beemer on the drive." Rachel was smiling from ear-to-ear.

"Well listen, even if it is temporary housing, it's still fucking amazing! This is the sort of house I'd get if me numbers come up. I'm proper jealous! Green with envy, I'm not gonna lie!" Johnny was staring admiringly at the brand new five bedroom property, as he parked on the double drive-way. He pulled the hand brake on and turned off the engine. Mick opened the passenger door, jumped out, before helping Rachel down the step from the cab.

"Cheers love." She gave him a kiss on the lips. "So,

here we are!" A tear formed in her eye which she was fast to wipe with her sleeve. They laughed and hugged one another. This moment had seemed a long time in coming, since the fire that had gutted the family home eighteen months earlier.

"I can't wait until the kids come. What time's your mam dropping them off tomorrow?" asked Mick.

"She said when she's had enough of them, so probably six in the morning!"

"Come on you two, I'm not unloading it on my own you cheeky bastards!" shouted Johnny from around the back of the van. "We need to get this washing machine out first, I've got to drop it off at our Diane's later."

"Alright, chillax – I'm coming," said Mick as he gave Rachel another kiss. This was a fantastic day.

*****

Across the road, Graham Ashworth was watching the new tenants unload the van. He was a portly man, just on the edge of becoming elderly looking. He was standing in his bay window, glaring at the activities across the way, holding a cup of earl grey in one hand, and the saucer in the other.

"Suzanne, they're here." He said, his tone was flat. "Oh, I can't believe my God damn eyes, they've been here half a minute and there's a fucking washing machine dumped on the front lawn. You couldn't make this up!"

In the kitchen, Suzanne Ashworth rolled her eyes to the ceiling. She clutched the black granite worktop and stared for a moment out of the window, at the rolling valley that meandered off to the horizon, with Manchester city centre at the very bottom. She exhaled quietly out of the side of her mouth.

"What's that darling?" she asked. She had been dreading this moment all week, since the couple had been and viewed the property, and she had foolishly mentioned it to her husband on his arrival home from work.

"I'm sure you're going deaf!" he bellowed. "I said they're here. Straight from filming Jeremy fucking Kyle by the looks of them."

"Oh, the new neighbours? Let's have a look."

"Have a look? You can probably smell them as well!" replied Graham without any hint of humour. Suzanne waltzed through the lounge and over to her husband who was staring out of the window at the three people who were laughing and joking as they walked in and out of the house with black bin bags in their hands.

"That's all they've got in there - bin liners. It doesn't look like they've brought a single item of furniture with them. Can you believe that?"

"They look nice enough Graham. At least give them a chance, eh? We haven't even spoken to them yet." Suzanne thought that the lady looked very nice, and the two men that were unloading didn't look any different to any normal blokes in their early thirties. They were quite handsome actually, she thought.

"Just give them a chance? Listen to Mother Theresa here. You won't be saying that when they're nicking your pegs off the washing line. Look at her, with her greasy black roots and bottle blonde hair. And those two chavs look like they've been kicked out of borstal. I bet they sell drugs. Look at his tattoos. Moron. You want me to give them a chance? I'll give them a chance alright Suzanne - first chance I get, I'll ring the bloody police on them."

Suzanne could see that her husband was getting worked up. Rather than reply, and potentially stress him out further, she decided to put her arm around him and rub his shoulder gently.

"At the first opportunity Suzanne, I'll be phoning the police. I'm not putting up with any hassle, and you can mark my words. Look at them, bin bag after bin bag of belongings. It's quite ridiculous! Fact!"

*****

"Just shove all the bags in that cupboard under the stairs for now. We don't want to make the place look untidy already! God, look at it - everything is so new and gleaming. I love it!" Rachel was stood in the hall ordering her two volunteer removal men around, knowing that they wouldn't answer back just yet, at least not until the brews were served.

"Hoi, listen, do you know that bloke?" asked Johnny.

Mick wondered who he was talking about. "Who?"

"The one who's moving in a few doors up from you," said Johnny quietly as he neared Mick and threw his two bin bags of clothes into the vast cupboard space below the pine staircase. "Next door but one."

"Not seen him, don't know who you're on about Johnny."

"Well, get a good look when you go out. He used to live over Hattersley, years ago, but he had to move, rumour had it that he was a grass. Since then, he's become a bit of a pain in the arse all over Manchester. He's got about eight kids, all of them have been put in care. He thinks he's a bit of a main head. Just watch him, he's a proper snide fucker."

"Right, yeah, nice one Johnny." Said Mick, grateful for the heads up from his oldest friend, a man who, through his family connections rather than through choice, knew most of the criminal underclass of Manchester, if not most of the north west's.

"What are you two whispering about?" said Rachel as she returned from the van with more bin bags. Johnny changed the subject swiftly, there was another neighbour that had caught his attention.

"Rach, come here," he said. "When you next go out to the van, yeah, check out the bloke directly across the road, proper giving us evils from his window. Don't make it obvious, but have a look and see if it's just me imagining it."

"Which house, that one facing?" asked Mick.

"Yeah, number nine. Take a look on the snide. He's giving me the heeby jeebies."

Mick and Rachel burst out laughing.

"The heeby jeebies? Ha ha ha I haven't heard that for time!" Rachel slapped Johnny on the arm.

"Serious. Come on," muttered Johnny as he led the way back out towards his van. Rachel and Mick followed him, giggling.

"See?" said Johnny through clenched teeth as he neared the back of the transit.

"Yeah, he doesn't like us much, does he?" Mick looked annoyed.

"Oh, forget it. They're expecting Rab C Nesbitt to move in, or thingy, what's his name off Shameless?"

"Frank Gallagher!" said Johnny, smiling.

"We know how to throw a party!" added Mick, laughing.

"Yeah, well. It's been on the telly news, North West Tonight, Granada Reports - all the neighbours have been doing petitions and stuff to stop us coming. God knows what they think we're gonna be like." Rachel had fully anticipated a frosty reception, following all of the negative news coverage about "social housing service users" in recent weeks.

"Well they're stuck up pricks then Rach, just ignore them!" offered Johnny, who seemed shocked to hear about this. Having been brought up on a council estate, and still living on one now, he couldn't understand what all the fuss was about.

"It'll be reet. As soon as they see we're alright, they'll be cool." Rachel smiled, brushing it aside, and seemingly not too worried about it.

"Is that his bird or his daughter that's stood with him?" asked Mick as he grabbed a couple more bags from the van and turned to face his new neighbours.

"Don't stare Mick - you're as bad as them!" hissed Rachel. Mick walked off sulkily with the bags, annoyed that Johnny's observation had been so correct.

"Dicks aren't they?" muttered Johnny to Rachel.

"I'm not sure yet. I'll tell you after I've been over for a cup of sugar. It's always the best way of finding out."

*****

Rachel was determined to put a stop to any unpleasantness before it had chance to begin. She believed in nipping things in the bud, and that was her sole intention as she strode confidently across the road, and up to the doorway of her neighbours house. With total confidence, she pressed the doorbell and waited. After a minute or so the young woman came to the door, looking quite nervous, and holding the door to her hip.

"Hiya! Are you alright? I'm Rachel - your new neighbour across the road! Are you alright?"

"Oh, hi," said Suzanne, in as friendly a manner as she could muster under the circumstances. The circumstances being that her husband was stood out of view a few feet behind her, and had just forbidden her to open the door.

"So, I just thought I'd come and say hello, and let you know we're not the absolute scum of the earth! It was a bit strong what they were saying on the news. So, I just want you to know, we don't have any criminal convictions, my fellah works two jobs, and our kids are all doing really well at school, my oldest lad is a school prefect. I volunteer for the RSPCA charity shop on Mondays and Tuesdays, and I help at the Citizen's Advice on Fridays while the kids are at school, and I'm a member of the PTA. Treasurer, actually." Rachel was smiling as she said it, and Suzanne couldn't help but instantly warm to her friendly, and forthright nature. "Although, in saying all that, I'm far from perfect - I have no idea where the sugar is. So I just wondered if you might be able to lend me some until I can get down to the shop please?"

"Oh, right, well yes - of course. And we weren't thinking..." Suzanne felt it necessary to explain that she didn't believe the reports in the media. But her eyelids flickered intensely as she spoke, giving away her insincerity.

"Listen, don't worry about it. I'd feel exactly the same if the shoe was on the other foot. But it's hurtful what the papers were saying, and I just want you to know that even though we might only be here for a matter of weeks, or months, you'll get no trouble from my family. We've never caused any grief before, and we're not about to start now. I want to be very specific about that."

"Suzanne," shouted Graham from behind her. "Can you hurry up please, I need a lift to the club."

"Oh, right darling, one moment. What did you need..."

"Rachel."

"Yes, of course, Rachel. Was it sugar?"

"Do you not mind? Those two are on a go-slow until I get them a brew on." Rachel rolled her eyes, forcing Suzanne to laugh.

"One moment, I'll grab you some." Suzanne turned and walked into the house. She had a brilliant figure, thought Rachel as she pushed the door very lightly with her finger, forcing it to open a little more. She saw somebody stood in the hallway. It was the man from the window.

"Hello," said Rachel, awkwardly. Graham looked away and walked over towards the stairs, completely ignoring his new neighbour.

"Suzanne, for God's sake hurry up woman!" he shouted as he began walking up the staircase that was identical to the one in Rachel's house.

"I'm coming!" shouted Suzanne nervously, as the top of the sugar tin fell out of her hand and clanged loudly as it met the ceramic floor tiles. Rachel watched Graham disappear into a room at the top of the stairs, just as Suzanne came back with a Tupperware container filled with sugar.

"Here you go, Rachel." Suzanne handed her the tub. She had a beaming smile.

"Thanks. Sorry to intrude. I'll get back, get this brew sorted." Rachel brushed her hair behind her ear as she spoke. "Please, mention what I've said to your...."

"Graham. He's my husband. I will, and thank you for coming. It's been ever so lovely to meet you."

*****

"So what was said?" asked Mick, leaning against the sink with his brew between his hands. Johnny was stood beside him, but facing the opposite way, gawping out of the window at the back garden as Rachel put her steaming tea bag on the edge of the sink.

"I just said, don't worry, we're not the scum of the earth. And asked her for a cup of sugar." Johnny began laughing loudly.

"You didn't!" said Mick.

"I did. I told her we're alright us, and we bloody are! I wasn't lying. She seems alright, but that husband of hers..."

"Husband? Fucking hell. He looks old enough to be her dad!"

"Grandfather more like!" said Mick. Johnny laughed loudly.

"Well, I don't think he's that old, but he's a bit of a knob-head anyway. He just blanked me when I let on to him. He was stood behind the door while she was talking to me. And he talks to her like she's a piece of shit."

"Right, well don't worry about it. We'll just stay out of their way, I'm not letting any stuck up toss-pots ruin our big day."

"Amen to that!" Rachel bashed her cup against Mick's. "Cheers"

"Cheers."

"Right, hurry up with that brew and then get your arses down to Argos. I've reserved the stuff, here, take this reservation number in with you. It comes to four hundred and sixty seven quid."

"Is that all?" asked Mick, looking surprised that Rachel had ordered so much stuff for such a small amount of money.

"I've got most of the stuff in the sale. And don't forget, there'll be more to get tomorrow. But it's saved us a fortune with having fitted wardrobes and that. We'll still have to get some wardrobes and drawers and stuff for when we get our proper house."

"And what about summat to sit on?" asked Mick.

"I've ordered some fold out garden chairs. They'll have to do for now Mick. They're only a fiver each."

Rachel and Mick had been saving hard since the fire. The fire brigade said it was a fault on the drier that had started it. Luckily, it was only possessions that were harmed, all of the family were out at school or work. It had been a massive trauma for the family, returning home to find that the house they'd left that morning, had been completely gutted by the fire and the smoke damage. Neighbours had seen the smoke, but had just assumed it was a back garden bonfire. By the time the fire brigade had been alerted, Rachel and Mick's home had been destroyed. But it didn't take long to get over, as Rachel reminded everybody time after time, "We can replace the stuff, that's easy. Toys, bikes and computers and all that shit is easy to replace. But I could never replace any of you, so if that's our bad luck, if that's our nightmare - thank God it happened when it did, and none of you were hurt. We're the luckiest people in town." Liam, Britney, Noel and Shania had no real understanding of what their mum was talking about, but had nodded anyway.

The family home had been on the Gameshawe estate where the couple had grown up, a huge council estate with a population of fifteen thousand people in the north of Manchester. Like all council estates in Britain, Gameshawe had its fair share of social problems. But it wasn't all drugs, burglaries, alcoholism and anti-social behaviour - the estate had plenty of hard working families who wanted better for their kids, and worked hard to set a good example and maybe one day, move away into privately rented homes. A few had even bought their homes off the council under the "right-to-buy" scheme. Mick and Rachel had themselves applied to the council for a valuation on their property, just weeks before the fire.

Their biggest regret was the fact that they hadn't had contents insurance. After the fire had been assessed, and the cause was confirmed as accidental due to an unforeseen electrical fault, it seemed that the twenty four pound a month premium was worth it. But before the fire, as they struggled to make ends meet each month with rocketing gas and electric prices, the insurance had been ditched. They didn't dwell on it, Rachel believed that life was too short to go on a downer about things that couldn't be changed. The family made plenty of jokes about their rotten luck, but Rachel was always quick to put it in perspective.

"And what if your dad had been on nights, and was in bed on his sleeping tablets? There's no insurance that would have got us your ugly dad back."

Mick had taken on a second job, washing up at night in a Chinese restaurant in town. It was a cash-in-hand job, in between his shifts at the wallpaper factory where he worked full time. He was making twenty five pounds for each four hour shift, and every penny was put into the family's savings fund, ready for the day that a new house came up, to replace the claustrophobic static caravan that the family had been provided in the meantime.

The meantime had lasted a lot longer than anybody had anticipated, and the family of six had had to endure the cramped conditions for the previous eighteen months. The council had been extremely supportive, and appeared very sympathetic to the difficulties they faced with six people sharing a static caravan - but like most local authorities, Bury Borough was facing social housing demand like never before, due to the lack of affordable homes available.

With all of that finally behind them now, and thanks to the sudden availability of the homes on Haughton Park, it was now finally time for Rachel and Mick to start spending the savings, and to start re-building their lives in their new place. On this first, joyful day in the luxurious temporary home - things seemed, finally, to be getting back on track.

But if Mick and Rachel could have had any idea of what lay in store - they'd have stayed put in the caravan indefinitely.

Chapter Two

Mick and Johnny had been working late, building the beds, constructing the bedside cabinets, putting together shelving units and other items of furniture that they had collected earlier in the day from Argos. Rachel had also been kept busy, sorting through the dozens of bin bags that contained all of the family's possessions, then ironing and putting the clothes away in each of the four kid's bedrooms. It was gone two in the morning when Johnny had left and the couple finally turned in for their first night at the property.

"They'd better not get too used to having a bedroom each, with en-suite facilities," joked Rachel as she got into her pyjamas and got into the new double bed.

"As long as they don't start thinking I'm their bloody butler." Said Mick, smiling - but he was quite concerned, and thought it was a better idea for the girls to share a room, and for the boys to share too. He was worried that the kids might get a little too used to the luxury and it will be difficult for them to re-adjust when they finally got a council house back home on the Gameshawe estate.

"Oh give over!" said Rachel, "They've been cooped up in that bloody caravan for nearly two years. And they'll probably never live anywhere like this again. Just leave them be. And this bed's shite, I can feel the springs already."

"You bought it. I've told you, if you buy shit, you buy twice."

"It's still better than that fold down crap in the caravan." Rachel puffed up her pillows. "Night love, thanks for your hard work today."

"It's alright. We'll have to get Johnny a crate or summat. I offered him fifty quid before for using his van and that, but he was having none of it."

"Aw, he's a good egg isn't he? He made me piss today, do you remember when he said he had the heebie jeebies!" Mick and Rachel started laughing loudly at the memory. "I swear down, I've not heard anyone say that since I was about five!" added Rachel giggling. Mick was still laughing, the phrase was a real blast from the past.

"Seriously though Rach, that guy over the road seems like a right dick. I hope he's not going to cause us any shit. Remember what the council said - if we cause any hassle, we'll be straight back in the mobile home, and struck off the waiting list."

As part of the tenancy agreement on Haughton Park, the council had issued a strict code of conduct. It stopped short of demanding that any unexpected farts should be itemised, but only just. In their desperation to get a real home for their children, and themselves - they'd agreed to all of the terms and conditions laid down.

"I know. Don't worry about him. If we just keep out of his face, he'll forget we're even here in a few days. It's like my Gran used to say, life is like toilet paper. Most of the time you're on a roll, but every so often some arsehole comes along and starts giving you shit."

"Well, we can't have some stuck up bastard like that jeopardising our future Rach. If he looks like he's going to start, we need to go and tell them down at the council to chuck us in another house." Mick was deadly serious, but Rachel was a bit more relaxed about everything.

"Trust me Mick, it'll be right. I'll make them a cake or summat tomorrow. I've already said, it's the bloody papers and telly people who've got him stressed out. He'll soon see that we're just a normal family. It'll be right. Now shut up, I want to finish my
book before my eye lids shut for the day."

"What you reading?"

"It's a crime book, about a police man who is killing the suspects in a murder case."

"Any good?"

"No, it's pretty boring to be honest." Said Rachel, who amazed Mick with her ability to keep reading books even if she found them rubbish. She still needed to know what happened, she'd always say.

"Well I wouldn't mind, you know, trying this new bed out. Check the springs and that," Mick nudged Rachel in the kidney. "Bit of jiggy jiggy would be..."

"Mick," said Rachel softly as she stared dispassionately at her novel.

"Yeah babe?"

"Turn over and shut up you idiot."

Chapter Three

"Mick, wake up. Can you hear that?" Rachel was shaking Mick's shoulder.

"What?"

"It's kicking off." Rachel leapt up out of bed and darted across the bedroom to the window, opening it wide as she pushed her head through, trying to see where all the noise was coming from. It quickly became clear that there was a commotion further up the avenue. Adults were shouting, arguing. There was a lot of swearing, but she couldn't make out what exactly it was that was being said. It was still night time, and Rachel was struggling to see what was happening with only the light from the street lamp that obscured the view.

"Mick, it's that new family we let onto yesterday, those that were moving in at the same time as us, a few doors up. They're arguing with that creepy bloke from across the road."

Mick didn't seem interested. There was always something kicking off back home on the estate, and he had never taken any notice of that either.

"Shut up love. Stop waking me up." Mick pulled a pillow off Rachel's side of the bed and put it over his face.

"Mick, get up. He's going to get leathered. Please love, go and sort it out." Rachel was worried that the man who had been so frosty to her the previous day was about to get beaten up. The man and woman were shouting and swearing at him extremely aggressively. She knew that this was going to end with violence, any moment.

"Hurry up Mick."

"Rach, shut up man."

"Right, fuck you then, I'll sort it." Rachel put the big light on and looked for some shoes to put on her feet. This was enough for Mick, who reluctantly stretched out of bed and put his feet on the floor.

"Hurry up!" said Rachel as she raced out of the room.

"I thought we were supposed to be keeping our heads

down?" shouted Mick as his partner raced down the stairs. "Rach! Wait for me." Mick rushed after her, following her footsteps out into the street in bare feet. Rachel was already at the scene of the disturbance, and was gently pushing the man whose house it was back from the edge of his drive.

It was the goon from over the road, and that grass from Hattersley that Johnny had been going on about earlier, thought Mick. "Fuck's sake," he muttered as he hobbled on the tiny stones on the street.

"Just calm down love, what's going on?" asked Rachel as the man's partner was hurling abuse back at the man from across the road.

"This fucking tool, banging on my fucking door, waking us all up - saying I'm playing my music too fucking loud! It was the fucking telly, and I was asleep on the couch, so it weren't that fucking loud!" The neighbour was well built, and was clearly angry, but the man who had given Mick and Rachel's friend Johnny the heebie jeebies seemed oblivious to the danger he was in as he continued to antagonise the couple.

"If I could hear your bloody noise in my house, it was too bloody loud. Fact!" he announced, with a smug, almost psychotic expression on his face.

"It wasn't fucking loud at all." Interjected the man's wife. "This prick is just looking for some shit to flick at us. Well, you'd better tell him to watch his back, he's just come here to cause a load of fucking shit."

Rachel had seen and heard enough. She had sussed out what was going on. She whispered to Mick to go and ask the creepy guy for his version of events, then quietly and calmly she stepped back across the lawn and spoke to the two furious neighbours, in a bid to try and calm them.

"Sssh, just shush a sec," she said quietly. "That guy is a fucking wrong 'un, right, just listen, I'll bet you two a fucking tenner he's already phoned the police right, so the best thing you can do is go inside, turn everything off and pretend you're in bed. Don't give the council an excuse to fire you off before you've even unpacked."

"You reckon?" said the wife, as her husband still looked hyped and ready to attack.

"Serious. Just leave him to it, he'll look a right cock when the dibble turn up to a sleeping street." Rachel was talking sense, and had calmed them both down in no time. This was her main job at the Citizen's Advice and she knew how it was done. All of the time she was speaking to the furious couple, Mick had inadvertently become the subject of the abuse, and was beginning to raise his voice at his tormentor.

The wife was much calmer now, and looked over at her husband, who nodded his understanding of Rachel's advice. She looked back at Rachel. "Nice one love. We'll sort this knob-head out another day. Cheers." With that, they quietly turned, went into their house and within a minute, the downstairs of the house was in complete darkness.

"Right, Mick, home." Rachel grabbed her husband's arm and began dragging him back towards their own house, a couple of houses away.

"Oh, home? Ha ha brilliant! Is that what you spongers have called it? Home? Good God, give me strength! It is not your *home*, it's a halfway house for useless losers who can't afford to buy their own house. Please don't call it home. It insults my intelligence." The man had also turned away from the house where he'd started his verbal assault and was casually following Rachel and Mick. They carried on walking, Mick limping slightly as his bare feet stepped on the loose stones and chippings on the ground.

"Ignore him Mick, he's trying to get a reaction, just get in the house, the police will be here any second." Said Rachel quietly as she continued pulling her man along the street as the abuse continued behind them.

"Look at you both, can't stand the truth so you walk away, pretending you can't hear it. Pathetic."

Rachel nipped Mick's arm, just as a warning to him to keep walking and ignore the bait. Within seconds they were inside the house and Rachel had closed the door behind them, locking their would-be tormentor outside.

"Come on Mick, straight upstairs, the police will be here any second."

"He's off his fucking nugget him. He's as pissed as a

fart." Said Mick as he went up the stairs, glad to feel the luxury of the carpet under his feet, in place of the hard gritty stones and the cold of the street.

"Just get in bed love, I've got a feeling he rang the police before he went kicking off, they'll probably be here any second."

"If you say that one more time, I'm going to throttle you."

"What was he saying to you?"

"Nowt much, just going on about how much he fucking hates scrubbers and he can't believe that filth like us are living on this street. He's a right dick."

"Seriously? Fucking hell. He wants to watch what he's saying. And thanks for not hitting him Mick!"

"Seriously love, what do you take me for? I'm working two jobs to try and dig us out of the shit since the fire, and you think I'm about to fuck everything up by hitting a fat old bastard like that? Jesus, give me some credit love." Mick looked hurt by the suggestion, and Rachel felt bad for saying it. But then he laughed,

"Ha ha, you won't believe what else he said, I've just remembered!" Mick was sat in bed, grinning from ear to ear as Rachel knocked off the bedroom light.

"Go on!" she said, as she made her way over to the bed, keen to know what was amusing Mick so much.

"Honest to God right, he said "What do your tattoo's say? Are they your kids names in case you forget them when you're down the dole office?" Mick laughed again. Rachel wasn't amused.

"Are you serious? What a cheeky bastard. Why does he think you go down the dole office anyway?"

"He obviously thinks that if you have a council house, you're on the dole. He's a typical Daily Mail reader. He wants to watch his mouth though, not everyone is going to brush it off. He'll be getting a good kicking if he says stuff like that to the wrong bloke."

"Or woman!" added Rachel snappily. "God that's really pissed me off!"

"Don't give it any thought love. Fuck him, and his

trophy bride. Right, I'm going back to sleep."

"Yeah, night Mick. Love ya."

Within a few minutes, Mick was snoring again. Rachel was too wound up to sleep just yet. The comments that the neighbour had made to Mick, and to her as they walked away had really bothered her. She lay in bed, mulling things over, trying to think of a positive way to resolve matters, considering what to say to the council about the bizarre confrontation and wondering whether the arrival of the kids in the morning would create any further problems.

And then the blue revolving lights illuminated the room. Rachel got out of the bed and went nearer to the window to listen and watch from behind the curtain. It was a police van, it drove slowly up the avenue, around onto the adjoining cul-de-sac, and cruised back towards Rachel's house. The revolving lights had been switched off now, a sign that the police officers hadn't discovered whatever it was they'd be sent up here to find. Then she heard a man's voice.

"Officer!"

It was that dreaded guy from over the road, thought Rachel. The van stopped outside Rachel's house and an officer got out of the passenger side of the vehicle.

"Thanks for coming - it's these new neighbours, they were having a rave up, but they're all pretending to be asleep now."

"What's your name, Sir?" asked the police officer as his colleague got out of the driver's side.

"Graham Ashworth, I was the one who rang you."

"And you say that there was a party going on?" asked the second officer.

"Yes, I challenged them about it. But they just started threatening me. I knew this would happen, these spongers should never have been allowed up here in the first place..." said Graham. Rachel was listening intently, cursing under her breath.

"Have you been drinking Sir?" asked the second officer, sounding extremely disinterested by Graham's social observations.

"No, not really. Well, yes - but well, it's not like..."

It sounded to Rachel as though Graham's confidence was slipping.

"Sir, we were given a priority call to respond to a disturbance here. And there is nothing but silence. We currently have five priority calls to attend to. So why have you flagged us down?"

"You do realise that it is a criminal offence to make hoax calls to the emergency services don't you Sir?" added the other officer. Graham stood by the van, looking a little bit overwhelmed by the situation. This clearly wasn't the reception that he had anticipated. He mumbled quietly to himself, Rachel couldn't make out what he said, but the police officer nearest to him, the one who had got out of the driving seat certainly did.

"Can you repeat that statement please Sir?" he asked, shining a torch at Graham Ashworth.

"I said, you people are all in it together. And you know it's true, you fucking useless twenty-three-thousand-pound-a-year retarded pleb PIG! So what do you think about that?" Graham began walking away from the police officers, laughing mockingly as he went. The officers laughed to one another as they followed him up his drive.

"Do you want to do it or shall I?" asked the first constable.

"You can do it, I did the last one."

"Sir, I am arresting you on suspicion of making hoax calls to the emergency services, and also for a breach of the peace, and for insulting a police officer in a threatening and aggressive manner. You do not have to say anything, but anything that you do say will be taken down and could be used in evidence against you. Do you understand?"

"Forget it. Do you know who I am you stupid bastards? You'll never prove it. This will cost you your jobs."

"Graham!" His wife appeared at the front door, she was tying her dressing gown as she walked towards her husband who was being handcuffed. "What a mess!"

"It's these bloody plods, they're on the side of the fucking scum! DO YOU HEAR THAT? YOU'RE FUCKING SCUM!" He bellowed across the neighbourhood as loudly as he could, his words echoed around the houses as he was led away to the van. The officers were quick to push him into the back of the van, and slam the gate shut. They then slammed the door of the van, drowning out Graham's continued shouting and ranting.

"What will happen to him?" asked Suzanne Ashworth.

"Sorry Madam, but we can't tolerate anti-social behaviour like that. We'll give him a few hours to sober up and calm down, and then speak to him in the morning." Said the arresting officer as he got into the drivers seat and closed the door. He turned the ignition and wound down the window. "Don't worry about him, he'll be fine."

"Thank you." Suzanne looked helpless as tears rolled down her face.

"Good night Madam." Said the officer as he eased the clutch and the van began moving. Graham's muffled abuse continued as the van left the avenue.

"Good grief," said the officer who was driving. "His wife's pretty fit!"

"You're not wrong! I wonder what first attracted her to this rich, fat ugly bastard!" laughed the other policeman.

"YOU'LL BE FUCKING SACKED FOR THIS!" shouted Graham Ashworth from the back of the police van. "DO YOU HEAR ME? SACKED!"

Chapter Four

Rachel knocked lightly on the door. Suzanne's silhouette appeared in the light from the kitchen doorway and she walked quickly towards the door. The patterned glass was obscuring her shape slightly as she got closer. She opened the door without hesitation, and Rachel saw straight away that she was still crying.

"Hiya love. Are you okay?" asked Rachel. This compassion from a virtual stranger welled up a fresh surge of tears.

"No. Not really." Said Suzanne as she wiped away her tears with her sleeve. The street lights highlighted how upset she was, the whites of her eyes were red and bloodshot, her eyelids were puffy. She was in a state.

"Can I come in? I can sit with you for a minute." Rachel put her arm out and touched Suzanne's forearm tenderly.

"How can you be so nice? I heard what he said about you!" said Suzanne. She opened the door wide and invited Rachel to step inside.

"Thanks. Let me make you a brew." Said Rachel as she stepped into the house. It was immaculate inside, and gave Rachel the impression that the couple didn't have any kids.

"It's alright, honestly," said Suzanne, "I've just poured a glass of wine. Would you like one?"

"No, I'm fine thanks. I've given it up."

"God, I wish Graham would. He's drinking more and more. That's not him, that behaviour. It's like the devil has got inside him when he's had a drink." Suzanne started walking back towards the kitchen, and she was shaking slightly, as though she'd had a shock. The new neighbour followed her host as she grabbed her glass of wine and sat on a stool at the granite topped island in the centre of the room. "What a mess." She said after a few seconds. She took a good gulp of her wine and stared at the glass.

"He'll be alright. They'll not do anything to him for that. He'll get a sixty quid fine in the morning love, that's all."

The wine seemed to help calm Suzanne's nerves. It also helped her to loosen up, though Rachel suspected that the freedom from her over-bearing husband was probably a major factor in helping with that too. This didn't seem like the same, nervous, timid looking woman that she had met at the door just sixteen hours earlier.

"He's in a lot more trouble than that if the council hear about it."

"The council?" asked Rachel. "What've they got to do with it?" She continued, thinking that it was the tenants, not the home-owners who had to fear the council.

"Graham works for the council. He's quite high up in the Chief Exec's department. If they hear about this, well, well I don't know. They don't take kindly to officers being in trouble with the law."

"They won't find out love. Not unless he tells them. Police can't say nothing - not about minor offences."

"Are you sure?" asked Suzanne, visibly encouraged by the news.

"Honestly. I know this from the Citizens Advice. Things like this happen all the time - mostly to MP's and police officers!" The pair laughed, and for the first time, Rachel saw that her words were beginning to help her neighbour, who she had felt deeply sorry for as she'd watched the van drive away with her irrational, shameful husband inside. But the smiles were short-lived, as another concern popped into Suzanne's mind.

"He's had a warning at work. He's worked there for more than thirty years, and he got his first disciplinary a week ago. He's been really stressed about, this..."

"About the council houses?" asked Rachel, nodding sympathetically.

"Well, yes. He thinks that the deal will de-value his property. Our property." Suzanne's eyes flicked up at Rachel. That tiny slip of the tongue covered a thousand words, and Suzanne knew it. "He wrote a really nasty e-mail to all of the councillors involved in the discussions about the deal. He was given a warning that he'll be sacked if he ever does anything like that again. He feels absolutely stupid, and his reputation has taken a real nose-dive because of it." Suzanne looked sad, as well as concerned.

"Well, he obviously feels strongly about this. Are all of the neighbours feeling the same way?" asked Rachel, her eyes were locked onto the side of Suzanne's face.

"Some of the people are, it hasn't helped with the news coverage." Suzanne exhaled heavily and took another large gulp of her wine. "It's been handled really badly to be honest. If we hadn't heard anything about it, I doubt there would be an issue. It could have all just been kept a secret - but instead, it's caused a media storm and all the TV crews and newspapers have really made things... well, impossible."

Rachel was listening intently, and she found this perspective very interesting, particularly the point about keeping it secret. Rachel found herself nodding in agreement as she began to speak. "I shouldn't tell you this, right, but there won't be any trouble up here - certainly not from the families that have been given temporary housing. We've had to apply for consideration, write massive application forms out with letters about why we deserve a chance. Then we had two preliminary interviews with council staff, then a final interview with the bosses of the building company who built them. We've signed contracts that say if we cause any hassle at all, or any damage to the properties, we'll be evicted within days, and taken off the waiting list for permanent housing."

"Honestly? Gosh, that all sounds quite thorough!" said Suzanne, visibly shocked by the depth of selection.

"They are going to come and do weekly inspections inside and out and everything. Trust me, if there is going to be any hassle - it will be the owners, not us who create it." Rachel was still fuming about what Suzanne's husband had been saying before the police took him. But she wanted to comfort Suzanne, she felt genuinely sorry for her and didn't really want to touch on what her husband had been saying. She stopped there, confident that she'd said enough to try and give her new neighbour some perspective on the matter.

"I'm really sorry about..."

"Forget it. Honestly. It's just prejudice, it happens

on every street in every town. It even happens on council estates, rumours fly about this, that and the other everywhere. Where we used to live, every week a paedophile had moved in, terrorists were making bombs in their downstairs loo, somebody had even been arrested for murder and it turned out they'd just been down the shops for a loaf and some gravy granules." Suzanne laughed politely at Rachel's reassuring words. "But just try and convince your hubby that he has nothing to fear. Well, except my cooking if you ever fancy coming over for tea!"

Rachel smiled as Suzanne laughed once again and it seemed that her mood was improving.

"Well, I'll leave you to it," said Rachel, standing up from the stool.

"No, please. Stay, let me make you a hot drink." Suzanne stood, and headed across the kitchen to the kettle.

"I should get back. I'm up early, unpacking and ironing and…"

"Please, just stay five minutes. It's lovely to have somebody to talk to."

Rachel looked at her neighbour again, thinking it would be best to leave it at that for tonight. "I'll have a tea, one sugar. Thanks."

Chapter Five

Graham Ashworth was led into the police station wearing handcuffs on his wrists. His indignant attitude remained unaltered, the twenty minute ride in the back of the police van had done nothing to calm his sense of outrage at the monumental miscarriage of justice that he found himself at the centre of.

"This is a complete and utter scandal! You have brought the police into disrepute!" he shouted at the officer who led him into the custody suite.

"Oh shut your minging face you fucking muppet!" shouted a drunken woman who was waiting by the desk. Graham looked across at her, then back at his arresting officer.

"Are you going to arrest her officer? You've arrested me for saying less. Now arrest her! De-arrest me. I demand that you arrest this woman!" He started struggling with the handcuffs, attracting a look of indifference from the police staff within the custody suite.

"Ignore him lads. He's just upset because he's got a tiny dick." Said the woman, waggling her little finger at Graham Ashworth. The custody area erupted into laughter, both the male and female staff found this outburst hilarious.

"And you'd know would you Sheila?" asked the custody Sergeant of his regular inmate, grinning at the harshness of her abuse towards the new inmate.

"Yeah, we all know him on the street - his nickname is noodle dick!"

"Right, come on Sheila, cell five, we'll see you in the morning love." Said the Sergeant.

"Night Sheila," said another officer from behind the huge custody desk that towered high above the inmates that were waiting to be checked in.

"Night everyone. Love you all! Get me up at six with a brew," shouted Sheila as she was led away by a female officer. She pointed at Graham Ashworth and did a drunken cackle as she passed him. "Night night noodle!"

"Right, officer Danson, who have we here please?"

asked the Sergeant, summonsing PC Danson and his prisoner across to the desk.

"Thank you Sergeant. This is Graham Ashworth, from number nine Fir Trees Grove on the Haughton Park development. He phoned us to alert us to a disturbance. When we arrived, there was no disturbance Sir, just this man who was threatening and aggressive, and who also called us some very naughty names indeed. The likes of which I have never heard before in all of my service, Sir."

Graham Ashworth remained silent. Sheila had done a good job in quietening him down for the first time since the officers first came into contact with the man. He looked as though he was having a moment of clarity, and that the reality of his situation was emerging through the fog of drink and anger.

"What naughty names did he call you PC Danson? It must have been bad," asked the Sergeant in a very sarcastic and dead-pan manner as he looked away from the prisoner and across at his computer screen. PC Danson took out his notebook and began to read out his notes.

"It's very disturbing stuff Sir. He said that we are plods,"

The Sergeant's eyes flicked across at his colleague, and he tut-tutted as he fixed his gaze on Graham Ashworth.

"He also said we are stupid bastards…"

"I've heard enough. This is too much for me to bear," said the Sergeant, shaking his head, and quite blatantly taking the mick out of the situation with his constable.

"No, please Sergeant, I must tell you the worst part."

"Go on," he said, slowly raising one eyebrow and fixing his eyes on the prisoner.

"I said you are fucking pleb pigs!" snapped Graham, his fury and contempt was back for all to see. He got no reaction. A few seconds passed before PC Danson spoke again.

"No, I don't think you did."

"I fucking did!" snapped the prisoner.

"Nope, I don't recall that. You must be mistaken. I'd have remembered that."

"I did and you know it! So fuck off!" hissed Graham,

to a chorus of laughter from the Sergeant and PC Danson.

"Anyway, he's drunk and disorderly Sir, and a night in the cells will give his neighbours a nice rest from him shouting "You're all effing scum," down the street at the top of his voice at two thirty five in the morning, evidence of which I have recorded on my body cam, Sarge."

"I'm appalled, I really am," said the Sergeant.

"Is this funny to you? Is it? You think that arresting me is funny. Well we'll see what the Chief Constable has to say about this. We'll see if you're smirking then!" Graham Ashworth was red in the face as he expressed his fury at being in this situation which he considered to be absolutely ridiculous. The Sergeant paid him no attention as he filled out his custody sheet.

"Are you on any medication, Sir?" asked the Sergeant.

"No."

"Are you on any other drugs?"

"No."

"How many sugars in your tea?"

"None."

"Okay PC Danson, cell six, thank you."

The PC grabbed Graham by the arm and began leading him away. The prisoner offered no resistance, but turned to face the desk as he was led away.

"You've not heard the last of this Mr Plod. Fact."

Chapter Six

Rachel was knackered. She'd had to get up at half past seven, and felt that she hadn't had any sleep at all. She had been at the Ashworth house for almost an hour when she had finally managed to get herself away at 3.30. In that time, she had learnt a great deal about her new neighbours - in fact, she thought that she had probably learnt everything that there was to know. Every so often, as Mick was wandering about the house doing various last minute jobs before the kids were due to arrive, she would deliver another nugget of information as their paths crossed.

"Oh aye, she's from Wythenshawe you know. So he's getting himself all worked up because council house scum are moving in. And he's only bloody married to one of us." Rachel laughed at the expression that Mick pulled. It was probably the exact same as her own, when Suzanne had made the bizarre announcement a few hours earlier. "She torks terribly porsh though, she must have gone to electrocution lessons."

"What's that?" asked Mick.

"Electrocution. It's where all the posh folk go to learn how to talk proper. Like that advert from years ago, the water in Majorca one." Said Rachel as she hung a pair of her son's jeans on a hanger."

"I thought it was where hairy women had to go to get their moustaches chopped off. Anyway, how did some fat old posh bloke end up with a lass from Withenshawe if he thinks he's such a big deal? Doesn't add up."

"They met when she started an office job at the council. He works there, one of the bosses apparently. She's only twenty eight, he's fifty!"

"She's seriously fit though. She looks well maintained!"

Rachel threw a t - shirt at Mick. "You keep your boggley eyes off!"

"You know what I mean Rach - he must have a bob or two to keep her in tow. He's not exactly George Clooney to look at. His face looks like a broken egg."

"Hey, mister - you sound as judgemental as him. You

can't just make remarks and assumptions like that about people. Sometimes love knows no boundaries." Rachel gave Mick a stern look, but he just laughed in response.

"You're the one going on about her life history. I'm just looking for my hammer. I couldn't give a shit about it. You're boring me to death about them. They're a pair of bell whiffs if you ask me. Have you seen my hammer?"

"I think it's on the stairs. Don't be making any holes in the walls, it's strictly prohibited!"

"I'm not. I'm just trying to put the back on a bookshelf." Mick walked over to the staircase and found his hammer. "Oh, here you go, your mate's going off in her car. I bet she's picking Victor Meldrew up from his porridge."

Rachel jumped away from the ironing board and across to the lounge window to see Suzanne getting into her car.

"God, look at her - she looks fresh as a daisy. I look like I'm out of the Thriller video and I wasn't even drinking! Hey, she was knocking them back as well last night you know. She'll be well over the limit. I better go and say summat." She started walking towards the door but Mick grabbed her arm.

"Nah love, leave it. It's her problem. Besides, she'll think you're a right dick."

Rachel considered what Mick had said and realised that it was a bit over-familiar.

"You're right. Cheers love."

"Anyway, you can change the record now. We've wasted enough gas on them two fucking loons. Let's get back to talking about us, and the house - and the kids." Mick looked at the clock on his phone. It read 8.06. "They'll be here soon! Can't wait to see their faces! They'll be buzzing when they see this place!"

"Aw, I know, yeah." Said Rachel, the idea forced a giddy wave to flutter through her belly.

Just as Mick began heading back up the stairs, the doorbell rang, three times in quick succession and whoever it was, was knocking loudly too. Rachel answered the door as Mick came back down the stairs to see who was visiting at such a ridiculous hour on a Sunday morning, particularly with such an over-the-top knock. It took a second, but Rachel realised that it was the couple from a few doors up, the couple who had been caught up in the trouble the previous night.

"Oh, hiya." She said. The couple looked unhappy.

"Can we come in a minute?" asked the man. His wife looked like she was seriously stressed out, and neither of them looked as though they'd slept very much, if at all.

"Yeah, course, come in." said Rachel, who introduced herself, and then Mick as the couple stepped inside.

"Alright. I'm Kev, this is Tania. From number twenty." He looked like a stereotypical nineteen-nineties wannabe hard-man. He was standing at the door wearing a three quarter length leather coat and two fistfuls of sovereign rings. His chest was sticking out and his shoulders were back. Mick didn't recognise him from anywhere, but he thought the man was a knob-head straight away. His wife looked like she'd fallen in a vat of tanning lotion, she lit up the room.

"Well, come in, have a seat in the lounge. Excuse the deck chairs - the sofa is on order!" said Rachel, blushing slightly and feeling mildly embarrassed by the fold out chairs. "Do you want a brew?"

"No, it's alright," said Tania. "Thanks, but we're only passing. Just wanted to thank you for last night. It was exactly what you said, he was trying to get a smack so the police would lift us. His fucking face when they put him in the van!" said Tania, forcing a fake, humourless laugh.

"Anyway," interrupted Kev, "He's getting a warning for that, yeah. I'm not having none of that shit. So, just make sure yous are not about tomorrow night. We appreciate you stepping in last night, it was good of yous. But leave it down to me now, yeah? Just go out for the night, and make sure you're seen by plenty of people. I don't want yous getting accused of anything. Alright?" Kev looked deadly serious. Mick was standing by the door, holding his hammer, looking a bit confused by what was being said.

"We just don't want yous getting caught up in it, we don't want that fucking wrong 'un saying yous had anything to do with it." Added Tania.

The conversation was over. Kev reached out and took Tania's arm and led her to the door.

"And it's nice meeting yous. We'll try and get to know yous properly once all this shit has settled down a bit alright? Cheers." They headed for the door.

"Alright, well, er, thanks for coming." Rachel looked quite nervous. She closed the door behind them.

"What the fuck?" she mouthed to Mick as she watched the silhouette of the couple walk down the drive through the doppled glass on the front door.

"Does he still think its nineteen ninety two? That's the last time I saw a coat like that." Mick was smiling, shaking his head. "I bet he thinks he's MC Tunes."

"I know yeah, all he needs now is a pit bull and some nun-chakas?" replied Rachel, mockingly.

"An alcoholic Victor Meldrew over the road, a fuck-wit Tony Soprano next door but one. Fuck me." Said Mick, shaking his head as he wandered off once again with his hammer. "The next neighbour I meet had better be a sane one, I'm telling you now."

Chapter Seven

Suzanne was sitting on one of the solid steel waiting room chairs in the police station reception area, when her husband was released from custody. He was led through into the public area by a uniformed officer. Although she had been anxiously dreading the moment, she was also extremely relieved to see him, and to see that he was okay.

A young man in a tracksuit had been shouting "I want my fucking dog back!" over and over again for the past ten minutes, and was being very professionally ignored by the police staff who were sitting behind the glass counter. Although the waiting room had several other people inside, it was still a very intimidating and volatile place - and Suzanne couldn't wait to get out of there.

"Darling!" she shouted as he walked into the public space. "How are you?" she asked as she warmly embraced her man. He just looked through her as he spoke.

"Don't make a fuss Suzanne. Let's just go, thank you very much." Graham was in the worst of moods, and Suzanne realised at that moment, that it would be a lot nicer if he was still inside the police station.

"Of course darling. I've parked just around the corner, by the chip shop. Do you want to go and get something to eat? A nice big breakfast somewhere?" asked Suzanne as the couple walked out into the street. She was trying her best to be as cheerful as she possibly could.

"Please stop wittering on. Just give me some quiet please Suzanne, I must insist!" snapped Graham.

The walk to the car was silent. Suzanne hated these occasions where she felt that she was walking on eggshells. She was only trying to be nice, and welcoming, she thought. He'd have had a right cob on if she'd just said "hello" she considered, as they neared the car. He was completely out of order, not just last night, but now as well, she thought, as they approached the car.

"I'll drive." Said Graham, holding his hand out for the car key. "You smell like an alcoholic." added Graham, seemingly unaware of how much he had personally drank the previous evening. Suzanne handed the key fob over as requested, and got into the passenger seat once Graham had deactivated the lock.

The drive back was silent. Graham just drove, occasionally blowing out an exasperated breath, whilst Suzanne just kept her eyes on the road ahead. She really wanted to give her husband a good yelling at for his crazy behaviour the previous night, but knew better of it. She would only make matters worse for both of them if she spoke her mind.

Eventually, Graham spoke. "I need to get a shower and get some clean clothes on. I feel itchy. All I had was a piss stinking cold plastic mattress, in a shit stinking cell. That was the most disgusting thing I have ever experienced." He sounded as though he was feeling sorry for himself.

Suzanne didn't know what to say. The voice in her mind was saying "it serves you right, you bloody pig headed idiot." But her real voice had nothing to say.

"Did you just hear what I said to you?" said Graham, his tone was sharper this time, and he'd turned his head to look at his wife as the car hurtled along the by-pass at sixty miles per hour.

"Yes, of course I heard you. I just thought that you wanted quiet." Said Suzanne, feeling a familiar tension bubble up from the very pit of her stomach.

"Are you being sarcastic Suzanne? Because if you are, I will pull this car over to the side of the road right now, and you can walk the rest of the way home." Graham had an angry, crazy expression on his face. An expression that only Suzanne was familiar with.

"Darling, don't be silly, of course I am not being sarcastic. You're scaring me, please stop." Suzanne started crying.

"How am I scaring you? HOW? Are you deliberately trying to force me to be angry with you? And what was that you said to me last night, in front of those police men?"

"I, I don't know. What *did* I say?" Suzanne looked genuinely confused. She tried to cast her mind back to the incident. She had no idea what she had said.

Graham let out a loud, humourless laugh. He blew out a big breath again, and waited a few seconds before speaking. "You said that I have made of mess of everything! You have a bloody nerve, belittling me like that in front of those moronic fucking plods. I'll never forgive you for that Suzanne. In fact, just get out." He started indicating and pulled the car over by the side of the road. "You can find your own way home."

"Graham, please." Pleaded Suzanne, though her voice gave away that she knew that his mind was set. "Can we just talk about this…"

"You had your chance to talk last night. You had your chance to tell those bloody Nazi police men what was happening. Instead, you just took the opportunity to humiliate me."

"Graham! I did not!" said Suzanne forcefully, between sobs. Tears were streaming down her face. Graham just smirked, and nodded.

"You ungrateful little bitch. Get out of my car, go on." Graham's voice was shaking with rage.

"No Graham, please don't make me." She pleaded.

"GET OUT!" he shouted, his face had turned a violent shade of red in an instant, and beads of sweat had begun pouring down his brow. Suzanne realised that it would be the best option to just open the car door and go. Obedience was key when Graham was being like this, she reasoned with herself. She unclipped her seat belt and opened the door as the car came to a complete stop. As she did so, her husband lashed out at her, shoving the back of her head violently as she turned to get out. Suzanne's face smashed with a thud into the window, and she howled in pain as she stumbled from the car, landing in a heap on the grass verge by the side of the road. She tried her best to stand, but fell to her knees in the wet grass. Her vision had become a mixture of huge white dots and shooting stars, as she groaned in pain. Suzanne put her hand up and felt her face where her cheekbone had taken the full force of the impact against the rigid glass of the Range Rover window. As the pain throbbed through her face, and her vision cleared slightly, she saw Graham leaning over, looking at her, as she sat in a heap on the floor. Blood was pouring from her face.

"Close the door, please Suzanne," was all he said. She did as she was asked and pushed the half opened door shut. Graham indicated right, looked over his shoulder and began driving off. Suzanne was left sitting in a heap in the long, wet grass, her face throbbing with pain, and feeling the familiar mixture of relief, sorrow and despair.

Chapter Eight

"Rach, they're here!" shouted Mick from upstairs as he saw his mother-in-law's car heading up the avenue towards the house.

"Aw, are they?" screeched Rachel, running towards the door. "About bloody time!" She threw open the front door and ran down the drive to greet her mum and the children.

"Hiiii," she shrieked in the kind of really high pitched way that only women can say it. The kids burst out of the car.

"Hi mum, let's have a look then!" Her eldest, Liam was first out of the car. He seemed to have got even taller in the twenty four hours since she had last seen him, too.

"Hiya mum! I've well missed you!" said her youngest, eight year old Shania, giving her mum a big cuddle.

"Hello mum!" hollered her other son, eleven year old Noel, as he slammed the car door closed.

"Noel, you knob-end!" shouted fourteen year old Britney, as she opened the car door and appeared, looking furious. "You nearly smashed my face in then you little mong. Hi mum!"

"Hiya guys, have you all been good?" Rachel was laughing as the children hurried past to get inside their new home and have a look around it for the very first time.

"Course we have!" said Noel as his walk developed into an enthusiastic jog towards the door.

"A'right Dad!" wheezed Noel as he dashed past.

"Hiiiii" said Britney in the high pitched tone to her dad, walking casually towards the house, checking her phone for any new notifications since she'd got out of the car.

"Alright love! Come inside and have a look around!"

The children were quickly running from room to room shouting things like "wow!" and "no way!" and "sick!" as they entered each room.

Rachel was still laughing as she hugged her mum.

"Bloody hell Rachel, love, I know you said it was posh up here, but bugger me! I had no idea it was this posh! Can I move in as well? It's gorgeous love! It's absolutely gorgeous love!" Maureen had a tear in her eye as she looked up at the property. "God, I'm so proud of you, love."

"Oh give over, mum." Rachel was feeling quite emotional too.

"How's it been going with the moving and unpacking anyway love?" asked Maureen.

"Aw, I'm knackered! Honest mum, I'm in and out like a blue arsed fly, up and down those stairs like a bleeding yo-yo."

"Well, it's one of the most stressful things you can do, moving house."

"I know mum, but thanks for having the kids. We wouldn't have got anything done with these little buggers here as well!"

"It's my pleasure. Here, I've brought you a Vienetta to celebrate." Maureen handed the carrier bag that she was carrying to Rachel.

"Aw, thanks mum!" Rachel kissed her mum on the cheek again.

"Alright Maureen?" asked Mick as he came to give his mother-in-law a hug.

"Bloody hell Mick, this is fantastic!" she said, looking as though she was over the moon for her family. "But look at my car on this posh street! I'll go and park it down the road, it's bringing the place down!"

Mick laughed. "Don't be so bloody daft Maureen! At least you've got a car, there's plenty that haven't. Besides, you're not up to your eyes in debt on yours. At least you own it. All these on here are on HP, the bank own them, not the folk driving them! Leave it where it is."

"Have they been good, mum?" asked Rachel.

"Erm. Excited. Let's just say that!" said Maureen with a twinkle in her eye. Rachel smiled and handed the carrier bag to Mick.

"Put that in the freezer – mum's got us a Vienetta. Don't let the kids see it."

"Right, nice one," said Mick, quietly.

"Come on mum, let's give you the grand tour!" Rachel began dragging her mum up the drive.

"Okay love, let me just lock the car up."

"You don't need to lock the car around here Maureen. Too posh for car thieves up here, don't you know." Said Mick, using an awkwardly delivered posh accent for the last part of his sentence. Rachel and Maureen laughed out loud as they entered the house.

"Right, well, show me around. It must be heaven coming here after the caravan. God bless you all, you really do deserve a break." Maureen looked as though she was close to tears again.

"Do you want a brew Maureen?" asked Mick, as he followed his partner and his mother-in-law inside the house. The kids were still wailing and running about like morons inside.

"Oh my God! Look at it! Oh for the love of Christ this is absolutely stunning!"

"Come and look at the en-suite bathroom mum, they even have those things to wash your bits." Rachel gestured down to her groin.

"It's absolutely stunning! It's beautiful. Yes, I will have a brew Mick, but get Britney to do it, she makes a cracking cup of tea. I can't drink your brews love, sorry."

"This is the front room. Sorry, the lounge. We haven't got a settee yet, so we're just making a do with these deck chairs for now. Mick's going to look on Manchester buy and sell for one, we've still got about two hundred and fifty quid left. But we've bought brand new beds and furniture for the bedrooms."

"Aw, you've done really well. We had bean bags when you were a baby love, do you remember? I quite missed them when we got a proper settee." Said Maureen.

"Britney, come and do your Granny a brew."

"Don't call me Granny Mick. I hate that. It makes me sound dead old."

"You are dead old Maureen!" laughed Mick.

"You cheeky likkle bastard. I'm only forty five!" Maureen stared sternly at Mick as she spoke.

"Ha ha! You're so full of it!"

"Right mum, come on. Britney, make your Grandma a brew please love. Right, so, kitchen first…"

After a good, fun half an hour of looking around and testing out the various devices such as the automatic garage doors, the garden sprinkler and the bidet, Rachel sat all of the children down on the deck-chairs in the lounge.

"Right, I know you're all dead excited about everything, but me and your dad need five minutes with you to talk about things." Said Rachel, to a chorus of snoring noises and groans.

"Bor - ing!" shouted Liam.

"Kill me now!" groaned Britney.

"Shut up right, listen right," said Mick. "Hands up if you like the house."

All four of the children, as well as their grandmother placed a hand up in the air.

"Right, good. I thought you'd all say that. Now hands up who wants to go back and live in that mouldy old caravan?" asked Mick, smiling. He laughed as all of the family kept their hands firmly on their laps.

"No way!" said the youngest of the group, Shania in her small, cute voice.

"Nah, you're alright dad," said Liam.

"Well, listen up," said Rachel, pulling an A4 paper booklet out of her bag. "This big massive book is a list of all the rules that we are basically going to have to follow one hundred per cent, or we'll be back in that caravan for good. I'm being serious - it even says that if we do something that forces us to get kicked out - it'll happen in twenty four hours, honest, there's absolutely no messing about with these guys." Said Rachel, pleased to see how seriously her family were taking it, as they all sat quietly, paying attention to their parents and not arguing amongst themselves.

"Most of it's proper logical to be honest," offered Mick, as he realised that the kids looked quite scared and upset at the option of having all this taken away from them, before they'd even stayed a night.

"Don't look sad," Rachel smiled at everyone. "I just want you all to know the rules, so we don't make a mistake and get kicked out. Bottom line is this - best behaviour at all times. That means no fighting or arguing. If someone is doing your head in, just go and chill out by yourself in your room. We could get evicted if a neighbour complains about a loud argument. It's that strict. I shit you not." Rachel tried to press home the seriousness of the rules with a gentle shake of the head, letting her children know that it wasn't just them that thought it was all a bit harsh.

"Thing is," interrupted Mick, in a bid to help his missus out, "if anybody started giving you any jip, say a neighbour came over and said "hoi, your football just touched a blade of my grass," the kids all laughed at Mick's sarcastic expression, "you need to just say sorry, and walk away. No cheek, no back chat. Hands up if you all understand that."

Everybody put their hand in the air once again, though Britney made it look like it took tremendous effort.

"Right, Britney, come here a minute." Mick gestured her with his hand.

"Why?" she asked in her typical teenage, stroppy manner. She was becoming a real pain in the arse, thought Mick, but he was determined to get her to cheer up a bit.

"Because I want to practise this out, right. So, say I'm a neighbour. And you're you."

"Right dad, get on with it. You're starting to grate on me." Britney wobbled her head from side to side as she spoke, to demonstrate that she was being serious.

"Don't be like that love," said Rachel.

"I know but it's dumb. I get it. Don't do anything wrong, I don't need to role play with you like I'm some kind of a retard."

"Come on Britney, don't be a dip-shit." Mick was smiling.

"Oh my God dad, who even says that now. Shut up!"

"I'll do it dad." Noel stood and walked over to his father. He loved taking part in these kind of family meetings.

"Right, good lad. So, I'm a neighbour right, and I've just nearly knocked you off your bike. So I'm going to start bollocking you, and you have to be really nice and just say sorry, yeah?" Mick looked encouragingly at his son.

"Yeah, bring it on." Said Noel, grinning. His older brother Liam burst out laughing loudly.

"Hey, you! You little twerp! I almost killed you then." Said Mick, looking really angry, which made the others laugh.

"Oh, so you did. That was absolutely foolish of me Sir, and I cannot explain my actions. I am eternally sorry." Replied Noel, bowing slightly before his father, to a chorus of laughter from his gran, his mum and siblings.

"No, stop. That's too sarcastic right Noel. Tone it down right. Start again," said Mick.

"Go on then," said Noel, smiling at his elder brother Liam.

"I say, young man, I almost ran you over there."

"You didn't. You can't drive dad!"

"Aw, he's spoiling it," Mick looked at Rachel and she laughed out loud at his mard expression.

"Sorry dad. Right, so, take two."

"Go on then,""

"I am so very sorry about that, it was my fault entirely. Please don't tell my parents though or I'll tell them that you touched my willy."

The whole family were in fits of laughter at Noel's unexpected ad-lib. It took a minute or so for everybody to settle down. Eventually, Mick spoke. "No, I don't think that's a good idea Noel, you absolute loon!"

"No, dad, right, what if our Noel hadn't done nowt wrong though?" asked Britney, secretly gutted that she hadn't taken part, now that she had been reminded of how funny and silly these kind of family conversations could be.

"Doesn't matter!" said Mick, holding his palms open and shaking his head. "If he's right, or wrong, you just say sorry, and that's it. Try me right, so say I'm you, and you be the car driver."

"Okay dad," said Noel. "Hoi, you there. What on earth were you thinking you muppet. Do you have a mental problem or something? You look like you do, you look like a window licker!" said Noel, pretending to be angry whilst trying not to laugh as his family chuckled along.

"You are quite right Sir, I am the one who was in the wrong, and I'm so, so sorry." Mick looked down at his feet, clasped his hands by his groin and looked as apologetic and angelic as he possibly could.

"You sound more sarcastic than him Mick!" squealed Rachel as the kids mocked their dad.

"You will never be forgiven!" shouted Maureen, cackling hysterically at Mick's sad and embarrassed face.

"And the Oscar goes to..." shouted Britney, encouraging more laughter from everybody.

Outside, Mick heard the unmistakable sound of a car door slamming shut. He glanced out of the window and saw the weird guy from across the road march away from his car and into his house. He slammed the house door too. Mick looked back at his family who were still making jokes about him, his acting skills and his general uselessness.

"Right, let's leave it there, I don't want to bore you. All I'm saying is, best behaviour, don't be giving anyone any shit. If you do, we'll be straight back on the caravan site. Any problems, just come and talk directly to me or mum, right?"

"Yeah, don't worry mum and dad," said Liam. "We'll be good as gold."

"And no holes in the walls!" said Rachel. "Under any circumstances."

"Your mate's back." Said Mick, pointing his thumb out of the window towards the house opposite. Rachel rolled her eyes to the ceiling.

"No seriously, that guy who lives over the road is just waiting for one chance, and he'll report us." Rachel spoke in a more sobering voice, after seeing the dreaded man again.

"Honestly love? How do you know?" asked Maureen, visibly troubled by this solemn announcement.

"I'll tell you over a fag mum, come on, back door."

"Right, cheers kids, end of meeting," Mick clapped his hands together. "All the rules are in this book so give it a read. Oh, and remember, if you use the last of the toilet roll, tell me or your mum. I hate finding out that there's none left when I'm halfway through a dump."

Chapter Nine

Graham had arrived home a couple of minutes after leaving his wife by the side of the road. He was still in a fury when he reversed the white Range Rover Evoque onto his drive and slammed the car door shut. He went straight into his house, slamming his front door shut also. Inside, he headed upstairs, where he turned on the shower, and began quickly undressing. He literally could not wait to be out of the clothes that he could still smell that awful police station on.

Graham spent ten minutes in the shower, and still didn't feel that he had thoroughly washed the odour of urine, industrial strength disinfectant and poor people off himself. He had been given a caution by the police Sergeant, a different officer than the one who had dealt with him on his arrival. Rather than exacerbate matters there and then, he quietly accepted the police caution, knowing full well that he would be appealing this gross injustice at the first possible opportunity.

The opportunity came as soon as he had dried and dressed. He turned his computer on in his home office, before going downstairs to make a cup of earl grey. He realised that he felt very hungry all of a sudden, and cursed Suzanne for not being there to make him something. With his cup in his hand, and a head full of incensed ideas of what should be contained in his letter, he returned upstairs to the office, and began typing furiously on his keyboard.

As Graham vented his anger at the "inadequate judgement" of the officers, the "simply disgusting conditions within the cell facility," the "infantile and despicable behaviour of the Sergeant," and had finally concluded that "the police force requires a top down reorganisation with immediate effect if any faith is to be restored," he realised that he didn't feel half as satisfied as he had expected that he would, when he began writing his letter to the Chief Constable, who he had met once or twice at various functions. He began reading through it again, looking for opportunities to amplify his points. Eventually, he was satisfied and pressed the printer icon on the screen. A few seconds later, he scribbled his signature at the bottom, and put his letter into an envelope, hand writing the address, and marking it for the personal attention of the Chief Constable.

After going downstairs and drinking a generous portion of his 18 year old single malt whisky, Graham went back upstairs and got into bed, to catch up on his sleep after that appalling night in the police cell, Graham wondered how long it had been since he'd been forced to lose his temper and made Suzanne get out of the car. He looked at his watch, and remembered that it was about 10.20 when the police had finally let him go home. It had been almost an hour and half since he'd arrived home, and he began to wonder why Suzanne was taking such a long time to get home, figuring that it was only a fifteen or twenty minute walk. Half an hour at the very most.

"Ungrateful little scrubber." He muttered as he turned his phone off and put his eye mask over his face, before drifting peacefully into a deep, satisfying sleep.

*****

Rachel and Maureen were having a good old natter in the back garden when they heard something rattling the back fence.

"There's bloody thousands of cats around here as well, they'd better not shit on my lawn! There's nowt worse than breaking the skin of a cat shit with the lawn-mower," said Rachel. "Do you want another brew mum?"

"Rachel. Look!" said Maureen as her daughter stood to go inside and put the kettle on. Maureen was watching a young woman's head appear, she was climbing over the six foot high fence. Rachel turned around and saw Suzanne, struggling to get over the fence, looking wild, feral, her eyes were wide with fear, and she looked like she was crying.

"Suzanne!" she said as she ran across the grass. "What's wrong love?"

Suzanne fell into a bush, the weight and momentum of her legs following through after she had managed to get them over the top of the fence caused her to lose balance. She scrambled up out of the bush, feeling relieved to be in the relative safety of her new neighbours garden.

"What's going on? Are you alright love?" Rachel was visibly concerned by this extraordinary situation. Suzanne was sobbing uncontrollably and held her arms out for a hug. As Rachel got closer, she could see that Suzanne had a wound on her face, and was shaking uncontrollably. She gave her neighbour a hug and whispered "ssshhh," into her ear, quietly trying to reassure her.

Britney had appeared at the back door. She looked at the woman, and then at her gran.

"Okay, that's random," she said, searching her gran's face for clues as to what on earth was happening. Maureen looked back, with an equally confused expression.

"Daaad!" shouted Britney, "it's all getting a bit weird in the garden. Mum's going all lesbian with a zombie."

"Shut up Britney!" shouted Rachel. "Are you alright love? What's happened?" She kept repeating, but Suzanne was just clinging onto her, crying, and making a moaning noise. There was snot everywhere.

"Is everything alright?" asked Maureen, who was completely baffled by the situation. Mick appeared in the door way and added his own look of astonishment.

"Come on Suzanne, calm down love. What's happened?" said Rachel, starting to feel the grip on her back loosen slightly.

"Help me!" pleaded Suzanne, just.

"Come on love, come inside. Let's look at that face. What's happened? Have you been in an accident?" Rachel started walking Suzanne towards the house. By now all of the children were stood in the door way, confused and bemused by the unfolding drama in their new back garden.

"Move out of the way guys, please," ordered Rachel as she approached her family, clutching the hysterical woman.

"It's that woman from over the road." Mick looked thoroughly pissed off as he realised who the woman was.

"MOVE!" shouted Rachel at her family as they stayed put, gawping and blocking a way into the house.

Everybody parted and a pathway into the house appeared. Rachel pulled her new neighbour through the small crowd of onlookers and took her inside. "Do you want a cup of tea, Suzanne? Have a brew love, it'll settle you down."

"He can't know I'm here. Please?" she said, making the please sound more like a question than a request. In that sentence, Rachel understood everything.

"Britney! Make a brew for Suzanne. Sweet, plenty of sugars, she's had a shock."

"Alright mum, but I am going to start charging, it is becoming a full time job this you know." Britney was only trying to lighten the mood, but her timing was just a bit off.

"Not now Britney love. Come on Suzanne, come up to my room, let's get you washed up." Rachel was leading her neighbour towards the stairs.

"He mustn't know I'm here. I'm begging you." Pleaded Suzanne.

"Ssshhh just calm down love, you're safe now, you're alright." The two of them went upstairs slowly and the bedroom door was closed behind them.

"Fuck my life!" said Mick to his mother-in-law. He was standing with her at the bottom of the stairs. "Why does this kind of shit always happen to us?"

"Come on," said Liam, to Noel. "Let's go and listen."

"No, bollocks to that lads - go and play out. And no trouble! Right?" Mick's happy, excitable mood had disappeared completely. He was snappy and irritable. The boys took off through the front door without any hassle. They were keen to explore the new estate anyway.

"What the hell is going on Mick?" asked Maureen, by now she was desperate to find out what all this was about.

"I'm not sure. But I don't like it. We're meant to be keeping our heads down, and we've not even got the kids bedding on, but already the police have been round, and now the wife of the guy who called the police is in the house crying her arse off. This is a disaster Maureen love, I'm not kidding you."

"Shit! Is that who she is?" whispered Maureen, loudly. "Shit the bed!" she said, now that she had a better understanding of what was going on. Rachel had already filled Maureen in with the details of the previous night's activities. "I'm not having this Mick. I'll go round there now and I'll bleeding tell him straight!" Maureen looked ready for a fight. "You don't deserve any of this bull-shit!" she snarled.

"No, love, don't do anything. Just leave it. We'll talk to Rachel in a bit. She'll go off her nut if you do something without checking with her first. Please Maureen, it's good of you and that, but just put your foot in your mouth 'til in a bit."

"Mick, love - if you two lose this house, you're knackered. Our Rachel has got a big heart - but you've got to look after number one here lad. Seriously, look at me. I don't give a shit about that girl upstairs, all I care about is you lot. Now I can go and tell this prick to pack it in, and he fucking well will."

"He won't Maureen. Trust me, you've not seen him. He's a proper stuck up toff. But let's go upstairs and tell his wife to piss off. Tell them we don't want nowt to do with them."

"Yes, Alright Mick. That's what we'll do. But let's give them five minutes up there. She looked in a right state and our Rachel will sort her head out. Then, we'll both go up and tell her that she needs to do one, and stay well away. And you need to put your foot down Mick, tell our Rachel that she needs to leave this woman to it. Right?"

"Right. Sorted. Nice one." Mick was glad that he had the support of Maureen.

Upstairs, Rachel had taken Suzanne into the bathroom and had sat her down on the toilet seat. She was still shaking uncontrollably, but was visibly calmer than she had been when she'd first appeared in the garden.

"Just hold still love. That's it." Said Rachel who was stood over her neighbour, gently dabbing the wound on her cheek with cold water and cotton wool. "It's going to be a shiner that Suzanne, I can see it coming up." It went quiet, and Rachel became a little uncomfortable in the silence. She began chattering away about nothing in particular, just waffling on about her mum coming, and the kids' reaction to the house. Apart from the occasional "ooh" or "ow" Suzanne had remained silent for the past five minutes or so. Maureen knocked on the bedroom door, and then appeared holding a cup of tea. She wandered through to the en suite bathroom.

"Are you decent?" she asked.

"Yeah, come on in mum. Aw, have you brought a brew? Here you go Suzanne. That'll be the best brew you've ever tasted that love, trust me!" said Rachel, still very much in the waffling frame of mind.

"Are you okay love?" asked Maureen as she handed Suzanne the brew. Mick appeared just behind her and stood in the door way.

"Who?" asked Rachel. "Oh, Suzanne - yes I think she's alright, don't think it needs any stitches. What do you think mum?" Rachel gently lifted Suzanne's chin up.

Maureen looked at Suzanne's face and screwed her face up. "Nah, it won't need stitching that. It's going to swell up like a gonad that though."

"Who's done that to you?" asked Mick, without very much affection in his voice. The question certainly threw the cat amongst the pigeons. Rachel turned and gave Mick the look. Maureen leapt straight in.

"Don't look at him like that Rachel love. We've come up here to tell you both that whatever is going on, it has got to stop right now. If this couple have problems over the road, it's got to stay over the road love. I'm sorry."

"Mum, that's completely out of order that. Now you can just go down, that's really pissed me off that has."

"No, Rachel," said Mick, "We're going to be made homeless with these fucking weirdo's over the road. I'm not having it. I'm sorry if you're having trouble love, but it's not our fault, and we don't want to get involved, right."

Suzanne was just staring straight ahead, her vision was fixed on her reflection in the towel holder bar that faced her.

"You two had better get out of my sight right now, it's not the time or the place."

Rachel was quite clearly furious, but was desperately trying to keep a lid on it for Suzanne's benefit.

"Your trouble is - you're too nice Rachel love, you always have been. But this affair could have you in the caravan again tomorrow! You need to be aware how much danger you're putting yourself in. Not just you love, we're talking about everybody else as well. You said yourself - if you fart wrong you'll be turfed out." Maureen was rarely confrontational, especially where Rachel was concerned. But she was sticking to her guns on this matter. Rachel looked at them both for a couple of seconds, her feelings were quite obvious, but if her closest family members were in any doubt, she made herself perfectly clear when she eventually spoke.

"Mum, Mick, you can say all this shit later. But not in front of her, right? Are you both on summat? I've never known you to be so fucking rude, she's in bits here, her husband's just caved her face in and you come in here giving it all this. Now get out of my toilet this minute, or I swear down, I'll go outside and I'll smash every single fucking window on the estate. Get out, and you owe Suzanne an apology before you go, you pair of shit heads." Rachel was holding aloft a piece of wet, bloodied cotton wool as though it was a weapon.

"Sorry." Mick turned to leave. He knew that look, and knew not to proceed. Maureen also got the distinct impression that she'd misjudged this one too.

"Sorry Suzanne, but…"

"Get out mum, you've said enough."

"No, no, please, don't go. I totally get it. I understand what you are saying. I should never have come here." Suzanne sounded quite embarrassed, but her voice was clear and confident. "I didn't think of the consequences of me coming here. You are absolutely right. I'm sorry. He won't find out that I've been here." Suzanne looked up at Mick and Maureen, and they saw just how vulnerable she was for the first time.

"Ignore them Suzanne. They've lost their bloody manners. Now, can you two get out like I said. I'll speak to you both later."

"They are right though," said Suzanne as Mick and Maureen walked out quietly and closed the bedroom door behind them. "I didn't consider the effect this could have on you Rachel. Really I didn't. How selfish of me. I'll go," Suzanne stood, and tried her give her neighbour a hug.

"No, you're not going anywhere. Them two have got a point, fair enough. But I'm not going to be evicted because a battered wife has come to me for help."

Suddenly, Suzanne's eyes flicked up, and Rachel saw that a very raw nerve had been pressed.

"I'm not a …"

"You're not a battered wife? Is that what he's told you?"

"It's not…"

"It's not what?"

"It's not all the time. He just has this temper."

"So does he go boxing? Is he part of a martial arts group? Does he go and do a bit of fighting at the football on a Saturday to keep his aggression occupied? Or is he just a bully who thumps his little wife?" Rachel was stood face to face with Suzanne, and was searching her eyes for the truth.

"He hasn't done it for ages, it's just the stress of all this."

"You mean the houses being rented out to us?"

"Yes, it's really affected him."

"Forgive him then, it's fair enough, punching a woman because he doesn't like a decision that's been made by the local council. Tell you what, I might give my little daughter Shania a punch in the head tomorrow, if the bus is late, or the wind fucks my hair up."

"I'm not saying…"

"What was it last time he smacked you?"

"I, can't remember."

"Well, I'm sorry to say this to you love, but it won't change. You need to know that. Men like him, they can't help themselves. You need to get away from him." Suzanne suddenly looked very annoyed, and quite embarrassed. That comment had stamped on a raw nerve, and she didn't like Rachel speaking about Graham like this. She didn't even know him.

"He's a nice man most of the time. God, you're making him sound…"

"I'm not making him sound anything!" snapped Rachel. "You just climbed over my fence with blood pissing down your face. You just begged me to keep it secret that you're here. Don't start forgetting that already Suzanne. You might be in denial love, but I'm not, I know a battered wife when I see one."

Tears welled up in Suzanne's eyes. Different from the tears of fear from ten minutes earlier. These were the tears of emotional hurt. Suzanne just wasn't ready for the harsh brutality of what Rachel was saying.

"I think, well, I think I'd better go. Thanks for everything Rachel. I'm really sorry that I've got you involved."

"Where are you going to go?"

"I don't know. Home I guess."

"Can't you go to a mate's for a few days? What about family? You can't just go home after that Suzanne. You should be phoning the bloody police out on him."

"It's fine. I need to go, I'll leave you in peace."

"I'm not letting you go back there. I want someone to come and get you, and look after you for a few days, you need to do something, you can't live like this!"

"There isn't anybody," said Suzanne, as more tears began to well up in her eyes.

"What do you mean? There must be somebody, a mate or, what about your mum?"

"There is no-one, it's just me and Graham."

"Well, listen, I can get you numbers, phone numbers for charities that are there to help people like you. They can get you out of there, they can help you. You don't have to live like that Suzanne, nobody does."

"I'm sorry, Rachel, truly I am, I shouldn't have come here. Please, just let me go home. You've got the wrong end of the stick. I need to be with Graham, he'll be wondering where I am."

"And you don't think he'll hit you again?"

"No. He never does. He'll feel really bad about it now, he'll buy me loads of new things. Like I've said, he's not a wife beater."

"Well you promise me one thing please Suzanne. You let me know if he does. Because you can't live like that."

Rachel gave Suzanne a big hug, and insisted that she finish the cup of tea. She also insisted that Suzanne went through the front door this time.

Chapter Ten

Bez's Arms Pub
Salford

"Alright there now Kev? How're you now?" asked Seamus McCarthy, sitting down at the table opposite Kev, who had been sat, waiting patiently for a private word with the landlord for the previous thirty five minutes.

"Not bad, mate, not bad. Just moved into a new house over near Bury. It's nice, the wife and our Brett are loving it. Out in the country, loads of cows mooing and all that malarkey."

"Ah, I heard you talking about this last week, so I did. Wasn't it the place where the neighbours had a petition to stop you from moving in?" Seamus had a lovely big smile, and chuckled at the thought of council house folk moving in to a posh estate full of rich people. "It's a disaster waiting to unfold, surely to God it is, so it is." He said. Kev nodded. "Is this why you're sat here looking like you want your mammy?" laughed Seamus.

"Yeah, yeah, well, I need someone to get a good kicking to be honest. We moved in yesterday right, no hassle, no nothing. No one was out in the street welcoming us, but no one giving us any jip either. So me and the wife are like, doesn't matter, we'll just keep ourselves to ourselves and that. Say nothing more about it. Then, about three o clock this morning, this pissed up twat from down the road starts ringing on me bell, he's going on about my music being too loud and all this. I swear down, it was the telly, and I was asleep on the settee, so it can't have been that fucking loud if I was asleep could it?" Kev raised his upturned hands to the height of his shoulders.

"No, no, certainly not." Seamus nodded along to Kev's story.

"Anyway, big do's and little do's, it turns out, he phoned the police before he came over, so he was obviously hoping I'd give him a smack and then we'll get kicked out of the house. Honest Seamus, it was that blatant."

"He's a fucking grass, so he is." Seamus seemed genuinely annoyed by Kev's problems.

"I know! But he's worse than that! He's grassing about shit that hasn't even gone on! We've got all these strict rules to follow, and if we break any, then we're fucked. This guy knows this, so he's headed straight at me, trying to make me hit him in the face."

Seamus looked sympathetic, as he often did when somebody approached him with such difficulties. He looked down at the table top for a long time before speaking again.

"Well, I can see how this can be distressing for you. You've come to the right place so you have. Now, you know the terms of business here Kev, and I'm never one to turn my back when a friend is in an arsehole. I can get this fixed for you for five hundred pound, and you know my code of practice, you pay before the event, and there's a cash back guarantee that you won't get any more shite off of this fellah." Seamus displayed his charming smile again and held out his hand for a shake.

"Nice one. No, I really appreciate this Seamus. I'm a reasonable guy, you know that, but this chap, he just wants us gone and he'll say anything to get us out. So it's a case of who needs it most. He needs telling to calm the fuck down. But the trouble is, he can't know who is saying it."

"Ah, no problem at all. We can be very discreet here, so we can. So just leave me an envelope with the money in and fill out one of these," Seamus pulled a questionnaire out of his pocket and handed it across the table. "This helps us to do an efficient job. You'll need to fill out all the necessary details in the fields marked A to F and then as you can see, there's a section for you to describe the person you wish for us to discuss matters with, and put as much detail as you can in that section, what car he has, what colour front door, any tattoos on his face, that kind of thing. Any kids involved, do you want a certain marking leaving on him, you know the score Kev, so you do. We don't like anything going arseways."

Kev was staring hard at the paperwork. He was clearly impressed with the professionalism. It had been quite some time since Kev had needed a situation sorting out, and he thought that the questionnaire really gave the Bez's Arms operation a certain je ne sais quoi.

"Alright there now, I'll leave you with that. Did you have an appointment time in mind?" Seamus was talking in a very matter-of-fact way, as he always did at these kinds of meetings.

"Well, the sooner the better, I was hoping tomorrow night, say tea time? In fact, that would be best 'cos I've warned the other neighbours to be out of the way."

"That should be fine."

"Nothing too upsetting, he can keep all his body parts and that." Kev grinned menacingly.

"Ah, well that's very noble of you Kev. Great! Well, pop back over to the bar when you've got all this paperwork filled out. And I'll need the payment before we can process the paperwork."

"Yeah, yeah, no worries Seamus, I've got it on me. We was going to get a new bed but fuck it! I'd rather get this shit sorted out to tell you the truth. I'd rather have a house with a shit bed, than a comfy bed with no house – you get me?"

"Well, that's very logical of you to think. Just take your time, there's no hurry. I'll be across at the bar, so I will."

Chapter Eleven

MONDAY

Rachel met her eldest kids at the bus station in town as arranged that morning, after she'd picked Shania up from her primary school over on the Gameshawe estate.

"Right, listen, best behaviour in here, I've got to go in and see the council about this new house. And I swear down, I want the staff in there thinking that you four were the Royal family or summat, right?" Rachel took a long drag on her cigarette and waited for a response.

"Yes, mum," said Britney in her typically sarcastic way, rolling her eyes away slowly, producing an expression that she personally thought was quite enchanting and intellectual. It always reminded Rachel of Rik Mayall's TV face, just before he would hit somebody over the head with a frying pan, and she always struggled not to laugh at her daughter whenever she did it.

"What's in it for us?" laughed Noel.

"What's in it for you, you cocky little shit, is that you'll hopefully keep your house!"

"I'll stay outside mum, if that's alright. I'll just hang about in JD and that, text me when you've finished." Said Liam.

Rachel nodded. "Yeah, fair enough love. Alright. Don't be going too far though, and keep your phone on." She knew that Liam was getting a bit too old to be seen hanging around the council offices. Kids get picked on for anything nowadays, she thought.

"In a bit!" muttered Liam as he strutted off towards the shopping centre.

"Aw no way! I want to as well!" Britney looked as though she was about to start one of her sulks.

"No love, I want you to come in with me. I'll have to start crying and I need you to say "Don't cry mum" and pass me a tissue, and rub my back a bit."

"Fair enough." Britney looked quite pleased that she had a purpose in the meeting.

"In fact, it would be amazing if you could cry too, and say you're sick of seeing me crying all the time." Added Rachel, determined to go in and make heavy weather of the situation.

"Yeah, no worries, as long as I can go to the bogs after and sort my eye-liner out before we leave?" asked Britney, suddenly feeling quite empowered by the responsibility that had been handed to her.

"Cheers love. Are you alright Shania?" asked Rachel of her youngest, who was stood amongst the small group by the bus station entrance, looking quite fed up.

"Yes, I'm alright." She said in her cute little voice. Rachel rubbed her shoulder gently.

"Alright, well, once we've got sorted in here, we're meeting your dad and we're having tea out as a special treat." Said Rachel. The children were instantly excited.

"Yes!" hissed Noel.

"McDonalds!" suggested Shania, this news had perked her up dramatically.

"K.F.C. It's got to be!" shouted Noel.

"No, we're having a posh tea, so best behaviour. Your dad's taking us to Wetherspoons. So you'd better be good or you'll be given a bag of chips to share on the bench outside! And I'm not even joking."

Rachel pulled on the handle of the huge glass door and held the door open while her children walked through into the familiar surroundings of the Town Hall offices.

"Hiya," said Rachel as she approached the glass window where the receptionist greeted her with a tilted head and a plastic smile. "Is there anybody available in the Housing? Preferably Daniel or Nicole?" Rachel smiled as she spoke to the lady behind the glass.

"Do you have an appointment? The department does work on an allocated appointments basis you see." Explained the receptionist, her eyes were dead, her heart just wasn't in it, but the smile remained.

"No, I'm sorry, I haven't got an appointment, but it's urgent actually. So if you could just ring up and see if anybody is available, that would be great." Rachel knew that any of the housing staff would be happy to speak to her. If she wasn't talking to them none stop about her own domestic situation, she was on first name terms with everybody in the department through her Citizens Advice Bureau work.

"I can ask, but you should really have booked an appointment, they might all be in meetings. What's your name please?"

"Rachel Birdsworth. It is urgent. Thanks."

The receptionist pressed some buttons on her desk and held the phone to her ear, trying to look very important. After a few seconds, she began speaking into the telephone. "Hello, it's Barbara on front desk, hiya. I've got a lady in reception who wants to speak to somebody urgently. No, she hasn't got an appointment but she says that Daniel or Nicole will know what it's about…"

"Anybody will," pleaded Rachel, through the glass. "Just tell them my name, it's Rachel Birdsworth."

"Yes, she's called Rachel Birdsworth," said the receptionist into the phone, while staring off into the distance. "Okay, I'll tell her, thank you." After placing the phone down on its cradle, Barbara looked at Rachel and announced that somebody would be down shortly to see her. Rachel and the children were sent to sit on the chairs in the waiting room.

After five minutes or so, Daniel Parker, one of the housing officers walked across and greeted the family.

"Hello, are you alright guys?" he asked, surprised to see them back here so soon after being given a new property. Daniel had been involved with the family's rehousing requirements since the fire, and had got to know them all quite well.

"Aw, Dan, hiya. Thanks for coming down, I know I didn't have an appointment."

"Don't worry about it – you've got me out of checking accounts for late rent, that's all the management care about - so I'm really grateful to be honest. Anyway, come on, we'll grab an empty room and you can tell me how it's going. I'm dying to know what you think of the house!" Dan smiled as he held open the door for Shania, Britney and Noel.

They wandered past him into a large open office area

that was full of serious looking people tapping on computer keyboards or talking into phones.

"Thanks Dan." Rachel followed her children and entered the offices.

"Right, no probs, just go in that little room there on the left. Yeah, that's it, just pull the door Britney."

It took five minutes for Rachel to fill Dan in with all of the details of the family's experience over the previous two days, from arriving at the house, to having the lady from across the road climbing over her fence and begging for shelter.

"In ten years at the old house, we never had any trouble at our door. We've been here ten minutes and we're wondering what's going to happen next. I'm scared Dan. If we get reported by anybody, we're finished. If he's prepared to make stories up – it's just too risky."

Dan looked really concerned. He hadn't for one moment considered that the new tenants up on Haughton Park would be in any danger of the home-owners causing them any aggravation. But now that Rachel was here, explaining the situation, it became obvious that this should have been anticipated.

"We've got a set of rules there that are like bloody, I don't know, a mental home and if we set one foot wrong, we're out on our rear! So I just want us to go back to the caravan Dan. We can just wait a bit longer in there for a house."

"Aw, no way mum, are you being serious?" asked Britney, the look of horror at this suggestion was the most genuine expression that Rachel had seen on her daughter's face for a very long time.

"No way mum! That's proper snide that," replied Noel. Shania began to cry and Rachel put her arm around her youngest.

"Aw, come on love, don't cry. It's for the best. We can manage a bit longer in the van, we've come this far!" Rachel was filling up too, but was trying to fight the tears. She hadn't said everything that she wanted to get off her chest yet.

Dan looked at the family, he was wearing an

unusually serious expression, and blew out a massive gust of air. "Well, guys, I'm in shock. I really am. You lot were chosen to go up there because we know you, we know what a good family you are. We have only re-housed people that we are really confident about on the development. This is unbelievable really. I'm going to have to speak to my superiors, and I'll have to speak to the developers as well, we need to get this sorted. Can you hang on a few minutes while I just pop upstairs?"

Rachel was still fighting back tears as she replied. "Dan, there's no point. I don't want to be put in any danger of not getting a proper house. We're being treated like the scum of the earth, just because we don't earn enough money to buy our own house. How can people be so judgemental?"

"Well, please, Rachel. Just stay here a minute." Dan stood and placed a comforting hand on Rachel's shoulder. "We never anticipated this. I need to ask for some assistance with this. Hang on here." Dan stood and bolted out of the little room. Rachel felt the tears begin to loosen and slide down her face. She was hugging Shania close, rocking in her chair and rubbing her back gently.

"I've got to make a big deal about these problems we've been having. I don't think we'll end up at the caravan, but I'm just watching our backs. I know it doesn't seem like it. But I'm just watching out for us all, right?" Rachel was talking quietly, but the emotion was clear in her voice.

"Don't want to go back in that caravan mum, it's rank." Said Noel, he too looked close to tears. Rachel leant across and put her arm around him.

"Well, hopefully, that guy over the road will pipe down and buck up his ideas once these lot have had a word. But like I have said all the time, a proper house could come up at anytime, on the old estate, so we're only temporary in the big posh house anyway. We all knew that, didn't we?"

The kids nodded, and it was clear that they didn't like the idea of leaving the new house at any time.

The door opened, and Dan reappeared. He had brought a colleague with him, another officer who was well known to the family.

"Hiya Rachel, hi guys," said Nicole. "Dan's just told me briefly. We're going to go up there tomorrow and sort this out. Now, please don't worry about going back to the caravan, it's not going to be an option."

Noel and Britney raised a fist and said "yesss" as though it was a well rehearsed and choreographed move.

"Thanks Nicole, but if that guy who owns the estate says we're out – that's the end of the road for us, so we really need it sorting out properly." It was clear from the state of Rachel's make up that she'd been crying. Nicole looked genuinely sympathetic. She knew Rachel well enough to know that she wasn't a trouble causer.

"Don't worry, it will be sorted properly. It's us who are doing the developers the favour you know, not the other way round. We'll get onto this first thing in the morning. And thanks so much for coming in to see us about it. This was supposed to be a really happy time for you lot, after all that time in the caravan," said Nicole. "Don't pay it any more thought – we'll sort it out tomorrow." Nicole was lovely, as was Dan, and they had been really good with Rachel and the family. It was moving for Rachel to see how seriously they were treating her concerns.

"Thanks, honestly. I've been going out of my mind with worry all day you know."

"You don't know what number house it is, do you?" asked Dan.

"I think it's number nine. But it's the one straight facing us. He was stood, staring at us the minute we turned up with the van on Saturday. It was like he'd been waiting for us. And he started trying to abuse us on Saturday night, when the other neighbours had shut the door on him. He's not right, honestly."

"Right. I think we've heard enough haven't we Dan?" asked Nicole. "We'll do some digging, and I'll give you a phone tomorrow Rachel, alright?"

"Thanks. I really appreciate how supportive you've been." Said Rachel as she left the little room, with her children in tow. As she made her way out of the building, and back towards the bus station, she wondered whether she had been right to avoid mentioning Kev and Tania's visit, and the threat that they had made about teaching Graham a lesson. The thought troubled her as she wondered just what kind of hassle Kev had planned. But straight away, another thought about what happens to grasses crossed her mind too. It was a dead end, and it was best to forget about it. The foundations were laid, at least she'd had the opportunity to put her side of the story across, and she felt confident that they had taken her concerns seriously. All in all, it was a very good meeting.

"Come on, let's go and meet your dad. His bus will be here any minute."

Chapter Twelve

Around at number twenty, Kev and Tania's fifteen year old son Brett had been given the very simple but important task in what his father had been referring to as "the warning."

Brett's objective was to stand near the front door, and watch for the neighbour who had disrespected his father to arrive home. Once the neighbour arrived and went inside his house, Brett's simple chore was to update his Facebook status with the words "God I'm starving and all there is in the house to eat is peanut butter and a mouldy fucking pitta bread!"

This simple message would alert Kev that it was time to post his own Facebook message, which read, "Are Brett's moaning that there's nowt to eat. Should have come with us to Little India for tea! Ha ha #dickhead" The message ended with a check - in tag to the famous Rusholme restaurant, six miles east of Haughton Park.

That seemingly innocent message was the red light for Graham Ashworth's "warning" to commence, whilst also providing a watertight alibi for Kev and Tania's movements while the incident took place.

Within minutes of Kev's status update, a silver Vauxhall Astra containing four black-hat wearing men pulled up outside Graham and Suzanne's house. They got out, and walked straight over to the front door, rolling down the hats, turning them into balaclavas, and stretching them over their faces as they reached the door.

Bing Bong.

One of them had pressed the bell. Within seconds, Suzanne answered the door and was thrown to the floor by the force of the door being shoved open violently. The men followed inside and the last of the group closed the door very calmly behind himself as two of the raiders began wrapping duct tape around Suzanne's wrists, clasping them together, and also placing a piece over her mouth. She was quickly pushed into the lounge, and thrown onto the sofa. It had all happened so quickly and quietly, that Graham Ashworth was taken completely by surprise as he stepped through from the kitchen to see who was at the door.

"Right, that's him," said one of the masked men, as he ran over and shoved Graham violently against the wall by the staircase. Graham went down straight away, offering nothing of a fight. The three masked men began kicking and punching him as he lay curled up in a ball. He was screaming, pleading for them to stop. He was getting kicks to his body, arms and legs, while the occasional blow got through to his face which was being protected by his curled up arms and hands.

One of the men was standing guard over Suzanne in the lounge. She couldn't see anything that was happening, but she could certainly hear the violence that was being delivered, and her husband's pitiful screams and pleas for mercy. She was shaking uncontrollably, but not crying. This was just too unbelievable and she was in a state of deep shock. The man who was stood over her kept his finger up to his mouth, and stared directly at her throughout the ordeal.

Within no time, the punching, kicking and struggling sounds had stopped. The noise in the hall had ceased. It was completely silent, but for Graham's whimpers. A masked man appeared at the doorway to the lounge.

"Are you right?" he asked.

"Done?" asked the man who had been stood over Suzanne.

"Yeah, we're done. He'll fuckin' die or summat if we carry on. He's a big fat fuckin' shitbag."

"Yeah, I know. Look at his bird's black eye."

"Fuckin' hell is that his bird? You're too good for that knob-head love, you need to fuck him off. Right, come on, time to bounce."

The masked man walked calmly past Suzanne, stepped out into the hall way and started making a strange "pssst" noise as the remaining men marched out of the house. The noise continued for fifteen seconds or maybe longer and Suzanne was desperate to jump up off the sofa and investigate it, but she was frozen rigid with fear. She just couldn't move.

Suddenly, the strange hissing noise stopped and the

man spoke.

"Can you hear me mate?" he asked.

Suzanne heard Graham snivel and reply with a simple, tearful "yes."

"Right, well sort your fucking head out, or we'll be back, and we'll set your big ugly head on fire. You've been warned, right. Don't get the police involved yeah. If you need hospital, say you fell down the stairs. Did you understand that?"

"Yes," whimpered Graham.

"Alright, no problem. See you now."

With that, the man walked out very quietly and closed the door menacingly quietly behind him as he left. A second or two passed before Suzanne heard a car door close and a vehicle pull away from outside the house.

At that moment, the full terror of the past unimaginable minute or so hit her with overwhelming force, and she began trembling and sobbing uncontrollably. She managed to pull the tape off her mouth and tried her best to wriggle her wrists free of the tape. She couldn't break free. Whimpering, she tried to stand but her legs wouldn't hold her weight, they felt like jelly. It took her a good minute to compose herself and try again to stand. Graham was weeping and gargling, it sounded as though he was in great pain, and she wanted desperately to go and see if he was okay. She wanted to comfort her husband, she was scared by the sounds that he was making, and had absolutely no idea what state she would find him in. The violence that he had been served had sounded vicious and relentless. Through all of the jumbled up emotions; horror, shock, outrage and delirious thoughts about what had just happened - her main confusion was about why.

Was it a case of mistaken identity? It must have been. Graham wasn't involved in anything like drugs or money lending. He never came into contact with the kind of people who behaved in this way anymore. It was all just too extraordinary, too unbelievable to take in and despite the fact that her hands were fastened together with tape, and her husband was wheezing and gargling in a ball in the hallway, it was all too surreal to comprehend.

"Suzanne," whimpered Graham. "Suzanne, are you... hurt?" he managed to ask, it sounded as though he was having difficulty talking. "Suzanne?"

Suzanne was frozen. She was sitting on the sofa, just staring out of the window, staring at nothing, shaking violently. She could smell something strange, it was like pear drop sweets.

"Suzanne." Said her husband again. "Why have... you done this?"

Chapter 13

"Yes, that one there mate, the only one with no car on the drive!" said Mick, pointing his house out to the minibus driver.

"Cheers mate!" said Rachel from just over Mick's shoulder. "How much is that?" she asked.

"Eight pound." Said the taxi driver, without much enthusiasm. He looked like he was impressed by the properties on Haughton Park though.

"Eight quid! Bloody hell, what's your name? Dick bleedin' Turpin?" said Mick, to an explosion of laughter from his family. They all loved him when he'd had a few beers, he could be quite outrageous. "It'd be a fiver if it weren't a big posh house wouldn't it you sleazebag!"

"No, eight pound, it's the correct price."

"Pull the other one, it's got bells on!" added Rachel, trying to capitalise on the situation for the kids amusement.

"I'm only kidding pal. Eight quid is a very fine price for all of us lot to get home. Here's a tenner, you can keep the change!" said Mick with a big, drunken grin all across his face.

"Are you feeling alright Dad?" asked Britney as she slid the back door open and jumped out of the vehicle.

"Course I am. I feel on top of the world me love!" Mick was still grinning weirdly as he got out of the cab.

"Your dad's drunk!" Said Rachel at the top of her voice as she followed Britney out of the back. "He's just tipped the taxi driver!"

"Shania, get your birthday present request in now!" laughed Liam.

"Hey! I'm not bloody drunk, right. It's only half eight! It's good manners to give a tip. Here, mate, here's another tip – whatever you want to do, do it now, right now. Because life is time and time is all there is."

Liam and Noel were laughing loudly at their dad as Rachel grabbed her partner and started dragging him away from the vehicle.

"Come on you, you can't take your ale!"

The taxi driver smiled politely, he had spent a great

many hours in the company of drunken people as he drove them around Manchester. Mick was one of the easier ones to cope with.

"Okay, thank you. I'll certainly do that!" He replied as Mick slammed the passenger door shut.

"You only get one shot! Make it count!" shouted Mick as the minibus pulled away. Mick stood and watched it pull off the avenue as Rachel stood by his side.

"Take a snide look over the road," she muttered out of the corner of her mouth.

"Where?" asked Mick, as he waved to the taxi as though it was his mum driving off.

"At Suzanne and Graham's. Can you see anything?" Rachel was talking really quietly.

"What like a roadblock, a crime scene investigation, Granada Reports cameras and all police helicopters circling overhead?" asked Mick sarcastically.

"It all looks quiet doesn't it?"

"There's no one in that's why you great galah."

"How do you know?" whispered Rachel.

"Because the piggin' lights are off and the car's not there you donkey! Right, come on, let's get kettle on!"

"Do you think anything's happened?" asked Rachel, a little louder than a whisper. she had expected to see some clue as to what had gone on, and was very frustrated and a bit cheesed off to see nothing after spending all of her night in the pub listening to the kids slag each other off and Mick talking about how Maine Road was a proper ground for proper working men.

"Don't know love to be honest. Come on, let's get in and get the bloody kettle on."

*****

Suzanne was sitting in a side room cubicle with Graham, who had been crying off and on for the past three hours, since arriving at Accident and Emergency by car. She had helped her husband to get into the car at home, and out again at the doors of the hospital. She'd managed to find him a wheelchair and gently helped him to get into it from the passenger seat that he had violently forced her out of, just a day earlier.

Graham was convinced that he had broken ribs, and possibly a fractured skull, and was awaiting the results of x-rays to come back. His constant sobbing and self pitying was really grating on his wife, who was still very edgy from the ordeal, feeling quite distressed and violated by the hostile, nastiness of the men. She wasn't used to gangsters and people like that. As Graham continued to sob and snivel, all she wanted to do was scream at her pathetic, hopeless husband and tell him "to shut the fuck up!"

But she couldn't do that. The question that Graham had asked her as he lay in a heap on the floor was playing very heavily on her mind. How could he think that she was behind it? And how was she going to explain that it had nothing to do with her. The question kept looping around and around in her head, and Suzanne realised that she had never felt any kind of stress like this before in her entire life. It was all consuming, from her head to her toes, there seemed to be this buzzing feeling, getting stronger and more intense, throbbing with the beat of her heart.

Graham's pathetic whinings were not helping either.

Eventually, the doctor who had last been in about an hour earlier, reappeared clutching an armful of papers and reports.

"Nothing's broken, everything is fine. You have some bruising on your chest, very consistent with falling down some stairs. You've been very lucky. You just need to take it easy for a few days, I'll prescribe you some strong pain killers, have you had codeine before?" asked the young Chinese looking doctor.

Graham looked across at his wife, once more adopting the expression of a scared child. He was really irritating Suzanne with this extraordinarily weedy performance. She just wanted to tell him to man up. It was making her feel angry that she had suffered so many occasions of abuse and assault from him, never really knowing that he was just a big, soft, wimp.

"You can take codeine can't you, Graham?" asked Suzanne, feeling embarrassed, and also bad for holding the doctor up.

"I don't know," he whined. "I think so."

"Well, there's nothing on your notes that would suggest that you've had any problems in the past. So I'll prescribe you one week's worth, you take two caplets, three times a day – but no more. They can cause constipation. If you get your things together, the prescription will be ready in a few minutes at the front desk."

"You, you're discharging me?" asked Graham.

"Yes, you're fine. It will hurt slightly, but you don't need to stay here."

"Thank you very much Doctor," said Suzanne. Graham just looked up at the ceiling tiles in despair, it seemed that this information came as a shock.

"No problem. I'll go and do this prescription," said the doctor as he wiped GRAHAM ASHWORTH off the wipe board on the cubicle door. He made it obvious that he wanted the room back urgently, as he looked back in at Graham, before walking quickly away.

"Come on, love. I'll help you onto your feet."

Graham started sobbing again. "I can't believe this Suzanne. I just do not believe it." He screwed his face up as he tried to pull his weight up off the bed.

"Here, grab my hands," said Suzanne, more out of embarrassment than a real desire to help him. She extended her hands and Graham gripped them hard. She pulled him up and he howled in pain.

"Sorry! So sorry Graham! But you're up now. Come on, just swing your legs off the side and I'll go and get the wheelchair." Suzanne had adopted a frosty edge to her voice and Graham was acutely aware of it.

"You are such an ice-cold fucking bitch Suzanne. I'll never forgive you for this."

*****

"Here we go! They're back!" said Rachel, jabbing

Mick in his side as the car head-lights illuminated the bedroom, as Graham and Suzanne's car reversed onto the drive.

"Eh?" asked Mick who was in a drunken sleep.

"They're back!" whispered Rachel as she leapt out of bed and waited for the headlights to be switched off so she could have a nosey out of the window, and try and see what was going on. It quickly became apparent that Graham had indeed been given some food for thought from Kev, the wannabe gangster from a few doors up. The vile neighbour was grimacing in pain as Suzanne helped him out of the car and led him up their drive. He was limping quite badly and making lots of groaning noises. Rachel felt quite bad as she watched, he was clearly in a great deal of pain. But at the back of her mind, she felt that he did deserve it – if not for the stunt that he had pulled with Kev and Tania in the first place – certainly for assaulting Suzanne and getting her in the state that she was in the previous day.

"Fuck yer!" she muttered under her breath as Suzanne closed the door behind her husband.

"Eh? What's up?" asked Mick as Rachel got back in bed.

"He looks like he's had a right good twatting!" whispered Rachel as she placed her head on the pillow and kissed Mick's shoulder.

"Good. A good kicking never did anyone any harm." replied Mick, as he slipped back into his beer induced sleep.

"That's probably not a hundred per cent true Mick, but I get your point. Night love."

*****

From the moment that Suzanne closed the door behind Graham, the interrogation began. He'd made it clear from before they'd even left to go to the hospital that he had it in his head that she was responsible for what had happened.

In light of what she had increasingly considered to be Graham's pathetic and wimpy behaviour since it *had* happened, and in response to his idiotic suggestion that she was behind what had happened – Suzanne had finally had enough.

"Are you serious? Are you suggesting that this is to do with me?" she asked, with clear and direct anger present in her voice as she filled the kettle, and Graham limped across the hall to the lounge. She felt empowered, and it was a very strange moment for the both of them. She knew that Graham couldn't give her a smack in the condition he was in. And, he knew, that she knew it.

"How, ow. How dare you speak to me like that! You ungrateful little slag!"

"How dare you accuse me of getting you beaten up! Anyway, it's not nice is it? Hurts doesn't it? Maybe now you'll stop doing it to me, now that you've had a taste of it for yourself."

At this, Graham collapsed very slowly into the armchair in the living room and began sobbing uncontrollably.

"You really are a pathetic man, Graham. It's quite an education to see this. To see how you respond to being beaten up. That's what it's like for me you know. Like yesterday, bashing my head against the car door."

"Please, Suzanne, just shut the fuck up. Your voice is hateful. Now, go and get me a glass of whiskey, and some of those pain-killers, and then get the fuck out of my space." Graham was looking down at the floor, his face looked raw where the tears had burned the skin around his eyes. Suzanne placed one hand on her hip and laughed mockingly. The empowerment that she felt was intoxicating. It made her feel slightly dizzy, and she felt quite giddy too.

"Do you know what, get your own fucking whiskey and tablets Graham, and while you sit there, feeling sorry for yourself and getting pissed once again, why not write a list of all the people that you have pissed off recently – and we can work our way through that tomorrow."

"Fuck you Suzanne. I know you planned this with that awful fucking tramp across the road, so please, don't insult my intelligence."

"You're wrong. If I had done that, to be honest, I'd

be feeling pretty bloody smug right now. But I didn't Graham. So you need to have a good long chat with yourself and try and figure it out. And if you come anywhere near me tonight, I'll hit you back, now I know what a soft bastard you are. Good night."

Suzanne slammed the door shut with all of her strength, something that she'd never had the courage to do before.

Chapter 14

Rachel had only just arrived home from dropping Shania at school when the doorbell rang. She cursed under her breath, there was only half an hour to get the house tidied before she had to set off to do her volunteering at the RSPCA charity shop, where she would stay until going back on the school run. The last thing she needed right now was a visitor, especially as it was probably that Suzanne from over the road.

Rachel went to the door. She could see through the glass that it *was* Suzanne. It was going to be a bit awkward, the last time the two had spoken was when Mick had pretty much ejected her from the house, forcing her to leave, to face her abusive husband alone. It had made Rachel feel wretched, but she understood the reason why it was necessary, and she knew that it was sensible, regardless of how awful it made her feel personally. All Mick had said over and over on Sunday, after Suzanne had gone home was "it's all for the greater good, love."

Rachel reached out for the door handle, she could feel her heartbeat quickening, and she felt slightly breathless. She hoped that she wasn't about to start having an anxiety attack – these kinds of confrontations had led to them in the past. But she took a deep breath, reminding herself that she hadn't had an attack in years. She took another deep breath, and pulled down the handle. Rachel had been dreading this moment since arriving home the previous night, not knowing what exactly was meant by Kev's so called "warning" or what it would consist of. She sensed that she was about to find out as she opened the door.

"Hi," said Rachel, she sounded warm, friendly but her greeting clearly lacked very much enthusiasm.

"Hi," replied Suzanne. "Have you got a minute?" she asked, stepping forward a pace so that her feet were almost inside the house. "I, we need to talk."

"Well, I was just on my way out, sorry. I've got my volunteering to go to." Rachel was trying to play it cool, trying her very best to make it appear that everything was normal, but she was a dreadful actress and she was making a hash of it. Suzanne thought that she saw straight through it, but she was about to discover that things weren't quite as clear cut as she had been anticipating.

"Please Rachel. Just let me in, you can be five minutes late. We need to talk about that bloody stunt you pulled." Suzanne looked empowered, and she was certainly a lot more assertive than she had been, on the previous few encounters that the pair had shared.

"What? What do you mean by that? What stunt?" she asked, and all of a sudden, Suzanne looked a little bit less assertive. "What are you talking about?" she asked. Suddenly, it was Rachel who sounded the more confident of the two.

"Can you let me in? I don't want to discuss it out here on the avenue."

Rachel swung the door open and let Suzanne through. "Seriously, I have five minutes, and no more." She said as she closed the door behind her uninvited guest. "What stunt are you talking about? Do you mean on Sunday?" Rachel was searching Suzanne's eyes for answers.

"No, I don't mean about Sunday. Just forget Sunday alright? I was half pissed, I'd drank all night, and then I'd had a big swig of vodka to steady my nerves before I went to pick Graham up. It's not about Sunday." Suzanne was standing in the hallway, facing Rachel, who didn't respond. She just waited for Suzanne to continue.

"I'm talking about last night." Suzanne fixed her eyes on Rachel, and put her hands in her jogging bottoms pockets.

"Why, what happened last night? Has he hit you again or something? Is it my fault this time?"

"Don't play dumb Rachel. You know what happened, and I've come here to tell you that you were bang out of order, arranging that." Suzanne was staring deep into her neighbours eyes. Rachel was staring straight back.

"If I'm playing dumb, then at least give me a clue what it's about. You're starting to get on my tits now Suzanne, you're holding me up, I've got to go for my bus. So either tell me what the fuck it is you are here for, or just let me go on my way."

"Are you serious? You don't know what I'm talking about?" Suzanne looked annoyed, more than frustrated. This was her only theory, and it looked as though it had come to a dead end already.

"Haven't the foggiest. I swear down love, I don't have a clue what you are on about. I have been dreading seeing you, after what happened on Sunday, it wasn't my style that, I've been hating myself for letting you go back - but my mum and Mick were right – we can't get involved in your problems. God, that makes me sound so shit. But it's true."

"So, for the avoidance of all doubt – you didn't arrange for Graham to get beaten up for hitting me?"

"No. What? Wait a minute, fucking slow down. Why would I do that? You're the one who started defending him, saying he wasn't a bad person. For fucks sake Suzanne, what the hell is going on here?"

Suzanne leaned back against the wall and exhaled loudly. When she began to speak, it was at a volume noticeably quieter than it had been until now.

"Last night, after tea, four men... masked men, came to the house, and beat my husband up." Suzanne's eyes began to well up, and her colour drained slightly as the terror of the moment was relived in her mind.

"Seriously? Is he alright?" Rachel managed to sound and look genuinely surprised.

"He's shook up, he's got bruised ribs and what have you. His pride is damaged more than anything. But they were sick bastards who did it. Really nasty pieces of work."

"Oh, so automatically, it's my doing?"

"No – I'm not…." Suzanne looked shell-shocked, and a little scared – now that she realised that she had no idea who did it, if it wasn't Rachel – then who *did* do it? And why? She shuddered. This was a scary thought.

"Shut up. I'm sorry to hear that. It was absolutely jack shit to do with me, or us, any of us in this house. I can assure you of that. We need to stay out of any trouble while we are here, so arranging for people to get beaten up is not only stupid, it's also not our style. What have the police said?" Rachel's eyes were opened wide, her attention had been grabbed on this matter completely.

"We haven't got them involved. The ringleader said no police, or they'll set him on fire." This revelation rocked Suzanne's voice, and her emotion began to break. "They wrote in spray paint on the walls DON'T DO IT AGAIN!"

"Don't do what again?" asked Rachel, this detail clearly surprised her, and she wondered if this genuine surprise in her voice and face would give away her earlier, less genuine surprise, when she had first heard about Graham's kicking.

"Well, we, sorry I, assumed that you had organised it as a way of teaching Graham a lesson for hitting me."

"Suzanne, I swear down, on my baby Shania's life, it had nothing to do with us. Nothing."

"We just want to move on now, forget about it. And, well, I'm sorry for everything. God, you must think we're freaks. I'm sorry."

"Don't worry about it, I'm just sad that it's happened. You need to get the police involved though. Honestly Suzanne, you have to!"

"No. We can't risk it. These were serious people, dangerous men." Suzanne looked stressed, and worried, naturally. She held her index finger up to her mouth and glared at Rachel, and then grabbed her Bolton University hoody at the waist and began lifting it up, very slowly, revealing her well tanned tummy beneath. Rachel pulled her head back a few inches and raised her eyebrows, showing her visitor that she was puzzled. But Suzanne continued talking about how upset they had been as she continued pulling her top up slowly, to just below her boobs. Rachel bent down slightly to see what her neighbour was showing her. There, strapped across her ribs with some kind of elastic belt was an i-phone, and the screen was showing a recording icon, and waves were moving up and down on the screen as she spoke.

"So obviously, if it wasn't down to you, we've got to try and figure out who it was down to. And why? At least if it had been in response to Graham hitting me, it kind of makes a bit of sense." Suzanne seemed to be saying that remark deliberately to her i-phone. She was relieved that Graham's theory was snookered, and that she had some proof to take back to him. But at the same time, Suzanne was disappointed, because with the realisation that it wasn't Rachel who was behind the attack – she was reminded that there was no explanation for the attack, and the ominous message that had been graffiti painted all over the reception walls.

Despite the mystery, she was really pleased that Rachel, or "the scrubbers across the road" as Graham had been calling them, were not involved.

"I don't know love. Honestly, I'm really sorry to hear about it, but I have got to get going, people are relying on me."

"Of course, I'm sorry – I could give you a lift?" Suzanne looked really hopeful that Rachel would accept the offer.

"It's fine, honest. But I just need to leave right now." Rachel grabbed the door handle and opened it wide, stopping just short of waving Suzanne out.

"Okay, well, as I say, I'm sorry to bother you." Said Suzanne as she walked past Rachel as she left the house.

"Well, we just need to keep out of the limelight. We really do. So we're just going to keep our heads down, be invisible and silent until we get a new house sorted out. This has been the biggest nightmare I've ever known. So, thanks for coming round and that, but I think we need to keep our selves apart from now on." Rachel had an ability to talk quite candidly and assertively about things, and it was all thanks to her experience at the Citizen's Advice.

"Okay, well, I'm sorry. Thanks Rachel. You get going." Suzanne walked off quickly, down the drive and across the road. Rachel thought that she could hear her crying quietly.

"Fuck's sake," she said as she closed the door, rushed inside for her bag and keys and phone. It was a relief that the confrontation hadn't been too unpleasant, and to learn that the punishment had been quite lame by the sound of it. Most of all, Rachel was pleased that she had managed to cut her ties with Suzanne in such a relatively easy way.

As she left the house, locked the door and set off walking quickly towards the main road and the bus stop, Rachel believed that no matter how stressful it had been, the dreaded confrontation had been worthwhile. She felt glad that the ties to the new neighbours were severed and finally began to feel a little bit more relaxed about everything.

Her pace quickened as she broke into a power walk down the estate. As her thoughts wandered away from her recent problems and her mind began to focus on her other interests and concerns, Rachel could have had no idea that this was only the very beginning of her relationship with Suzanne. It most certainly was not the end.

Chapter 15

"God, it is bloody lovely up here though, isn't it?" Nicole was sat in the passenger seat beside Dan, her colleague from the council housing department. "I'd almost forgotten how nice this place was."

"Oh, no ta. It's not for me Nic, I couldn't be arsed with living up here. Can you imagine how pretentious you'd have to be to live on an estate that's been designed specifically for the filthy rich?" Dan shook his head as he looked through his windscreen, gazing nonchalantly at the extravagant properties as his battered little Ford Fiesta cruised along the newly built roads at the designated 10 mph speed limit.

"You little liar Daniel Parker! You're just jealous! You've got house envy!" Nicole laughed loudly and punched her junior colleague gently in the arm. "You'd move in here tomorrow if you had the cash!" she said, laughing again at Dan's unimpressed, sombre expression.

"Are you joking? Eurgh, you don't know me at all do you Nic? I couldn't stand it living here! I bet they're all competing for whose car cost the most, whose kid read the most books, who's got the best plastic surgeon. It's all so fake and predictable – a grotesque exhibition of material supremacy between the most bourgeois and superficial kind of people. It makes me sick in my mouth."

Nicole laughed again, and looked at Dan. He had been her colleague for the past four years. They had become quite good friends at work, often having a drink or two after work as well. Nicole had never before heard Dan say anything so negative, or thoughtful.

"Jesus, get you." She said, though the laughter had left her voice.

"Would you? Seriously I mean, would you want to live somewhere like this with your Jay and the girls?" asked Dan, his tone quite flat and depressed.

"Flipping heck Dan, have you been listening to The Smiths again?" asked Nicole. The question forced a laugh from her workmate, and she was relieved to see him smiling again.

Dan decided to cheer up a bit and began singing in a deliberately droney impression of Morrissey. "Please no, I couldn't bear to live here, I'd much rather live in a cold and lonely, desolate hole – without any arms or legs."

Nicole laughed loudly, and so did Dan as they continued along the endless turnings of almost identical avenues.

"It's like being on Scooby Doo, the same scene is going past over and over…"

"You could say that about any estate in the country. Oh, wait, stop – is that Rachel Birdsworth? It is – Dan, slow down." Nicole pressed the button and the window started rolling down as Dan's car pulled over to the kerb by the side of Rachel, who was walking at quite a pace.

"Hiya Rachel, are you alright?"

Rachel jumped with fright – she'd been lost in her own world.

"Oh, hiya, yeah, sorry I was miles away! I'm just on my way to catch my bus. It's a proper trek to the bus stop! They didn't think about buses when they built this estate did they?" she remarked, still moving slightly as she stood leaning into the car. "Mind you, I bet no-one on here used buses 'til us scrubbers turned up!"

"No, I never thought of that!"

Rachel looked eager to carry on towards the bus stop, but was embarrassed to say anything.

"Sorry, we won't keep you. Just wanted to say hello, and to let you know we're here to see what we can sort out, you know, about what we talked about yesterday."

"Oh right, nice one." Rachel looked pleased, "good luck!"

"Do you want a lift to the bus stop Rachel?" asked Dan, leaning over Nicole's chest in order to see Rachel's face.

"No, honest, I'm fine – but I'll have to get moving!" she smiled, looking friendly but feeling less so.

"Okay, go on, I'll phone you later, see you."

"See ya," said Rachel, as she began jogging away in the direction of the bus stop.

"Right," said Dan, "let's go and see why this

neighbour of theirs is being such a dick."

*****

Bing Bong.

"Graham," shouted Suzanne up the stairs, to where her husband was resting. "Are you expecting anybody?"

There was no reply. Graham was still in a dreadful mood with his wife, and it hadn't been helped since Suzanne had come home from Rachel's a few minutes earlier and played back the voice recording, smugly announcing that she had concrete evidence that the attack had nothing to do with her. It had come as a relief to Suzanne though, she was delighted by the outcome. She really wanted Rachel to become her best friend.

"Gra-ham!" she shouted again as the doorbell rang a second time. He ignored her once again. Suzanne opened the door, her first impression of the two visitors was that they were police, C.I.D officers, although they looked quite young. Straight away, she wondered how they knew about the attack, and worried that the perpetrators will be back now that the police are involved.

"Hello?" said Suzanne. She was smiling but she was quite visibly concerned by the presence of the unexpected visitors.

"Hello," said Nicole as Dan nodded his greeting, "We're very sorry to trouble you. We're from the council, we're just checking with everybody that things are okay with the new neighbours and everything?" Nicole was looking beyond Suzanne, into the house slightly as she spoke.

"Er, well – I, I guess so. I'm not really…" Suzanne began coughing and stuttering. This unexpected encounter had taken her by surprise and her mind began racing, wondering what Graham would want her to say. "Er, well if you, do you want to come in a minute?"

"That would be great, thank you." Nicole stepped inside. Dan followed and smiled at Suzanne as he stepped past her. The bruise and cut on her cheek made him do an embarrassing double-take as he stepped past, which made

Suzanne blush.

"I'll get my husband, he's probably the best person to speak to about this matter actually. Please, make yourselves comfortable in here," she showed the visitors through into the lounge. "I'll just go and get him. I won't be a tick."

The lounge was decorated beautifully, and Nicole was massively impressed. Her eyes were scanning the expensive furniture, the bright, fresh décor, the stylish ornaments and the carefully chosen artwork and pictures.

"It's gorgeous!" she whispered to Dan as she sat with her hands on her lap.

"It looks like DFS in here!" whispered Dan out of the side of his mouth.

"Don't be daft!" said Nicole, feeling the material of the sofa.

"Won't be a minute!" shouted Suzanne from the upstairs landing. She burst into the couple's bedroom. "Graham, you need to come downstairs. There are people from the council, they want to know that everything is okay with the new neighbours." Suzanne began pulling at Graham's duvet. "Come on."

"I'm not coming down. Are you insane woman?" asked Graham, he grimaced in pain from his bruised ribs as he spoke.

"This is your big chance to complain, you can tell them what's wrong with the new neighbours that are causing you such misery!" Suzanne was being sarcastic, and she was loving it – knowing that Graham was in no fit state to punish her physically.

"You know I can't go down there! I work in the fucking Chief Exec's department. They will know me from the Town Hall you mad woman!" Graham hissed the words, and the look of anger and disgust that was aimed at his wife was unmistakable.

"So?" said Suzanne, stood at the end of the bed with her arms folded. "You can still tell them about all the things that are stressing you out! Like that man having his TV on too loud on Saturday – or the family across the road bringing their luggage in bin liners. What else was it?"

"You know perfectly well what it is Suzanne!" Snapped Graham, staring impassively towards the wall.

"So come down stairs and tell them all about it. Come on, tell them how the new neighbours made you get yourself arrested, and how you spent a night in jail because of them!"

Graham was visibly becoming more and more agitated by Suzanne's pecking at him. "Suzanne, I already told you. I'm not coming down there. So drop it, you awful little bastard. I should have left you in the gutter where I found you."

"What do you want me to say then? That everything is okay?"

"Tell them, that I will write to them. And I will highlight all of my concerns in the letter." Graham once again scowled as the pain from his chest seared through his torso.

"Fine. Have it your way. They are here to ask you if you have any concerns and you are not prepared to see them. You are a very strange man Graham Ashworth." Suzanne stormed across the bedroom and opened the door, she used all of her will-power to close it gently as she left. Suzanne stepped gracefully down the stairs and breezed through into the lounge where her visitors were sat waiting patiently.

"I'm sorry. My husband isn't up to talking to you today, he isn't well. He said that he will write to you, and put his concerns down in writing."

Nicole looked at Dan, and raised an eyebrow. Dan took the expression as a prompt and began to explain the situation. "Sorry, Mrs..."

"Ashworth. Call me Suzanne."

"Sorry Suzanne. I think we've got ourselves muddled up. We're here to investigate a complaint that somebody has made..."

"Who?" asked Suzanne, the urgency in her voice alarmed her, as well as her guests.

"Well, I'm afraid that we have a duty of care, we can't tell you who has made the complaint, but it is a very serious concern to us, and that is the reason why we have come here today, to see what facts we can gather, and hopefully find a way of resolving matters going forward." Dan had adopted a more serious expression on his face.

Suzanne sat down and looked as though she was about to burst into tears.

"If your husband is ill, we can come back another time, or we can arrange for you to see us at the Town Hall. But it is imperative that we speak to you both and get to the bottom of the situation, and hopefully find a satisfactory resolution."

"Yes, well, of course. But…" Suzanne was stupefied by the revelation, even though she knew that it was her husband's irrational and unreasonable behaviour that had provoked this excruciatingly embarrassing visit.

"You see, our tenants are on a behaviour bond that is so strict, it's probably illegal to be honest, but all of the tenants who have moved into this development have signed the contract," explained Dan. Nicole saw an opportunity to assist her colleague, and took over.

"But what we hadn't bargained for, was the behaviour of the home-owners. Our cock-up, it has to be said. We will be talking to the developers about this matter. But naturally, we want to hear your side, and get a clear picture of what the issues are, if indeed there are any." Nicole ended her sentence with a patronising civil servant smile. Suzanne sat across from Dan and Nicole and looked embarrassed and ashamed. She desperately wanted to come clean, and explain that it had nothing to do with her, that it was her husband. That he's a knob. But she couldn't.

"Is your husband too ill to talk to us now?" asked Dan, hopeful to get something moving today.

"No, he won't come down. I'm really sorry." Suzanne's cheeks were reddening.

"Well, here is my card." said Nicole as she stretched across the coffee table with her business card between two fingers. Suzanne took it and nodded. She could not remember feeling so small and embarrassed, and she wanted nothing more than to confess that it was her husband that had started the trouble with the neighbours and that she had nothing to do with it. But she couldn't say that, she just continued sitting there, looking awkward and embarrassed.

"Give me a call when your husband is feeling better Mrs Ashworth. Can I just take your husband's name for my notes please?" asked Nicole.

"Erm, well just Mr Ashworth will be fine. I'll see that he calls you himself. It's not really got anything to do with me you see, I don't really…"

"Sorry, Mrs Ashworth. It does have something to do with you. We are investigating a complaint about a very serious matter, which could potentially result in people being made homeless through no fault of their own. I cannot impress on you the seriousness of this enough." Dan's tone was quite sharp and his manner abrupt. He was just one vocal notch off his dialogue sounding like a bollocking. It was just enough to make Suzanne snap.

"Right, okay. I've heard enough. To re-cap, it is *not* me that you need to speak to, and I can't make him come downstairs. Now, if you want to go up and talk to him in his bed, then I won't stand in your way – but I won't be spoken to like I've just walked dog dirt all over your new carpet, do you understand me?"

"Well just a sec…" said Nicole, but Suzanne continued to talk, and spoke directly over the housing officer.

"I'm not going to listen to anymore of your bloody lectures. So are you going upstairs, or are you going away?" Suzanne really wasn't in the mood for anything, let alone two irritating civil servants pecking her head about her knob-head of a husband's latest misadventure.

"Well, I…" Nicole was lost for words, Suzanne's outburst had come from nowhere, it was completely unexpected, and was quite conclusive.

"I think we should leave it there for today," said Dan, helping Nicole out. "But please, make sure that your husband gets in touch with us as soon as he is well enough. This matter really does need resolving before other agencies are involved."

"Other agencies, what's that supposed to mean?" asked Suzanne.

"All in good time Mrs Ashworth. We haven't heard

your husband's reasoning for the situation yet, have we?" said Nicole as she stood. "Are you ready Dan?" she asked of her colleague.

"Yes, sure." Dan got to his feet and the three of them stood in a triangle. Suzanne broke the shape up as she headed out of the lounge and into the reception, heading straight for the door and opening it, before Dan and Nicole had caught up with her.

"I'm sorry if you think I'm being objectionable, but when you meet my husband, you'll have a better understanding of the predicament." Said Suzanne as her uninvited guests left.

*****

"Fuck in hell," mumbled Dan as he reached his car.

"Fuck a doodle do," said Nicole as she opened the door and sat down in the passenger seat. Dan slammed his door as he jumped in.

"He won't come and talk to us about it, he leaves his wife, who quite clearly couldn't care less, to try and explain his situation. I'm convinced that stuck up folk live on another planet to the rest of us. No wonder they are so despised by most of the population!" Dan was fuming, he loosened his tie and grabbed a cigarette from his pack, offering one to Nicole. She took it and they both sat and quietly smoked as Dan drove the car back through the development towards the main road.

After a few minutes, Dan broke the silence.

"She knows that her husband's being a twat. What did she mean by "you'll understand once you've met my husband?" Dan asked, not really expecting a reply. Nicole was lost in thought. After a good long puff on her cigarette, she blew the smoke out of the window and replied. "I don't know. She was being really cagey about revealing his name as well, wasn't she?"

"Oh, shit, yeah, I'd forgot about that. What did she say, just call him Mr Ashworth?"

"Something like that. Rachel did say that they were

weird though, so we'll have to give them the benefit of the doubt, and talk to the developers." Nicole looked uneasy.

"Well, I'm not getting involved in that," said Dan. "Fuck that."

"Come on, I thought you were my wing man?" Nicole chucked her cigarette dimp out of the window.

"Bollocks. I'm not listening to that bell end Bill Heston kicking off. He's the scum of the earth and I can't believe the council have done this deal with him. It stinks."

"Please?"

"No, bollocks Nic, not happening. I hate the man. He looks at you like you just shat on his i-phone." Dan was shaking his head.

"Pleeeeease?"

"Forget it Nic. He'll just tell us to move Rachel and her family out. He's a wanker."

"Pleeeeeease?" Nicole's voice was now at its squeakiest. Dan laughed. "I'll do all the talking, please Dan. I want to phone Rachel up and tell her it's all been sorted. She's a bloody star and she doesn't need any of this stress. I really want to help her. But you're stopping me. Because you're nasty. You're doing it deliberately to upset me. You're a very nasty, selfish, mean, horrible man, with terrible personal hygiene issues!" Nicole was grinning and it did the trick. Dan cracked and burst into laughter.

"Good lad Dan! I knew you'd come." Nicole winked at him.

"I've not agreed yet!" said Dan. "I was just laughing at you going on with yourself."

"Yet! See, you said yet – so you've pretty much said that you are going to agree. So that means you've agreed really. Come on." Nicole was excellent at getting her own way, especially with Dan.

"Go on then. But you're buying the pies at dinner." Dan exhaled loudly. He hated Bill Heston with a passion.

"I'll buy you a pie, and I'll chuck in a can of dandelion and burdock."

"You're a right spoilt little cow you, always getting your own way. Your Dad has a lot to answer for."

*****

Dan parked his modest little car amongst the flashy Mercedes, Audi's and BMW's that filled the car park of Bright New Homes office HQ in Didsbury. The building was equally as extravagant as the developer's homes. Dan and Nicole had been here several times in the past few weeks, whilst organising the contracts and tenancy agreements, discussing details and all of the coal-face aspects of the deal. They hadn't had too many direct dealings with the managing director Bill Heston. The money matters were dealt with by officers slightly further up the food chain than Dan and Nicole – they were tasked with general housing officer matters.

"If I park my car at Tesco, it doesn't look that bad, but when I park it here, I get a full on, proper car inferiority complex. It's bonkers."

"It's alright your car, leave it alone. If you had enough money for one of these cars, you wouldn't buy one!" Nicole knew all too well that Dan's interests were travel and life experiences rather than material items, or "marques of distinction" as Auto-Trader labelled such vehicles.

"I know, still makes me feel a bit shite though." Dan held open the door and Nicole walked through.

"Hi Charlotte," said Nicole to the young lady on reception.

"Hi Nicole, Hi Dan, how are you both?"

"Not bad, well, stressed actually! We've got a bit of trouble up at Haughton Park, and we could really do with talking to someone, preferably Bill if he's in?" said Nicole. Dan just stood at the counter, admiring the pretty young receptionist.

"He is, just a sec, I'll give him a call."

"Thanks," said Nicole, as Dan continued to gaze at Charlotte.

"Bill, hi, it's Charlotte. I have Nicole and Dan from Bury Council in reception, they're wondering if you've got a few minutes? Okay, thanks." Charlotte put the phone down.

"Just go up, do you want a coffee?" she asked. Dan

nodded enthusiastically.

"Oh lovely, thanks Charlotte." Said Nicole as she and Dan started walking up the spiral staircase up to the first floor where the managing director's office was situated.

"You need to push your eyes back in!" whispered Nicole as they reached the top.

"I'm in love! Proper true love." Dan was grinning from ear to ear.

"Well, you'll need to park around the corner from now on!" said Nicole, laughing at her colleague's blatant infatuation.

"What are you two giggling about?" asked Bill Heston as they rounded the corner and reached his door.

"Oh. Hello Bill. How are you?" Nicole blushed slightly.

"Hi," said Dan.

"Hello, it's nice to see you, an unexpected pleasure!" said Bill, the comment clearly aimed exclusively to Nicole. He took her hand and kissed it very gently, very slowly. Nicole never meant to, but she made a flirty giggling sound. It made Dan blush with anger.

"Come on in, tell me what your tenants are saying, I bet they think they've won the lottery living at Haughton Park!" Bill laughed loudly as he gestured his visitors through into his office.

"Well actually," said Dan, "We've had an unexpected turn of events."

"Really?" said Bill, still looking up and down at Nicole, paying particular attention to her behind as he closed the door behind his guests.

"Yes. We'd not anticipated this, but the first problem of an anti-social nature that we've encountered has actually come from one of the home-owners."

Bill Heston sat down at his desk, and gestured for Nicole and Dan to sit on the chairs before his large modern smoked glass desk. "Go on," he said. Nicole spent the next few minutes describing the issues, and then told Bill about thereception that they had received at the house. Bill looked quite bemused. He wasn't annoyed, and he didn't appear very concerned.

Dan felt that Nicole had made a good job of explaining the situation, but he was frustrated that the multi-millionaire boss of Bright New Homes didn't appear to be taking the matter seriously enough. Charlotte came in and left a tray with three cups of coffee and some cookies, along with sugar and milk.

"Thanks pet." Said Bill Heston as the receptionist turned to leave.

"So, naturally, we're taking it very seriously." Said Dan, in a bid to get the problem of the weird home-owner back into discussion. "I mean, our tenants are on good behaviour bonds that read like they've just been let out of a mental hospital. But the home-owners themselves need to play fair if this is going to work." Dan didn't care much for the MD that he was talking to, and had little problem with speaking down to him. The way that he had delivered that line was a little too condescending for the businessman. Bill Heston suddenly looked enraged. His face turned a shocking shade of red as he sat up in his executive leather chair. The relaxed, happy-go-lucky style that he normally seemed to exude was gone. Bill looked like Dan had just called his mum an ugly slag.

"Whoa, whoa, whoa there young man!" he snapped. "Is it April the bloody first? Is this a joke?"

"I can assure you that it isn't a joke, Mr Heston," Nicole leapt in before Dan had the chance to make matters any worse with his typically tetchy style.

"Well, it sounds like a joke! And not a good joke either. Now, it seems to me that you're experiencing difficulties already, and you're turning it around on us, trying to frame my customers for anti-social behaviour on Haughton Park?" Bill did a loud, exaggerated, humourless laugh. There were a few seconds of awkward silence before Nicole tried to speak again, but Bill cut her up just as her mouth opened.

"You see, my customers are the opposite end of the social spectrum to your customers. Oh, sorry I meant your *service users*. My customers are the strivers, the winners, and go-getters. They all earn in excess of fifty thousand pounds per year, and they have highly skilled, highly regarded, professional occupations. Your service users sponge off the welfare state and lie around, smoking roll up cigarettes and watching Jeremy Kyle all day. The men all stand around in public with their hands down their trousers, playing with their genitals while the women go off to the shops in their pyjamas! These are basic facts that I'm saying to you. Now who am I supposed to believe here? Your people, or my people?" He glared furiously across his desk at the two dumbfounded council employees.

Dan and Nicole had never seen Bill Heston in anything but an amiable mood before, he had always been perfectly charming, displaying a very affable personality. But this outburst forced them both to rethink that impression. It was almost as though the man was displaying schizophrenic tendencies, his eyes didn't have that casual and carefree smile within them. He looked psychotic.

"You've taken this a bit too much to heart," Dan was quite stern in the way that he spoke.

"No I haven't!" snapped Bill Heston. As he said it, a tiny bit of spittle flew through the air and Dan saw that it had landed on him. Bill saw it too, but neither man acknowledged it.

"Mr Heston," said Nicole, quietly and calmly, attracting a glance from Bill, who still looked absolutely livid. "We have visited the home-owner responsible and he has flatly refused to talk to us, and he told his wife that he would write to us about it. We're here to ask you, for the sake of everybody at Haughton Park – not just our tenants, but your customers too, will you please try and have a chat with them? Just to relieve tensions. The police have actually arrested the man in question." Nicole knew that this information would shake things up. Bill Heston looked perfectly astounded at the revelation.

"What, wait a... just wait a minute. Slow down, this is all getting too much. Who exactly are we talking about?" Bill's aggression seemed to have reseeded, and the unhealthy colour in his face lessened slightly, suggesting that his blood pressure was dropping a little.

"We don't really know. His wife said he is called Mr Ashworth." Said Nicole. "As I say, they weren't too helpful, either of them."

"Well, he wouldn't even come down the stairs to talk to us," said Dan.

"Ashworth did you say? What was the address?" asked Bill Heston, by now looking quite intrigued by the situation, and as though he was trying to picture the Ashworth customer.

"It was… oh, er just wait, I have it here," Nicole flicked through her paperwork. "Number nine, Fir Trees Grove."

Bill Heston didn't have to think for very long. He was thinking about Suzanne Ashworth within an instant.

"Ah, yes, Suzanne and, er," Bill started to click his fingers as he tried to think of the man's name. "You should know him, he works at your place," said Bill. "He's a big knob."

"Yes, that's why we're here," muttered Dan.

"Graham! That's it, Graham Ashworth. He's been in trouble recently for sending inappropriate e-mails to councillors about this deal. God, it's all beginning to make sense now. No wonder he wouldn't see you." Bill began nodding, it was as though he wanted to start all over again with this conversation.

"I can't think who he is," said Nicole.

"I can," said Dan. "Top floor. He's in the Chief Exec's department. Fat, walks like he's shat himself. Total sleaze-bag. Looks at all the female staff a bit rapey."

"Alright, bloody hell Dan!" Nicole suppressed a laugh at her colleague's less than complimentary description.

"Right. Look. Can I apologise?" Bill stood up, as though to add greater sincerity to his apology. He had his arms spread open. "This is all beginning to make sense. The man is a thorn in our side. He has been since we suggested supporting the council with this scheme. Leave this to me, I'll have his colleagues put him right."

"Well, okay, this has all got very weird," said Nicole.

"Forget it, it's sorted. I'll have Graham Ashworth under no illusion that he had better buck his ideas up, or he'll be looking for a new employer. I'm not mucking around here." Bill Heston had returned to his usual, calm self. The character transition was bizarre, and it made Dan wonder if he could manage to get him to change back into a psycho again, not only for his own amusement, but for the sake of Rachel Birdsworth and her young family.

"Well, let's cut the crap Bill. We need to give assurances to our tenants, the ones who have made this complaint, that we have spoken to you, and that you are committed to putting a stop to it." Dan spoke with a sternness in his voice, but it did not cause a reaction. Bill just stayed silent for a few seconds, he stared out of the window beyond his visitors.

"Okay. You guys, get your coffee. I will type you a letter now, have a drink, have a biscuit, and I'll give you a written confirmation in a few minutes. What's the tenant called?"

"Rachel Birdsworth," replied Nicole.

With that, Bill sat back down at his desk and started typing furiously into his keyboard, completely ignoring the two council employees. After a few minutes, the typing got louder, and Dan began nudging Nicole, trying to make her laugh as Bill's typing got angrier and angrier with each new paragraph. Nicole managed to avoid eye contact with Dan, and sat looking at Bill's tropical fish tank. A few more minutes passed until Bill stood once again, and headed out of the room.

"That should just be coming out of the printer a round about now." He walked out of the office. When he came back, thirty seconds later, he signed the letter at the bottom and handed it across the desk to Nicole. She held it up for Dan to read.

Dear Rachel,
I have been informed by my colleagues at Bury Council of the unacceptable behaviour of one of our customers. I take this matter very seriously.

I will speak to this customer, and will endeavour to seek an immediate and definite end to the matter. I cannot apologise enough, and I am personally going to pay you the sum of £500 compensation for this unpleasantness. I believe that this figure equates to one month's rent.

Bright New Homes are committed to ensuring that the Haughton Park development is a happy and harmonius place to live. That was always my vision, and it is a vision that I take seriously, not only for my customers, but for the tenants too.

If you have any further problems, I will endeavour to deal with them zealously and dexterously.

Warm regards

Bill Heston
Managing Director
Bright New Homes

Nicole finished reading first and looked up at Bill.
"What do you think?" he asked, handing over the £500 cheque.
"You spelt harmonious wrong." Said Dan.

Chapter 16

It had been a long hard shift at the wallpaper factory, but Mick was pleased that he'd got three hours overtime in. The family really needed the money now that they'd spent most of the savings. Time and a half on eight pounds fifty an hour wasn't to be sniffed at, and Mick was pleased that next week's pay packet would have an extra thirty quid in it, at least. It was only Tuesday – there could well be more overtime available throughout the week, it certainly seemed busy enough.

Mick was enjoying the walk home in the sunshine, feeling quite optimistic about the future for the first time in quite a while. He was tired though, and glad to be nearing home, he was thirsty and ready for a rest.

"Alright mate?" shouted Kev along the avenue as he saw Mick approaching.

Fuck's sake, thought Mick as he looked up and saw his neighbour, stood with a can of Stella Artois in his hand. "Oh, yeah, alright." Mick showed little enthusiasm as he walked onto his own driveway, trying to leave it at that. But it was obvious that Kev wanted a word.

"Have you got a minute mate, I need a hand moving summat."

Mick made it pretty clear with his facial expression that he wasn't really interested. "I've just finished work mate. I'm done in." He shouted back across the lawn of the dividing house as he reached his front door.

"Aw come on. I only need an 'and for a minute. Come on, don't be a cunt," said Kev. Mick started walking reluctantly towards his neighbour, determined to nip any of this unwanted friendliness in the bud. He didn't need the aggravation of getting to know these kinds of people. The kind of people that boast that they used to be Hacienda bouncers. Manchester has many thousands of ex-Hacienda bouncers. To Mick, it seemed that more people claimed to have worked on the door of the city's infamous nightclub, than actually went inside the place.

"Not very nice, that." Said Kev, as Mick got closer to

him on the drive. He was wearing a sarcastic grin on his face, and he seemed pretty pleased with himself.

"You what?"

"You, being all moody. If that's the thanks I get for sorting that shithouse out over there, I can't believe I bothered." Kev's cheerful expression disappeared and he began to look really pissed off, staring aggressively at Mick.

Mick wasn't about to back down. He didn't know this Kev, but he wasn't going to back down from him. If this Kev character was testing the water, thought Mick, then he's going to get wet. Mick locked stares with his neighbour.

"Tell you what mate, if you call me a cunt again, I'll bite your fucking nose off." Mick banged two sturdy fingers against Kev's chest, tap-tapping him hard enough to let him know that if he wanted a fight, this was the time to throw a punch. If he didn't, it was time to shut the fuck up. Mick kept his stare locked as the force from his fingers forced Kev to step backwards. Mick's face was fixed, his glare was scary and the vein on his temple was pulsating, like a worm that was trying to wriggle off his face. Kev caught on very quickly that he'd started giving abuse to the wrong person. He'd received Mick's message loud and clear.

Kev broke the locked stares, smiled and then laughed, releasing his shoulders as he did so. It was a long, exaggerated laugh, and Mick knew the expression well enough to see that his neighbour was struggling to snap out of a "oh shit, what do I do now?" moment.

"Ha ha, see, I knew you was one of us. Just wanted to see if you had a bit of a back bone on ya mate. People like us, we don't take any shit do we? Nice one. Ha ha, you had me at it there pal. What did you say your name was?" Kev took a sip from his beer can, and his hand was shaking noticeably.

Mick kept his face locked, he wanted there to be no doubt in Kev's mind that he was a serious bloke. He genuinely didn't want any associations with this person whatsoever. This was a golden opportunity to break any connection with the dickhead before anything further could come of it. "I told you my name the other day. Anyway, I'm going home now.

Sort your head out speaking to me like that yeah? In fact, just don't talk to me at all. Right?"

"He ar mate, there's no need for all this. I've just got that fucking dick sorted out over there – and this is the appreciation you've showed me?"

"I don't know fuck all about that. I don't owe you fuck all, so whatever you're trying to blag me about, you can forget it." Mick turned, and started walking slowly away from Kev. He knew that if anything was going to come back at him, it would be now whilst his back was turned. He continued walking, expecting to be jumped, or punched, or to have that can of lager thrown at the back of his head. He was ready.

But nothing happened. Mick walked slowly up the avenue, swaggering past the house that divided them. As he reached his own drive, he turned to look at Kev, but he had gone inside. Mick sniggered to himself as he reached his front door and went inside.

*****

"He is a fucking dead man!" shouted Kev as he slammed his door shut. It shook the whole house.

"What? What the fuck is that, stop slamming the doors Kev, you egg belly bastard."

"Shut up you, you fat old boot."

"Hoi, I'll smash your fucking head in with this iron. You can't be slamming the doors, we've got to look after the house. Why are you such a twat Kev? Just answer me that. I think you need your head seeing to." Tania was fuming. She knew that it was going to be hard work living in a nice house with her idiot husband. She felt the anxiety suffocate her.

"Shut your face."

"No you shut your face Kev. I'm sick of it." Tania was stood right in front of her husband, holding the steaming hot iron. "Honestly, I am. Sick to death of you being a dick, slamming doors and all that. You'll get us kicked out for that, and then what are we meant to do? Just try and act normal for once in your life."

"They can't fucking kick us out for shutting a door loud. Get over it Tania, Jesus, you're doing me nut in."

"Well why was you slamming the door anyway?" It hadn't occurred to Tania to ask her husband what was wrong, she was so angry about the way he showed such disrespect to this beautiful new house.

"Nowt." Said Kev, grabbing another can of lager from the fridge. "Just that dick from next door but one. He's full of himself, thinks his shit smells like Lynx he does."

"Why, what's been said?" Tania looked concerned.

"Not much, he just offered me out."

"Aw for fucks sake Kev. Why are you such a knob?"

"Oh, so automatically it's my fault?" Kev looked hurt.

"Fucking right it is. Go in there and stay out of my face. I'm going to get you put down, you make me hate life."

"Fuck off."

"No, you fuck off. I wish you would, I wish you'd been knocked off Strangeways roof when they were firing those hose pipes at you!"

*****

"Hi honey, I'm home!" shouted Mick as he closed the door behind himself.

"Alright Dad?" shouted Liam.

"There you are!" Rachel marched through from the kitchen. "Where've you been love?" she asked.

"Got a bit of overtime in. It's dead busy, and a few lads have been off, so I got three hours in." Mick raised both of his hands in the air and mouthed "yes!"

"Aw, nice one love. That'll come in useful!"

"There's probably going to be more. Hope so anyway, need to sort out a better settee than those flipping chairs. They kill your arse after a bit. I just want summat I can flop out on after work."

"Do you wanna brew love?" she asked as she gave Mick a kiss on the lips and grabbed his butty bag off him.

"Na, do you know what, I'm gonna have a big

massive glass of cordial. My mouth's as dry as a nun's muff."

"Michael!" said Rachel, in exaggerated offence as she walked through into the kitchen. Mick followed.

"I have officially had the weirdest day of my life. Starting this morning, I had a visitor."

"Oh aye, her from across the road?" asked Mick, he was planning to ask Rachel if she knew anything about what had been going on with the weirdos over the road.

"Yeah, she came over, bold as brass, asking me why I'd arranged for her husband to get beaten up!" Rachel poured vimto into a glass and ran it under the cold tap.

"Get out! She thinks it were you?" he shook his head and wiped his hand over his face.

"Yeah, well, that's what she asked me. So I said it's got jack shit to do with us, and then guess what she did!" Rachel grinned as she handed the glass to Mick.

"Dunno?" said Mick, but Rachel could tell he was desperate to know from the bemused expression on his face.

"She lifted her top up right, and there was one of those straps, you know like what you put heart monitors and stuff on with, well there was a phone strapped to her chest, recording everything that we were saying – he'd obviously sent her over to get a confession! He must think his beating was down to us."

"What. Wait a sec." Mick looked completely puzzled by what Rachel was saying. It took him a few seconds to figure it out. After a short while, he continued speaking,

"So, if she's come over here, accusing you and trying to record you doing a confession – why would she lift her top up and show you?" Mick was still completely baffled by the story.

"I don't know! It doesn't make any sense!"

"Unless, he made her do it," Mick pointed over in the direction of their neighbours house.

"Well, yeah, clever dick. That's obvious – but why would she show it me – what's she trying to prove by that?"

"Well, I don't know. All I know is, they are as a mad as a bag of wasps. You have binned her off, haven't you love?"

"Yeah, I said to her as she was going, I said we need to stay apart from now on. She looked gutted. I think she was crying as she went home."

"Bunny boiler!"

"Aw, don't Mick, I really feel sorry for her. She's a lost soul." Rachel looked quite sad as she looked at Mick.

"Oh, no way, speaking of absolute dickheads, guess what that goon from up the road has just been saying!" Mick had a wide grin as he remembered his conversation with Kev.

"Who?"

"That cabbage from a few doors up. Kev Soprano."

"Oh, why what's he said?" Rachel suddenly looked worried.

"I was just walking up the street, and he's shouting "give us a lift to move summat," so I was like "leave it out mate, I've just finished work." So he shouts "don't be a cee word. So I went over and told him off. He shat himself." Mick laughed at the memory of Kev's face when he realised he'd cocked up.

"Aw Mick, what did you do?" Rachel looked really concerned.

"Nowt, just told him that I don't want nowt to do with him."

"Is that all you said?" Rachel knew that her partner had a bit of a temper at times. Mick downed the rest of the vimto and forced an appreciative burp out, then wiped his mouth with his sleeve before replying.

"Yeah, honest. I just advised him that if he calls me a cee word again, I'll bite his nose off." Mick laughed at Rachel's look of disapproval. "Don't be like that love, he was over stepping the mark. It's dealt with now, he knows where the line is, and he won't be crossing it again. Job done."

"Well," said Rachel, looking suddenly very stressed and anxious. "I think there's a problem. Shit."

"What?" asked Mick, folding his arms and leaning back against the kitchen worktop.

"They came round here earlier, him and his wife Tania. They said they've got the neighbour problem under control, but we owe them two hundred and fifty quid."

"You what?" Mick's face changed from humour to anger in the blink of an eye.

"They said they had to pay some people to sort it out, and as we're benefiting, we should give them half."

"What did you say?" Mick looked really annoyed.

"I said okay." Rachel looked down at the floor as she spoke.

"Aw, fuck off mate. You didn't did you love? That's what he'll have been going on about it for. Right, well fuck him. He's not having jack shit. If they come to the door again, tell them they need to speak to me." Mick placed his glass down and started walking out of the kitchen. "I'm going for a shower love, I smell like John McCririck's jock strap."

"Mick, wait. I gave him the money." The anxiety was clear in Rachel's voice. Mick stopped walking, paused a second or two, before turning around. His face had gone bright red.

"Are you being serious?" Mick was furious, there was absolutely no mistake about it.

"I just, well, I didn't think."

"I've been doing two bastard jobs to get the money together for this move, and you've given it to that dick? Why?" Mick hated being unpleasant to Rachel, but this had seriously annoyed him. He just couldn't keep his views silent.

"I just thought it would be best to keep the peace. I'll go round now and get it. It's fine."

"Nah, I'll go round and get it. That's an absolute fuck up that Rach. Seriously." Mick stomped off and slammed the front door behind him.

"Shit." Said Rachel, realising that she'd been so caught up in her story about what a weird day she'd had, that she'd forgotten to tell Mick about the random cheque for five hundred quid that had been posted through while she was at the RSPCA.

"Shit." She headed to the back door and lit a cigarette.

*****

"What a fucking idiot!" said Mick under his breath as he marched down his drive.

He walked quickly along the street, and then turned sharply as he reached Kev and Tania's driveway. He kept pressing the bell, and also banged on the door, in much the same way that Kev had knocked on Mick and Rachel's own door on Sunday morning. There was no answer, and Mick gave it another few bangs. There was still no answer after a further thirty seconds had passed. Mick saw that the car was on the drive, and it was only about five minutes since he'd been talking to Kev.

Mick tried the door handle. It offered no resistance as he pushed down on it. The door began to open, and Mick stepped confidently inside.

"Kev!" he shouted. "Kev!"

"Hey, what are you doing? You don't just walk into people's houses like that," said Tania as she appeared from the front room. Her voice was raised but she looked slightly scared. Her face was bright red.

"Didn't you hear me knocking on the door, and ringing the bell? Where's Kev?" said Mick, offering no doubt whatsoever that he was unhappy.

"He's gone out. He's not here." Tania was bulging her eyes out, trying to appear sincere. But it wasn't working, Mick knew that she was lying.

"I don't believe you. You know why I'm here. I want my money back, so just pass it here, or I swear down, you and Kev are going to wish you'd never seen me."

"Alright, I'll get you the money, it's no big deal – we just thought you'd want to chip in, since you're benefitting from it."

"I'm not benefitting from fuck all. Just give me back my money, and tell your bad man husband to stop hiding under the stairs or wherever he is."

"He's not, he's gone out. I swear down."

"Right, well, whatever. Has he left my money?"

"I'm looking for it now. That's what I was doing when you was knocking on. Kev told me you'd spat your dummy out. We was expecting you."

"So he is here?"

"He's not. For fucks sake – he's gone out."

"The car's still on the drive."

"He's gone to the shop."

"The shop's about two fucking miles away."

"He's not here love." Tania looked frustrated at having to keep repeating herself.

"Well, listen. I want my money back, and I don't want you thinking that we owe you anything."

"Wait, your missus was being sound about it. It's nothing snide, we just thought you'd want to put in."

"Well, I don't want to put in. I wish my missus hadn't got involved the other night. I just want my money back, give me my money back." Mick was getting angrier and his voice was getting louder – he was stressed out that he was having to have this argument with Kev's wife.

But right then, Kev appeared from the front room, and he was holding a carving knife.

"Tell you what mate, come and fucking get your money, yeah?" he said with a psychotic grin on his face.

"Kev! What the fuck are you doing, put that down you dickhead!" screamed Tania, as she walked across to the doorway and stood in Kev's way. "Fuck off, put it away you stupid twat." Screamed Tania.

"Get out of my way, if this fucker wants to come round here, giving us shit, he can have a stab mark." Kev looked a bit wobbly, a mixture of adrenaline and the strong lager that he'd been drinking were clearly having an effect.

Mick had one rule, which was to never back down. But this situation was escalating far too quickly and he realised that he needed to get out of there, he knew only too well that some of the worst things happen when drunks have hold of knives.

"Come on then, if you want your money, come and get it." Kev was shouting, his eyes were wild and it was clear that his nutter button had been flicked onto maximum. Tania was visibly scared as she stood in between her husband, and Mick who was stood in the doorway that separated the lounge and the hallway. Mick was panicked, he couldn't think straight. This knife changed everything, and his mind was racing – he was frozen, unsure of what to do.

"Come on, you fucking hard man, come and get your fuckin' money!" shouted Kev. He was moving forward, pushing against his wife who was battling to keep him restrained. He was waving the knife above her head, and it was pretty obvious that he'd lost the plot.

"Tell you what, yeah, I'm just going to go home. But I want my money back, and I will fucking get it back, make no mistake Kev."

"You can fuck off, alright pal. You ungrateful cunt! Fuck off!"

Mick walked backwards, out of the house and onto the doorstep. He grabbed the door handle and closed it slowly, calmly before he turned and ran quickly back to his house.

"Where's the key?" he shouted as he burst into the house and slammed the door behind him. Quick, we need to lock the door!"

"What's going on?" shouted Rachel from the backdoor step, holding a cigarette in her hand.

"He's pulled a fucking knife."

"Aw for fuck's sake!" she stubbed the cigarette out against the back wall and slammed the back door shut.

"I know. Are all the kids in?"

"Liam, Noel, Shania, Britney! Are you in?"

"Yes," shouted Noel.

"Who is?" shouted Rachel up the stairs.

"Where's my bat?" asked Mick, his eyes were wide and he was in a state of panic.

"I'm in," shouted Shania from the landing.

"Liam's playing football down the street." Shouted Noel.

"I'm on the toilet!" shouted Britney.

Mick unlocked the front door and inched out – looking out towards Kev's house. There was no sign of him, or Tania. It was all quiet on the street. He couldn't see Liam, there was no game of football taking place.

"Noel, phone our Liam, and ask him where he is please," shouted Mick up the stairs as he locked the front door again. "Make sure that back door's locked Rach." He shouted through into the kitchen.

"It is, shit! This is really bad. What the fuck is this place?" asked Rachel.

"It's alright, he's not come out. He's pissed up – just acting up. It's nothing." Said Mick, staring out of the front window in the direction of Kev's house, and looking down the street to see if Liam was wandering up the avenue.

"Dad, he's at that new mates house on the next avenue, do you want him home?" shouted Noel from the top of the stairs.

"Nah, it's alright – just tell him to stay there, tell him he's to phone you when he sets off coming home."

"Alright dad, no hassle."

Mick spent the next hour or so pacing around the house, constantly wandering in and out of the front door to see if Kev had come out.

*****

Tania was fuming.

"Aw Kev, why are you such a bell end? You're going to get us kicked out of here, and you're going to get a fucking thick lip as well, carrying on like that."

"Thick lip, have you heard yourself? Who's going to give me a fucking thick lip? You're going soft on me you." Kev laughed mockingly as he stood in the kitchen and drank the last of the lager in his can.

"And you better put that carving knife down as well, in case the dibble end up coming here."

"The dibble! Tania, you've lost it you. You're turning into one of them soft arses. Give yer head a wobble and get back to normal, I can't stand you acting like Princess fucking Diana."

"Princess Diana? What are you on about?" Tania was not impressed with Kev's attitude at present.

"You – you're acting like a fucking saint, it's proper weird."

"I'll tell you what's weird, you fat cunt. Weird is you

threatening Johnny Booth's mate with a carving knife."

"Johnny Booth?" Kev suddenly looked alert, though his drunken frown remained, making the crease of his forehead push down onto the bridge of his nose.

"You don't know your arse from your elbow! You're telling me that you didn't fucking notice Johnny Booth emptying that Mick's stuff out of his van on Saturday?"

"That weren't Johnny Booth, you…"

"Kev, shut the fuck up. You're pissed, and you're acting like a proper dick. Now shut your mouth, and give me that money. I'll go and take it round, and try to make the peace. You, go to bed or something. Try and choke to death in your sleep."

Tania was getting close to slapping her husband across the face, his behaviour since he'd been given this house was becoming more stupid by the day. It was as though he had conned himself that it was his house, not a bloody council rent, thought his wife.

"It wasn't Johnny Booth though…"

"It was. But let's just say I'm wrong, for the first time in my life. Are you going to chance it?"

Kev's smug grin was fading quickly. "Well, if you're dead certain?"

"Just give me the money, you twat."

*****

Tania knocked quietly and politely on Mick and Rachel's.

Mick ran upstairs and opened the bedroom window fully to see who it was, and more to the point, to see if it was Kev, and whether or not he was armed. He was relieved to see that it was Tania. She had an apologetic look on her face.

"Let us in a minute please love, I've brought your money." Tania held up the wad of notes in her hand. Mick just nodded, and then his head disappeared from the window.

Tania could hear his feet pounding down the stairs. Seconds later, the door opened, and Tania was welcomed into the house by a very tense looking Mick, and a very angry

Rachel.

"Look, I'm really sorry. He's losing it, honestly – that was bang out of order love. But he's been told, there'll be nothing else said about it." Tania handed the money over to Mick.

"He wants to watch it, pulling fucking knives out…" Mick was clearly unimpressed. Rachel on the other hand was glad that Tania had come round, and that she'd brought the money.

"Thanks, I really appreciate you coming."

Tania's eyes flicked up and locked on to Rachel's.

"It's alright, don't thank me. I just can't believe he's acting like this, he's losing the plot. Honestly." Tania was keen to distance herself from the actions of her husband.

"Right, listen yeah, thanks for the money. But let's just leave it at that. We're having a fucking nightmare on this street, and we don't want nowt to do with anyone." Mick was scowling at Tania, in much the same way that he had been when his head appeared at the bedroom window a moment earlier.

"Thing is," said Rachel, "I didn't think when I gave you that money. But Mick's right. We didn't ask you to pay people to sort anything out, and it's not like we're loaded." Rachel felt a lot more confident with Mick here. She had been too much of a push-over earlier, and she felt stupid for handing the money over.

"And it's not our problem, anyway!" added Mick, quite sarcastically. "I mean, if Rachel had just watched on from the window, and stopped you's from falling in the trap, you'd have got arrested and you'd have been kicked out by now anyway. So it's you who should be round here, owing us a fucking favour – not the other way around."

"I know, I know, seriously, honest. It's okay, I get it. He's been drinking beer in the garden all day. I understand, we just don't want any trouble ourselves. You know what I mean?" Tania was trying her best to be nice and make the peace but Mick and Rachel just couldn't warm to her at all.

"Yes, we know what you mean," said Rachel, "we

wish we'd never been picked for these houses to be honest. So, no offence but we're just keeping our heads down now."

"That means don't come back round here again, and tell your husband the same thing." Mick was talking in an aggressive and to-the-point manner.

"Well thanks for being so understanding about it. If he carries on acting like such a numpty, Kev will be out on his arse, and I mean that. I can't stand the fat bastard."

Mick opened the door and held it at the top. Tania walked through the gap, beneath his arm, and smiled awkwardly as she left.

"Seeya." Said Rachel, sombrely. Mick closed the door.

"Right. Sorted. And nobody got killed."

"Mick, I'm really sorry – but you only heard half of my story. I was telling you about my day,"

"Yeah, sorry, I got distracted when you said you'd given that dick two hundred and fifty quid!" said Mick, still looking annoyed at Rachel.

"Well, the reason I was so relaxed about giving that money over was because of this." She held the cheque out for Mick to get hold of. "This was the next bit of my story." Rachel handed Mick the letter. He stood and read it, and began laughing. Rachel burst out laughing too.

"Oh, you dick! You still shouldn't have give them that money though!"

"I know. Well, I was just giddy, but as soon as you pointed it out, I realised what a stupid thing it was to do. Soz Mick."

"Don't matter babe! We're fucking loaded! Ha ha mint! Come on, get the internet on and let's get a settee sorted out. I've been on that buy and sell page for the last few days and there's nowt good on them sites. Do they have loot anymore?"

"Loot? I doubt it. Look on eBay or try that Gumtree site."

"Finally, summat good's happened!" said Mick, sniffing his armpit and gagging at the smell. "I'm just going for a shower."

Chapter 17

A FEW WEEKS LATER

Rachel hated Saturday nights. Not too many years earlier, in the old house, it had been her favourite night of the week. All of the family would be sat around watching TV or films, piles of sweets, bottles of pop, bowls of crisps and popcorn, duvets and pillows were everywhere. Mick would have a few tins of beer and Rachel would have a bottle of red wine and it would be the most relaxing and fun night of the week. Saturdays had always been a really good laugh.

But as the kids had grown older, and found their own social engagements to attend on Saturday nights', and particularly since Mick had started his cash-in-hand job on weekend nights after the fire, Saturday evenings had become quite a lonely and miserable time for Rachel, and she dreaded it.

There was only her and Shania in the house, and Shania spent most of the time staring gormlessly at her tablet, so Saturday nights had slowly but surely become ironing and laundry night. And as Rachel hung the ironing on hangers all over the downstairs door handles, ready for the kids to take up to their respective wardrobes, she realised with a judder that this was her third Saturday in the house.

"God, that's flown!" she muttered to herself as she packed the ironing board away and stacked the undies on the stairs.

The boys, Liam and Noel were staying at their gran's overnight, as they'd been out with their friends back home on the Gameshawe Estate, and Maureen had no problem with them staying over. Britney, arrived home just after eleven. She looked like she'd had a sip or two of the cider or whatever it was that had been handed around.

"I'm juzz gonna go bed, really tired..." she said, in a small and quiet voice.

"Yes, you do look tired, love. Go on, get yourself up to bed, a good nights sleep will do you wonders!" said Rachel, deliberately encouraging and nurturing her teenage daughter's belief that her mother had been born yesterday. Rachel always thought that if she allowed the kids to think that she was as thick as pig shit, they wouldn't feel that they had to be too conniving or sly.

Once Britney had got herself upstairs and ready for bed, and Rachel had finished hanging the last load of washing on the radiators, Mick finally arrived home, just after midnight. After fixing him up with a can of lager, his favourite comedy on television and his tea on his lap, Rachel went out and stood on the doorstep to have her last cigarette of the day before turning in.

It was a cool, still night. There was no traffic, no aeroplanes were coming in to land, or taking off from the airport. It was just really still, and silent. It wasn't very often that you could enjoy complete peace and quiet in Greater Manchester, but this was a rare, satisfying moment, thought Rachel as she put her cigarette between her lips and flicked the wheel on her lighter, inhaling the satisfying smoke deeply and blowing it out slowly.

The street was eerily quiet, there wasn't a soul around and Rachel was determined to enjoy this moment of tranquillity as best she could, before going off to bed. She looked up as the bedroom light came on at the house across the road, and Suzanne looked like she was running past the window, which made Rachel smile. What the fuck is she up to now? She wondered as she blew the cigarette smoke out of her nose. Then Graham was right behind her, and he looked like he was running too. The shadows were flickering in the room and Rachel felt her insides somersault as it registered that this wasn't right. Graham was attacking Suzanne. Was he? Nah, they're just pissing about. No, he's properly kicking the shit out of her. Her mind was racing, but Rachel couldn't be sure what she was witnessing. She stood a few seconds longer, taking a long, deep draw on her cigarette, keeping her eyes fixed on the light from the upstairs window across the road. Right then, she saw Graham dragging his wife across the room by her hair. Rachel thought she heard a scream, a very short, muffled scream. Another shadow appeared, and it looked like a punch was being thrown.

Rachel felt sick, her adrenaline had kicked in and before she knew what was happening she was across the road, and she was trying to open the front door. It was locked. Rachel then found herself opening the gate at the side of the house, she was running around to the back door, in the next blink she was inside the house, there was banging, shouting, screaming, and she was running up the stairs.

Suzanne was sobbing. Graham was shouting, it wasn't clear what he was shouting, it was all just a noisey blur, Rachel's heart-beat was the loudest thing she could hear as she reached the top of the stairs. She saw a metal thing, holding one of the doors open, she bent down quietly and picked it up.

God, it's heavy, she thought. Her heart beat was booming in her chest, and twice as loud in her head. Graham was still shouting,

"You got me sacked you bitch!" he shouted as his wife struggled on the floor. Suzanne was sobbing and screaming and pleading and wriggling about hysterically beside the bed, trying to get away from her attacker.

Rachel entered the room silently. Suzanne was cowering at the side of the bed, one arm was raised above her head. That was when the kick went in. Graham kicked his wife in the face like he was kicking a football across a park. She was knocked out cold, long before she landed on her back in a pile on the floor. She looked dead. It looked as though Graham had killed her.

The squelching thud noise of the kick had made Rachel sick, it was an involuntary reaction, and she had vomit all down her chin and down her front as she reached Graham. She had raised the metal thing up and it was above his head. Just as she was about to pull the object down with full force against the back of his head, Graham heard the ghastly noises of vomit, choking and terror that were coming from Rachel. He turned slowly, and had a scared, startled look in his eyes as Rachel smashed the object against the side of his head. The impact made a horrific squishing, cracking noise. He fell to the floor, landing with a thunderous thump beside his wife.

Then there was nothing. Just silence. From a room filled with chaos, noise and violence just seconds earlier, now there was nothing but a very instant, very intense silence.

A thick, richly coloured stream of blood began pouring from Graham's ear.

"Holy fuck… holy… fuck… holy fuck. Shit." Rachel couldn't catch her breath. She was staring down at the scene that lay before her on the bedroom floor. She looked around the room, the place was a tip, clothes, duvets and pillows were scattered all over the floor. There was a suitcase open, on its side, more clothes were situated all around it and sticking out of the sides. Rachel looked up, and noticed that she was in full view of the street. Centre stage, stood in the spotlight. She walked over to the window and drew the curtains shut.

"Shit. Aw fucking hell, shit," she was muttering, her breathing was heavy and fast, Rachel sounded like she was having an asthma attack. Suddenly, without warning her legs gave way, and she fell down to her knees, and hunched over on all fours. She vomited. A big, deep thrust from way down in her guts forced out with a ferocious retching noise and then, with it followed a thick, violent burst of sick. Then came another retch.

"Fucking hell," she tried to say, as another intense blast of vomit threw her words off course. Rachel was on all fours, beside two bodies, puking her stomach contents out, with snot and tears and sweat running freely off her head and dripping onto the puddle of sick on the bedroom carpet.

She was already shivering and shaking uncontrollably as she waited for the next deep wave of nausea to come, but now she noticed that she felt cold. A freezing cloak of sweat had covered her, from her thighs to her shoulders, Rachel was trembling, she felt as though she was inside a freezer at Tesco. But her head and her face were burning up.

"Aw God. Wake up." She reached out and shook Suzanne's shoulder. There was nothing, just nothing. "Aw fuck. Shit!" Rachel managed to pull herself together slightly. She wiped her eyes with the sleeve of her sweater. She wiped again, across her mouth, and again over her nose. All she could smell and taste was the fetid, acidic vomit.

"Come on, come on," she said to herself, pushing her small frame up from the all fours position and trying to stand. Her legs were weak, her entire body was trembling and the snot kept pouring as though she was just stepping out from the surf of the Mediterranean sea.

"Come on," she continued saying to herself, fighting a new, fresh wave of nausea that was washing over her. Using the door frame for support, she could feel her lungs closing up, she couldn't feel any air going into her body. Her heartbeat was speeding up again, and that heat in her head, it was getting hotter. Rachel stood and closed her eyes, pushing her forehead against the cool frame, she started counting to ten. "Three… four … five …" She kept going, concentrating on nothing more than the next number, and she got up past forty.

Eventually, she realised that she had managed to calm herself down, fighting an anxiety attack off at the very onset. She stayed put, working hard to calm herself and to concentrate on nothing other than her own breathing.

One minute later, she was walking down the stairs, slowly, and carefully, surprising herself by how mindful of the trail of DNA evidence that her sweat and snot and vomit and hair was likely to be leaving behind her. She walked through the reception, into the kitchen and out of the back door, trying not to touch a thing. She tip toed down the ginnel at the side of the property, out through the gate and continued straight across the grass, across the road and into her house.

After closing the door behind her, Rachel collapsed to her bum, her legs stretched out before her and she started to cry, as quietly as she could.

*****

Mick thought that he had heard somebody come in, and paused the telly. After a few seconds had passed, he heard Rachel sniffing and wiping her face with her sleeves.

"Is that you love?" he shouted.

"Yeah," said Rachel, after a pause that lasted a good

few seconds, her voice was quiet, and emotional. Mick wriggled up off his seat and came through into the reception area.

"S'up love, you alright?" He looked a bit confused. He wasn't scared, or alarmed, but he was concerned. It didn't seem right. It wasn't like Rachel, she hated drama queens. He stood over her, holding his can of lager. "You okay?"

"No love. I'm fucked."

"Eh? What you going on about?" asked Mick, he was beginning to feel scared.

"I've just killed that Graham, over the road. He's killed Suzanne. And I've just killed him." Rachel was staring straight into his eyes as she spoke. It was just so unreal, so insane – Mick couldn't filter it in, it made no sense. He smiled.

"Right, sorry love. Say that again." He crouched down, leaning in towards his partner.

"I've just killed Graham."

"Right…" Mick began wondering if Rachel was drunk.

"I was having a cigarette, out here, and I saw him twatting Suzanne. Next thing I know, I'm in their house, I'm upstairs, and he's kicked her to death. I've picked summat up, summat heavy, and split his head open. They're both lay there." Rachel started sobbing, as quietly as she could. "I'm fucked Mick. I'm going to jail love." Rachel started crying properly, she let it all go. Mick leaned in again to comfort her, rubbing her shoulder, and trying to compute the information that he had just heard.

"They're both dead?"

"Yeah!" she said, stopping a sob to say it, wipe away her snot, before continuing. A door clicked closed upstairs, and Mick's head spun around to look up the stairs. There was nobody there.

"You're alright love, just settle down a minute."

"Mick, I'm fucking not alright." Rachel tried doing a sarcastic laugh but it didn't work out, she just sounded scared, and slightly crazy. It trailed off into a pathetic, scared sob.

"You'll be alright in a minute. Have a shower, you

stink, really bad. You're fucking minging Rach. Have a shower love." Mick was trying his best to comfort her, but he wasn't doing a great job of it.

"Mick, did you hear what I said? I've just killed Graham. I'm a murderer, I'm going to prison, I've... I've fucked... everything up." By saying it once again, the gravity of the situation began to hit home, not just to Rachel, but to Mick as well, finally.

Mick stood, and looked down at the shoulders of his best friend in the whole world, shivering and sobbing, her head was tucked away between her knees. In that moment, in that glance down at his pathetic looking partner, their entire history together flashed before his eyes. The flirty looks in school uniforms, the first dates at the roller skating, the birth of Liam, moving into the house on Gameshawe, the birth of Britney, right up to moving into the current, nightmare house that seemed to have cursed them so badly. It all flashed by in a matter of seconds, and then it all started over again, different memories and images, different happy scenes whizzing through his mind.

"Rach, love. You need to sort your head out babe. Go and get a shower, get some fresh clothes on, get your hair washed. Go on, ten minutes love, you'll feel a lot better."

"Mick, I don't know what to do..." She glanced up at him, looking lost. It wasn't an expression that Mick recognised. He held his hands out.

"Come on, let's get you washed up," he said, bending and touching her hands so that she would grip on to his and he could pull her up onto her feet.

"Rach, come on, I'm going to get fucking stressed in a minute. Come on." Mick's slightly harsh tone did the trick, and diverted Rachel from whatever distraction she had sidetracked herself with. She put her hands out and Mick lifted her to her feet. "Right, good, now, upstairs, you get all them clothes off and I'll get them in a bin bag, then, straight in the shower. Come on." He started pulling her towards the stairs and she followed, her mind not really taking on board what he was saying, but slowly replaying the frightened look on Graham's face in the millisecond before he was struck by Rachel's fatal blow. The urge to vomit was incredible, but there was nothing left inside her stomach that could come up. She still retched though, she couldn't do anything to stop that.

"I really need a shit," said Rachel, as she reached the top stair.

"Come on, you can have a shit, just keep going love, you're proper in shock. It's mad how it makes people feel, you'll be right in a minute, trust me." Mick was talking really quietly, mindful that the kids were asleep. The words he said still weren't being picked out properly by Rachel, but Mick felt he was making progress. As they walked into their bedroom, he knocked the door shut with his heel, and he continued walking her towards the en-suite bathroom.

"Here, give us your top," he said as he started pulling at the waist band. "Put your arms up you knob," he was smiling, and desperately wanting to see a smile come back to Rachel's face. But there was nothing, she just looked like an extra in a cheap horror film. She had a pale, scared looking face, and her sunken eyes were busy, elsewhere. They weren't connecting with his at all, regardless of how much he wanted them to. Mick managed to get her top over her head, and Rachel stood in her bra.

"Come on, lets get these keks off as well," he started pulling them down, he was on his knees as he pulled her sock off her foot and then pulled the jogging bottoms off her left foot, before repeating the process on the right leg. Rachel was stood in just her bra and knickers, shivering, and looking ready to cry again.

"Do you still need a dump?"

"Yeah," she managed to say. Her lips were trembling. Mick led her across to the lavatory and sat her down on the seat, taking her knickers off her feet as she went about her business. He unclipped her bra and pulled the straps off her arms, before throwing it onto the pile of stinking clothes that he had taken from her.

"Right, jump in the shower when you've finished shitting, I'm going to sort these out." Mick turned the shower on, bent down, scooped the pile of dirty, stinking clothes up and headed out of the bathroom, and then out of the bedroom before disappearing down the stairs. Rachel was just staring aimlessly, but feeling relieved to be on the toilet and relaxing her bowels. She pushed the toilet door closed as she realised how vulnerable she was.

Mick stuck the dirty clothes straight into the washing machine and filled the compartments with soap powder. He selected the dosser wash as they called it, the all forgiving ninety degree cycle that ruined more items of clothing than it cleaned. After setting the machine off, making Rachel a cup of sweet tea, and nipping into the children's bedrooms to try and figure out who had been on the landing when Rachel had arrived home, he went back to see how she was getting on.

Rachel was still on the toilet when he went back into the bedroom. His presence startled her, and reminded her that she was sat naked on a toilet, stinking and trembling after killing her neighbour ten minutes earlier.

"Where are the boys?" he asked. "And why aren't you in the shower? Come on love, get your self together." The question about the boys seemed to bring Rachel round a bit, her mind switched to her domestic obligations and it was almost as though a light had come on when she replied.

"The boys are at mums. I told you they were staying over again. Britney came in, pissed up and went straight to bed. Shania was in bed at nine, she didn't even watch the end of X factor."

Mick realised that he had distracted Rachel by mentioning the kids.

"So, was she proper pissed or just a bit merry?" Mick was aiming to keep Rachel focused. She finished her business and went to the sink to wash her hands.

"She was really tired she said." Rachel had a flicker of a tiny smile, but it lasted only a tenth of a second. "She just went straight up."

"So, did Shania have her tablet in bed?" he asked.

"Yeah, I think so. Why?"

"Nowt, its just it's still warm, that all, I just wondered how long she's been on it for. Here, jump in this shower and get yourself washed up."

"Then what. What am I doing after my shower? Are we phoning the police?" Rachel looked confused and lost. It scared Mick to see her looking so vulnerable. So fragile.

"We're going to go over the road and sort everything out."

*****

"You're not going to prison, love." Mick said it as he held Rachel's face in his hands. "No fucking deal."

Twenty five minutes had elapsed between Rachel arriving home from Graham and Suzanne's house, to setting off back there, this time with Mick.

It was almost one o'clock in the morning, and Mick had told Rachel that they weren't to creep, or hide in the shadows, but they had to walk confidently and normally across the road, talking as they went, they had to appear perfectly normal. And that was precisely what they did, just in case any of the neighbours were still up and about. They talked quietly as they closed their own front door, and continued chatting as they crossed the road, and reached the gate at the side of the house. Rachel and Mick had strolled across the road as though they didn't have a care in the world. If there had been a casual observer, Mick hoped that the couple would just look like they were popping across to their friend's house.

Once beyond the gate, and out of public view, both of them felt scared and panicky about what they were about to do.

The plan, that Mick had made up on the spot as Rachel slowly dressed after her shower was very simple. They were going to remove the metal thing that had killed Graham and then phone the police and ambulance, and leave it for the police to try and work out how the husband and wife ended up dead, with Rachel explaining that she saw them fighting, but was scared to get involved after the hassle that went with it all last time. It was going to be okay.

Mick explained that it was perfect that Rachel had been to the council, she had told them about Suzanne being beaten up by Graham. It was easy, Mick said. They just needed to clean the place up and get rid of the murder weapon.

As they reached the back of the house, and the back door that was still wide open following Rachel's speedy exit, the couple stopped.

"Right, here we go." Whispered Mick, as he crept in through the back door.

"I don't want to, I want to go home…" Rachel's tone of voice demonstrated how scared she was. Her bowels wanted more time on the toilet, and her guts were spinning as though there was zero gravity.

"Sshhh, come on." Mick pushed her into the house, and followed closely behind. There were two empty wine bottles on the side, near the door, and two glasses, one empty and the other a quarter filled with red wine.

"They were pissed," said Mick. "That's good."

"Why?" asked Rachel, also taking in the scene – and noticing another empty bottle on the dining table.

"Drunken chaos. The police can't work out what pissed up people have been doing, because it's always so mental. They don't try as hard to figure everything out. I saw something about it on Channel Five. Come on, we just need to get the weapon. Where is it?"

"It's upstairs, in the bedroom, I think. I don't remember putting it down." Rachel was trembling, and her teeth were chattering.

"Come on, listen right, we need to get the story straight right. You've come here, a few minutes ago, then seen them two lay there, then you've run over to the house, and fetched me, and then we've burst in here. Yeah?"

"Yeah."

"So touch the banister and door frames and that, you don't need to worry about leaving prints."

"Right."

"Listen to me. I know you've had a shock, but concentrate. You need to know this shit love, so concentrate really hard. It's five to one now. You came here five minutes ago, it was about ten to one. Yeah?"

"Ten to one, right, Mick, I've got it."

"Right, show me where you dumped the bodies." Mick was smiling, trying to make light of the situation, but the joke missed by a mile and Rachel just walked past Mick.

"This way." She started walking up the stairs. She was walking very slowly, almost creeping up the stairs when they heard a noise.

Rachel froze. Mick was following just behind her and he heard it too. It sounded like a toilet seat dropping shut.

"Shit." Said Mick. "I thought you said they were dead."

"They are."

"Well who the fuck is in the loo?"

As the couple stood there trembling, staring at each other, mouths hanging open and wondering what was happening, the toilet flushed and the bathroom door opened right before them.

Chapter 18

"There's something going on over the road you know," said Tania to Kev, as she stood in the dark at her bedroom window. Kev was in bed, trying to get to sleep.

"Shud up will yoh?" he said, slurring slightly.

"I don't know what's happening, but there's something very fucking weird going on between them lot. I bet they're swingers."

This comment caught Kev's attention. "Eh? Who are you on about?" he asked.

"Them over there, that Graham and Suzanne. Mick and Rachel are over there now, all the lights are on, it's nearly one in the morning!"

"Doesn't mean they're swinging, does it? God, you're a proper shit-stirrer you."

"They've just gone there now. And I seen Rachel coming out of there about half an hour ago, looking all upset."

"You're puddled you love. Is that all you do, watch what everyone else is up to? You need to stop being such a nosey bitch!" said Kev, somewhat disappointed that the swinging theory had been such a short lived and poorly researched suggestion.

"Well, if I can get some shit on them, I won't have to keep worrying all the time that we're going to get booted out, will I? So you just carry on doing what you always do Kev, fuck all." Tania was raising her voice slightly and had to remind herself that the window was open, and that she was supposed to be spying on what was going on over the road.

"Like I've said, you're a proper loon Tan, you need sectioning. Now shut your big wobbly face and let me go to sleep."

Tania ignored him. She stood and watched for a while longer, but there was nothing happening. Kev was snoring blissfully when she finally gave up waiting to see what time Mick and Rachel were going to leave the house. Tania got into bed beside her husband.

"I hope you die in your sleep you big fat ugly bastard. A brain haemorrhage would be ideal." She lay down and turned her back on him. Tania had gone past being tired now, she was wide awake, her head buzzing with thoughts that never normally troubled her during the day. Kev's snoring and farting was stressing her out further, and after fifteen minutes of tossing and turning, trying to get comfy, and trying her best to feel as tired as she had done when she'd come upstairs in the first place, she gave up.

Tania got out of bed, grabbed her dressing gown off the drawers and put it on. She checked that her cigarettes were in the dressing gown pocket, kicked on her slippers and headed downstairs, undecided whether to make a cup of tea or pour a glass of wine. By the time she'd got downstairs, and saw that Kev had finished her wine, she decided to have a cup of tea instead.

"Drinks all his fucking cans then has to finish my bastard wine. God, I fucking hate that man." She filled the kettle. Tears began to well up in her eyes, as she realised just how miserable she was. This move to a completely new area was supposed to be a fresh start. Wipe the slate clean. A new beginning. Instead, it had just been a load of aggro, right from the very first night.

Tania made her cup of tea and tried to stop feeling sorry for herself. She remembered that she'd been noseying on the neighbours over the road, and decided to go and have another look while she had her fag. She went outside with her brew and lit her cigarette. All the lights at the weirdo's house were still on.

"It's lit up like Blackpool bleeding illuminations!" said Tania under her breath as she watched the house. She was still really intrigued as to why Mick and Rachel were over there. She couldn't believe that they'd find anything in common with that nowty old dickhead and his bimbo, fake-as-fuck wife. She still thought it plausible that they were all swingers. Why else would a pretty young woman be shacked up with a sweaty, fat old man like that if they weren't a bit kinky, she thought as she stood and sipped her cup of tea and smoked the cigarette.

It was a still, calm night, and a lovely evening to be outdoors. Tania glanced at her watch, it was getting on for three o'clock in the morning, and it would be starting to get light soon, she thought. Her attention had been averted from her miserable marriage and the disastrous new start on Haughton Park by the goings-on across the road. She knew that she shouldn't, but she decided to go across the road and try and see what was going on. If they *were* swinging, she wanted to get a photo of them at it, on her phone.

Tania went into her house, put her cup in the kitchen, grabbed her phone off the side where it was charging, and then swapped her slippers for her trainers. Her heart beat was racing, she felt quite excited by the prospect of sneaking across the road and spying on the neighbours. It was easily justified in her mind, they'd tried to get her family kicked out on the very first night.

"Fuck 'em." She said, as she opened her front door, stepped out into the street and closed her door quietly. She crept as silently as she could, her phone was in her hand, already set on camera mode.

Tania couldn't see anything through the windows at the front, there was nobody about. She walked silently around the side, through the gate that was wide open, deciding that if she was caught, she'd just say she was looking for her cat. As she stepped closer to the back of the house, she could hear crying, and arguing. Her adrenaline was going full pelt now, and she was getting quite a thrill from this unexpected adventure in the dead of the night. The lights at the back of the house were all off, and Tania was struggling to see exactly what was going on inside.

She was crouching down by the back door to the property, which was open slightly. She stayed there and listened. Watching through the gap at the back door, she could see three people carrying something quite big. They were struggling to get it around the corner at the bottom of the stairs. In the dim light, it looked like a big roll of carpet. Or was it a mattress? They were shouting at each other, but she couldn't make out what they were saying, or even who the three people were. Her heart was beating rapidly, high up in her chest, and her palms were sweating.

She grabbed the phone and held it up at the glass. It

was shaking quite badly in her hands. There didn't seem to be much of a picture on the screen, she thought. She pressed the red button on the screen. She had no idea that the phone would do a big bright flash that lit up the whole kitchen, startling the three scared, angry looking faces that were holding the object.

"Fuck."

END OF PART ONE

PART TWO

Chapter 19

JUNE 25th

SERIOUS CRIMES INVESTIGATION OFFICE, MANCHESTER CITY POLICE HQ

D.C.I. Andrew Miller was staring gormlessly at the wall in the incident room. Keith Saunders, recently promoted to Detective Inspector following the murder of his previous superior, was giving a briefing to all of the S.C.I.U team.

Five A3 sized police mug shot pictures were pinned up on the incident room wall, placed around a map of Manchester city centre. Each face had a red line connecting their photograph to the part of the city centre where they had previously slept rough, prior to their deaths.

The five homeless people had been found dead in the last few weeks. As it was summer, it was quite unusual to have high numbers of homeless deaths, and the case had been handed to DCI Miller's team to look at, and hopefully, rule out any foul play.

It all seemed very straight forward. All of the dead people had been poisoned by alcohol, and their toxicology reports had shown extraordinarily high amounts of concentrated methanol in the blood. Alcohol poisoning was one of the most common causes of death in homeless people, but all five of the dead people had unprecedented levels in their systems. The strength of the drink that they had all taken was almost ten times the strength that it is possible to buy from a shop.

In the past decade, the rise in "fake" alcohol products had become a huge industry, particularly in Greater Manchester and other big cities in Britain. Entrepreneurs had invested huge sums of money into creating their own, secret distilleries that were hidden away in warehouses and incognito units on industrial estates where they brewed a cheaper, fake version of famous name spirits, which were then sold in dodgy backstreet off licenses, the kind of which Greater Manchester has a great many.

DI Saunders was addressing the S.C.I.U. team, explaining his theory that these deaths were not simply from a bad batch of dodgy spirits, as the death toll would be much greater. Local hospital trusts all around the city had been approached and asked if their Accident and Emergency departments had seen any particularly worrying alcohol poisoning cases in recent weeks, and the answer had been a resounding no.

"So, how have these five people met their deaths?" Asked Saunders. He stood and paused a minute, looking at the pictures. "We need to know where they managed to get hold of this alcohol, which is of the same strength as nail varnish remover, and has traces of car windscreen wash in it, along with bleach. It's pretty dirty stuff."

"Jesus! I bet it tastes awful!" said DCI Miller, pulling his face as though he'd just sucked a grapefruit.

"We'd be seeing a lot more deaths if this stuff was available from a shop. We need to work out where these five dossers have got it from!" said Bill Chapman, one of the department's Detective Constables.

"Sir," said Saunders in Miller's direction. "Could we get uniform to give out leaflets and flyers, warning the homeless about any suspicious drink they are offered?" he asked. Miller considered the question for a minute, sitting cross legged at the back of the small group of detectives. He was twiddling a paper-clip in his hands and he looked quite depressed. After a short time, he replied.

"It's not a bad idea that Detective Inspector. But we still don't know what it is that has been drank, do we? So we'd basically be sending out the message that we don't know what we're going on about. And that's not our style."

DI Saunders looked dejected.

"What if the dossers are mixing all this shit up themselves, and then drinking it?" offered another member of the team, DC Joanne Rudovsky. "Think about it – you can buy those ingredients from Poundland. Three quid would get you a big nail polish remover, two bottles of bleach and a big massive bottle of the windscreen wash. A cheap bottle of vodka is about a tenner – so for thirteen quid, you could produce a massive bucket of booze that will keep everyone buzzing for hours!"

The remark got a hearty laugh from the team.

"Scary thought Jo." Said Saunders.

"For all we know, they might have been doing this for years. But then maybe the strength of the ethanol ingredient has been changed recently, and they can't hack it?" added Jo.

"Okay," said DI Saunders. "Don't throw pens at me, but I think we're going to have to go out and talk to the street dwellers about this."

The room erupted with groans and swear words. It wasn't a popular suggestion by any stretch of the imagination.

"Only if we can wear fucking gas masks!" said Bill Chapman.

"Now, come on," said Miller from the back, stifling a grin.

"We need to know if anybody knows of a cheap home made drink that's going around. If so, who is selling it? We are not looking to prosecute anyone for making it, not yet anyway, we just need to try and work out if it is common knowledge that there is a concoction available that will get you off your tits for a few quid." Saunders began pointing at the map. "Chapman and Worthington – you can go around this area," he pointed at the Gay Village and the China Town district of the City Centre. "Rudovsky and Kenyon," He pointed to the team's other two Detective Constables, Peter Kenyon and Jo Rudovsky. "You two concentrate on this area please," Saunders tapped on map, on the opposite side of the city centre, around the Manchester Arena and Victoria train station. Hundreds of homeless people slept in the doorways, back exits and loading bays of the buildings in the City Centre, and many more lived underneath the railway arches at Castlefield, which is where Saunders intended to work with his boss DCI Andy Miller.

"I'm going to look around Castlefield with the gaffer."

"So, Sir, we are not saying there is anything

suspicious about the five deaths at this stage?" asked Peter Kenyon, his face suggested that he was unsure what the actual point of this inquiry was. Peter was an experienced detective, he'd been with the S.C.I.U. since its inception – but he couldn't remember a case so vague in terms of its actual point.

DCI Miller saw where this was headed and stood up to support Saunders. He walked to the front of the room, and stood by Saunders at the wall of photographs.

"That's a valid point Peter. This case is being viewed as "suspicious" at this stage. We don't have any understanding of why five homeless people are dead, other than that they all drank a massively toxic mixture of insanely strong alcohol. We need to figure out if the deaths were intentional, or just a bit of misadventure by desperate homeless alcoholics. The fact that the dead people all died on separate occasions, at separate locations, and that the hospitals haven't seen any other cases of alcohol poisoning suggests to me that there are reasonable grounds to be suspicious."

"Okay, so, if we all know what we're doing, I suggest we work late into the night, speak to these people while they are easy to find, and we can meet up and have a team brief at four pm tomorrow, giving us all a good lie-in." said Saunders, emphasising the lie-in bit, while knowing full well that spending a night talking to Manchester's homeless people was about as soul destroying as it could get for any detective. The mood was predictable as the team sullenly pushed their seats back to their desks and quietly got on with their work.

"DI Saunders, have you got two minutes?" Miller ushered Keith Saunders towards his office at the back of the incident room.

"Sir?" he said, as he started writing notes on the white-board.

"Two minutes, when you've done that. Cheers."

Miller walked across the incident room floor, smiling at the dejected faces of his SCIU colleagues.

"Cheer up. Talking to tramps is nothing! I had to go down into the sewers looking for a suitcase full of cocaine once. Shit and periods, piss and Johnny-bags swimming around in my wellies. I could still smell it six months later. Soft bastards!" he shouted as he closed his office door, and smirked to himself because only he knew that it was a complete lie that he'd just made up on the spot.

A minute or two later, Saunders knocked and came in.

"Sir?"

"Oh, sorry to bug you Keith, I know you're busy," Miller squinted at his computer screen. "It's about tonight – I'm not available, sorry – I'm on a night out. It's been on the calendar for two weeks, look." He pointed to his PC screen, and the staff rota calendar that the SCIU team used for booking days off and leave periods. It read MILLER OFF ALL NIGHT NO MATTER WHAT. AND I MEAN NO MATTER WHAT.

"Shit, I didn't see that Sir. Sorry." Saunders looked really annoyed with himself for not being as efficient as he ought to be.

"Don't apologise to me mate, I'm going out for dinner with friends. But give my regards to one-eyed Jack if he's still alive. He used to be a fantastic grass at one time – he knew everything there was to know about low-life scum in the city. That was in the days when they used to all sleep in Piccadilly Gardens. It was like a refugee camp, bodies everywhere." Miller grinned at the memory of the stinking, homeless drunk who could solve impenetrable cases in return for a bottle of Thunderbird and a pouch of Old Holborn. "Good old one-eyed Jack." Muttered Miller as he returned to his computer screen.

"Have a good night Sir, and please, don't rub it in tomorrow!"

"I'll try," smiled Miller, with a wink.

Chapter 20

"Well, I can't tell you how glad I am to be here, and on a school night as well!" said Andy Miller to his wife Clare, as he clinked glasses with her, and their friends, Ollie and Pippa. The group were eating at one of Manchester's finest restaurants, "Gaucho," on Deansgate in the city centre. It was a late birthday treat for Ollie who'd had to work through his birthday weekend.

"The rest of my team are out interviewing the homeless. Oh, I do feel guilty, sitting here in excellent surroundings with fine Argentinean food and great company – while they are walking around asking pissed up dossers if they've been offered any cheap spirits recently!" Andy laughed at his own caustic sarcasm and his guests chuckled along too.

Clare wasn't buying her husband's statement. "When you say you feel guilty, do you actually mean that you think it's absolutely hilarious?" she asked, sniggering away.

"Yes, sorry, yes. That's exactly what I meant." Replied Andy with a sly look on his face.

"Well, I'm glad you're not my boss!" said Pippa wearing a neutral looking "is she serious, isn't she serious" expression on her face.

"I'm glad I'm not your boss Pippa! The one thing I can't stand is trying to manage bossy, opinionated women!" retorted Andy to a shocked laugh from Pippa. Ollie and Clare were laughing hysterically too, mainly due to the sheer bravery of Andy's come-back.

Pippa and Ollie had lived a few doors away from Andy and Clare on Grosvenor Road in Worsley, until recently when they'd moved into their dream property across the Salford boundary at the exclusive new Haughton Park development in Bury, about four miles away from Worsley. It was nice for the four to get together, and to have a good catch up. Pippa was the head of the Primary Care Trust, and was regularly painted as a nasty, oppressive bitch in the local newspaper, especially when expensive cancer treatments were refused for people because of a lack of funding.

Ollie was a website designer and ran a hugely successful business which offered bespoke designs for such well known brands as Marks and Spencer and Next, among a long list littered with iconic retail names.

"So, how is life up your way?" asked Clare. "Is it all settling down now, after all the protests on the news?"

"Yes, well, to be honest," replied Ollie, "it was all a bit of a storm in a teacup. If the media hadn't got themselves involved, I doubt there would have been much of an issue at all, really."

"God, yeah it was a bit much all that, wasn't it? So are neighbour relations okay? The way Granada Reports were going on, it sounded like you'd moved into the middle of world war three!" Andy shook his head at the memory of the media frenzy from just a month or so earlier.

"No, honestly, it was nothing. The people who the council put in are fine – they're just ordinary people. It really was a strange story, it just showed the media up for what a snobby bunch they are – and it was all led by a couple of the most stuck up tossers you can possibly imagine!" said Pippa. "It's embarrassing really."

"The media are determined to demonise the poor – it's to take everybody's mind off the fact that the bankers have bankrupted the nation, and not a single one of them has been sent to jail for it. The story about your estate was perfect to remind everybody that they should hate the poor! That's all it was!" Clare looked as though she was getting quite angry.

"You're absolutely spot on," said Pippa. "At least one programme a night on the television is anti-poor propaganda. "Benefits Britain" or "Drunk dads on the dole" or "Honey I have eighteen kids and I've never worked a day in my whole life but I want a bigger house!" Pippa laughed mockingly as she said it, at the sheer tastelessness of the media's attack on the most demonised, neglected and overlooked section of society.

"Poor folk are the only people that we are allowed to openly hate now. Well, them and paedophiles. Think about it. We can't say anything without risk of offending some section or other of society – but we can all stick together and openly abuse poor people – in fact, it's bloody well encouraged by the television programmes that you're on about Pippa!" said Clare.

"Britain's biggest bums!" said Andy, laughing at the transparency of it all.

"Help! I spent all my giro on cider and pot!" offered Ollie to a loud, enthusiastic wave of laughter from around the table. It took a few seconds for the silliness to abate.

"Yes, well it was quite strange to start with. But it's all fine now, it works a treat." Said Pippa. "We do try to avoid inviting the poor over for barbeques though. It has the tendency to become so inadequately competitive. I raise your Asda value beef burgers with this tray of Waitrose king prawns!"

"Oh God, that's so inappropriate!" Clare found this bizarre conversation droll and distasteful at the same time.

"I think the lobster we keep in the freezer will always be our skud missile in that particular war!" said Pippa, pretending to be very pleased with herself.

"Oh, God, stop it Pippa – you're making us sound as bad as those bloody snobs on the news! Hey - that reminds me Andy – I wanted to pick your brains about something actually." Ollie looked slightly serious.

"Oh, right?" Andy took a large sip of his wine, still grinning at the poor people being abused so casually.

"Yeah, but – er, well it's not that entertaining really. I'll speak to you in a bit." Ollie blushed slightly, realising that what he wanted to talk about would be boring for everybody else.

"Tell you what, shall we go and have a smoke?"

"Oh, Andy! I thought you said you were trying to give up?" Clare's tone made it clear that she wanted to say something a lot more assertive, but was on her best behaviour.

"One can't do any harm." He stood, patting his jacket pocket to double check the cigarette packet was all set. Ollie stood too and Clare rolled her eyes at her husband, before making a face at Pippa.

"Oh leave them to it. We can discuss their inadequacies while they're away!" said Pippa, instantly cheering Clare up and diffusing the hovering bad vibes.

"Won't be long!" Andy brushed his hand across his wife's shoulder.

"We're discussing your inadequacies darling, so please, take as much time as you like."

*****

"I'm smoking about thirty a day at the minute," said Andy as he offered his pack to Ollie. "Clare thinks I'm only having the odd one here and there. I bet I'm smoking more now than I ever have done!"

"Why's that then?" Ollie lit his cigarette and sat down at one of the smoker's tables outside the busy restaurant.

"Dunno. Because I love them!" Andy smiled as he inhaled the smoke deep into his lungs.

"How long did you give up for?"

"Eighteen months. Tell you what though – it gets harder and harder the longer you go. In the few weeks before I started again, it was all I could bloody think about." Andy suddenly remembered the circumstances of him starting the habit again, and it made him feel sad.

"So, what's up?" he asked, forcing his voice to sound a bit happier than he actually felt at that moment. "What did you want to talk about?"

"Oh, well it was something I meant to give you a call about last week – but it completely slipped my mind." Ollie took another drag on his cigarette. "It's a bit weird really, and I probably just need to mind my own business."

"Oh?" asked Andy, raising an eyebrow. Ollie was the least "nosey" person he knew. All Ollie ever did was mind his own business.

"What we were talking about with the council moving tenants in – well one of our neighbours, he was making a big noise against it. Not publicly as he works at the council, but behind the scenes, he was being a right old bastard, no doubt orchestrating that media response."

"Right?"

"Yes, sorry – so anyway, he's not around anymore. I've not seen him for about three weeks, and when I was washing the car the other night, his wife was out, watering the flowers and I just mentioned that I'd not seen him. Graham he's called. And she started getting all jittery. I've never seen her like that before, she's usually really smiley and happy-go-lucky. But she seemed really, I don't know – nervous. It was really awkward."

"So where do you think he is?"

"Well that's what I'm saying, maybe I ought to mind my own business. There was talk that he was driven off in a police van, so I'm thinking that he might be in prison."

Andy burst out laughing. After a moment he stopped and looked across at Ollie. "So you want me to see if he's been banged up? Ha ha you nosey fucker Ollie, oh my days!"

Ollie laughed. "No, it's not just that. The neighbours across the road, they are council tenants, seem nice enough and everything, no problem or anything. But, they've started using his car."

"What?" Andy looked confused.

"Sorry, yeah. Right, the neighbour that I asked about her husband, the neighbours across the road have been using their car – but Graham – he's the guy I haven't seen for a while – he absolutely hates these council tenants. It's just got me really suspicious. Something seems a bit fishy."

Andy finished his cigarette and threw the dimp into the big ashtray and exhaled the last bit of smoke. "I can't just do a police check on someone, I need to have grounds for doing it Ollie."

Ollie raised an eyebrow and looked at Andy as if to say "pull the other one."

"Honestly! I shit you not, we have to be able to explain all police checks with notes in our pocket books. There has been a lot of corruption in the past, a lot of secrets sold to folk, journalists and gangsters and things. Black-mail stuff."

Andy was nodding to Ollie to confirm his sincerity.

"So I can't just do a search to find out if this

neighbour has been banged up. It's more than my job's worth!"

Ollie laughed at Andy's "jobs-worth" statement.

"Fair enough. It just seems a bit suspicious, that's all."

"What, being taken away in a police van, and then not being seen since? I think you should trust your gut instincts on this one Ollie. It certainly sounds to me like he's been banged up."

"Yeah, fair enough. That would explain his wife being a bit weird about it all too. But I still don't understand why she would be lending his car out to the neighbours across the road. None of it adds up."

"Well, you know what, one thing that I've learnt down the years is this. People do weird things. Now if you are telling me that you are genuinely worried about this neighbour – you could phone the police station and tell them your concerns. That's what I'd do, but as it stands right now – he could be in jail, or he could be away on business. He could have fucked off to get away from these new neighbours! For all you know Ollie, he might have moved in with his bit on the side. She's bound to act awkward if that's the case. And his wife is bound to do something that will piss him off. Like lending his car to the scruffy neighbours he hates."

"Fair enough. I'm just being stupid aren't I? But he is the kind of bloke you can imagine going missing."

"What's that supposed to mean?" Andy laughed, but was genuinely intrigued by such a bizarre statement, particularly coming from the mouth of Ollie.

"Oh, he's just your typical busy-body with a hate fuelled opinion on everything. His wife tends to sport a black eye every so often. She's drop-dead-gorgeous as well, and half his age. He's just one of those blokes that you try and avoid. It's just got my mind racing that he's the one who has created all this bad harmony up on the development, then he's suddenly disappeared without a trace."

Andy was staring off into the distance, watching people walking past, and staring out into space. After a long silence he grabbed his Benson and Hedges packet and offered

Ollie another cigarette.

"No, one's enough for me, thanks."

"I'll have one more. I won't get another chance now until after Clare's gone to bed. Even then she'll be kicking off in her sleep!"

Ollie laughed, as Andy lit his cigarette.

"Okay, I'll tell you what. You text me in the morning, give me this Graham's address and I'll have a poke about and see if I can find a rational explanation for him not being around. Give me the registration number of his car as well. What was it again?"

"What was what?"

"The car that the neighbours are using."

"Oh, it's a Range Rover Evoque. Nice car, only a year old - if that. That's what I mean, it's just so random that some new neighbours who've only moved in recently are going off for days out in it, going shopping and things!" Ollie was shaking his head, it really was eating at him. He sensed that something wasn't right. Regardless of his personal feelings towards Graham, he was genuinely concerned for the welfare of the man, and his gut was telling him that he wasn't in jail.

"When you moved up there, Clare was pretty gutted you know. She started trying to convince me that we should move up to Haughton Park as well."

"And?" Ollie looked intrigued.

"And then it came on the telly that half of Manchester's scummiest people were moving in and we just forgot all about it!"

"Ha ha, very good!"

"Okay, seeing as it's your birthday, I'll have a dig about. Alright?"

"Nice one! I'll bet you fifty quid that something fishy is going on. And please, don't try and make out that it's a birthday gift – you weren't remotely interested until I mentioned the attractive wife!" Ollie laughed loudly and Andy smiled too.

"Objection your honour!" he said as he smoked the last of his cigarette. "That's a slanderous remark."

"Over ruled!"

Chapter 21

"So, come on, what was Ollie talking about?" asked Clare as she changed into her pyjamas. Miller was stood by the chest of drawers reading text messages that had appeared on his phone when he'd plugged it into charge.

"Eh?" he asked as he scanned the details that Saunders had been sending through over the course of the evening.

"God, you're like a zombie when you're looking at that phone. What was Ollie talking to you about?" Clare pulled the duvet back and got into bed. Miller was completely absorbed in the texts that he was reading.

"Andy!"

"What? Oh sorry – what did you say?"

"I'm not talking to you until you put that bloody phone away." Clare gave her husband the half-closed eyes stare, so he knew that she was seriously pissed off with him ignoring her. He got the message and put the phone away, for the time being at least, Saunders had spent the night texting his every thought by the looks of things, thought Miller.

"Right, sorry love – you've had my undivided attention all night, and now – you're having a tantrum because I'm not gazing adoringly at you and hanging on your every word?"

"Correct."

"The Elton John of Manchester, that's you Clare Miller. High maintenance, super bitch!"

"I much prefer you calling me poppet!" she laughed as Miller began unbuttoning his shirt.

"I might get a shower. Unless, you know…"

"Don't be ridiculous. Anyway, answer my question. What did Ollie say?"

"God. You are a really, really nosey cow, aren't you?" Miller was laughing at his wife's extraordinary appetite to know other peoples business.

"Come on, don't be so coy!"

"No, it's private. If I told you what he said, you'd be texting Pippa. In fact, you'd probably ring her up straight away!" Miller had a dead-pan expression on his face.

"Why, what? Oh, come on, tell me Andy, don't be such a spoil-sport!" Clare was sat up in bed, with the duvet over her knees, looking really excited.

"No. It's men stuff. Sorry love, classified information."

"Go on, tell me."

"Okay, look, you mustn't repeat this to anyone. If this gets out, Ollie will know that it's come from me. So please, promise."

"Scout's honour!" said Clare. "You know I won't say anything."

"Well, you better not. He's thinking of leaving Pippa."

Clare was thunderstruck. That really was a bolt from the blue. "Shut up. What? Are you... why?" She had her hand over her mouth, and her eyes were wide.

"He's been hanging around with this guy from work called Barry. He's started developing feelings for him. Deep feelings." Andy was sat on the end of the bed, pulling his socks off. Clare looked absolutely gutted.

"I can't believe it. I can't bloody believe it!"

"He said that the way this Barry looks at him sends him crazy, and he's moving in with him on Friday."

"Oh, my, God! Does Pippa know? Has he told her?" She looked genuinely upset, but also mildly excited. This news was massive.

"Told her what?" Andy looked confused.

"Told her about moving in with Barry? Der!"

"Oh, that! I made all that up. You didn't believe me did you?" Andy started laughing. Clare threw her pillow at his head.

"Flipping heck Clare, you are so gullible! As if Ollie is gay, but even if he was, he wouldn't go out with a bloke called Barry would he? You moron!" Andy was stood, shaking his head and pointing at his wife.

"Aw Andy. You are such a weapon."

Andy walked off to the en-suite bathroom chuckling as he went.

"No wonder Pippa hates you."

"No wonder she turned Ollie gay! Ha ha! You're so funny Clare. I think you're great!" Andy closed the door, giggling away to himself as he took the rest of his clothes off and got into the shower.

"You bastard!" Clare smiled to herself as she picked up her Kindle from the bedside table. "Barry." She said, and laughed at her ridiculous gullibility.

Chapter 22

The following morning, Miller received the text from Ollie, as promised. It read; "Hi Andy, thanks for a lush night. The neighbour is called Graham Ashcroft. He's a big deal at Bury council, six figure salary I think. His registration is PN66 YDW. Address is 9 Fir Trees Grove, Haughton Park. Thanks again for a great night, really enjoyed it. Ol."

Miller read the message as he sat in traffic. The idea of looking into this missing neighbour of Ollie's was quite irritating for the D.C.I. He currently had three cases on the go, plus the alcohol poisoning investigation. "I could do without this Ollie, you big spanner." He said to himself as the traffic began to crawl through the Salford University district towards Manchester City Centre. And then the traffic stopped again, and all of the car drivers returned their attention to their mobiles. Including Miller who composed a reply before the lights changed to green. "No worries, and when he turns up safe and well, you owe me fifty quid."

Once at the office, Miller was reminded that Saunders had given the team a late start. The place was deserted.

"Good enough!" he was delighted at the prospect of a bit of peace and quiet. But then his boss strolled in, with an urgent look on his face.

"Morning Sir." Said Miller quite unenthusiastically, sensing that Detective Chief Superintendent Dixon was here with even more work.

"Only you in Andy?" His bushy white eyebrows that had gained him the nickname "Frosty," were riding high up on his forehead, making him look quite astonished that Miller was the only officer in the unit.

"They were all working late last night, interviewing dossers about the alcohol deaths. Saunders given them a late start… which means that I get some peace and quiet to get on with this." He extended both of his arms to highlight his overflowing in-tray in dramatic fashion.

"Oh. Well, don't shoot the messenger!" Dixon looked apologetic already.

"But?"

"We've had a murder in Longsight last night, the dead man is a community centre cleaner, fifty four years old, family man, cycling home at half past ten last night, stabbed in the back and in the side of the head. Longsight C.I.D. have upgraded it to an S.C.I.U job, you'll be delighted to know." Dixon handed the file over the desk to Miller.

Miller looked slightly pissed off, but not too much. It was becoming an almost weekly occurrence where jobs were being back-heeled his way by over-stretched C.I.D. departments that had lost all enthusiasm for their work due to the government's irresponsible cuts to the policing budget. Across the police service, morale was at an all time low. It didn't concern Miller greatly, the way that he viewed it - it just made his team look brilliant, and thus protected their budget.

"What was the justification for upgrading it?" asked Miller. A run-of-the-mill murder investigation would traditionally be handled by the divisional C.I.D. departments, but the more problematic cases usually ended up with the S.C.I.U involved quite early on, simply because they were the best detectives in the Manchester City Police force. This case didn't look particularly unusual at first glance.

"The dead man was threatened with a kicking two weeks ago on his way home from work, and his wife reported it. A statement was taken at the time, but he'd said that he had no idea who the people were. All the details are in there." Dixon nodded at the folder that Miller was holding between both hands.

"I'm sure they are, Sir. But that still doesn't explain why it has been upgraded to my desk?"

Dixon frowned slightly. "Precautionary, I'm afraid. Longsight C.I.D think it will end up being looked at by the IPCC, because the dead man had recently contacted police in fear of his life."

"Ah, okay. So it's being treated as a police custody death?" Miller was slightly perturbed that Longsight were so paranoid about a potential inquiry by the Independent Police Complaints Commission, that they had collapsed the whole inquiry and chucked it onto Miller's desk.

"I'll leave it with you, if that's okay?" Dixon looked eager to get away before he got talked into doing something.

"Yes Sir, but before you go, I wanted to mention something. It's almost a year since Karen's death."

"Good God! My, you're right." Dixon looked stunned by the announcement. It really had just seemed like a matter of weeks, or maybe months, but certainly not twelve. The year had passed by very quickly.

"So, I was just wondering if the force were planning anything, a memorial service or something. I think we need to do something."

"Absolutely Andy, you're spot on." Dixon looked embarrassed, and somewhat ashamed. He struggled to maintain eye-contact. "I'll get onto it right away. Thanks." He closed the door behind him as he left. Miller exhaled loudly and began reading through the file. He started scratching his head, deciding that his desk was looking too untidy and that he urgently needed to write a priority list and sort out a better functioning incident room. This new file had suddenly found itself right at the top of the list, so everything else would need re-scheduling.

"Fuck's sake." Miller blew out loudly again, wondering at what point in his career had the murdered people stopped being victims that deserved justice, and had become little more than an irritation.

Reading through the case file for the incident in Longsight, Miller quickly began to realise that he'd been stitched up with this one. He picked up the phone and rang Dixon. It went to voice-mail, which was a blessing as it meant there was no discussion required. Miller could simply leave his message without getting into an argument.

"Sir, can you get on to Longsight and tell them that S.C.I.U. aren't taking this on. I will supervise the handling of their enquiry if they want, but I can't see any justification for this being sent our way. If their only excuse is the potential for an I.P.C.C inquiry, then I'll oversee that they are following procedure – but it just looks like a cop-out, can't-be-arsed, back-heel to me. I see it is D.S. Faulkner who has signed it off, tell him to phone me directly if he has any issues, but under no circumstances are we doing his job for him. And yes, you can repeat that word-for-word. In fact, just play this message down the phone to him if you want. Cheers Sir." He put the phone down heavily, knowing that it would leave a really annoying noise on the end of Dixon's message. The slammed down phone noise was meant for Faulkner, if Dixon decided to play it back to the D.S.

Saunders arrived into the office at 10.30am, and looked full of beans as Miller observed him walking around the incident room hurriedly and excitedly. Miller threw his pen down on the desk and decided to go and see how the young DI had got on with the street dwellers the previous evening. He stood, indulged himself in a rewarding, fully stretched yawn before popping out of his glass walled office and across the incident room floor.

"Alright Keith? Got a result?"

"Hi Sir, alright?" Saunders didn't look up from the file he was rapidly flicking through. "Not a result, but I might have a couple of leads. One in particular that I'm pretty buzzing about."

Miller loved seeing Saunders like this, completely focused, enthused and driven.

"Good, good. I'll leave you to it, then…"

"Sorry Sir, I'm not being rude. I've not even had a brew yet, I wanted to get in and check this. Two minutes and I'll come and see you. I'm not being ignorant." Saunders face was fixed, and his eyes didn't move from what he was reading for the entire time that he was speaking. Miller smiled and set off walking back across the open-plan office space towards his little "gold-fish bowl" office in the corner. He stopped at the little kitchen area and made himself and Saunders a coffee, taking the cups through to his office and sitting down beside the tall pile of paperwork that needed making into smaller piles.

A few minutes passed until Saunders leapt up off his chair, like a jack-in-the-box and practically jogged across the office floor before bursting into Miller's office.

"Sir!" he said, "got a theory on the alcoholics. One of them I talked to last night, he said "I'll bet it's the street angel." So I was like, who is the street angel, you know, going along with it, thinking it was drink or drugs talking. Anyway, check this out, the homeless in Manchester have a guardian angel who walks about checking they're okay, that they're tucked in at night!" Saunders was grinning.

"Shut up!" Miller laughed at the preposterous statement that Saunders had come out with. "Here, sit down, I've done you a brew."

Saunders pulled out a chair facing Miller and took a slurp of the coffee. "Cheers, nice one. Right, listen to this. This guy I was talking to, he was only about thirty, but he looked fifty at least. Smelt even older. He was pissed, and I mean, completely hammered, couldn't focus his eyes, he was slurring his words, but I could still understand him. He said that the five dead have probably been put to sleep, to help them." Saunders was wearing his creepy "I've got this one in the bag" grin, the expression that he always wore when he was in the final furlong of cracking a case.

"Bollocks!" said Miller loudly, then laughed manically.

"We'll see!" replied Saunders, with a cocky wink. "I need to check the post mortem and medical records, see if there was any underlying health conditions. We've not even considered this."

"We're only supposed to be working out if the deaths are suspicious, not solving a mass-murder inquiry before it's begun Keith. You're getting ahead of yourself!" Miller was suitably impressed with the usual level of enthusiasm from his DI.

"Well, I've checked the first case. That was the woman who was found behind the bins under the railway arches in Castlefield. She had a serious infection in her groin, from injecting. She was probably very poorly when she died. I'm not betting anything too big yet until I've checked the other post-mortem reports. I'll get on with it."

"Right, well, nice one. I'll leave you to crack on."

"Cheers. Thanks for the brew as well. I didn't know you knew how to brew up Sir."

"Oh, shut up. And close the door on your way out,

you ungrateful bastard."

"Cheers." Saunders left the office, laughing to himself as he walked briskly back across the office to his desk. He grabbed a piece of A4 paper from the printer tray and wrote in black marker pen "Untreated infection in groin area." He blu-tacked it beneath the large, sad looking photograph of the young woman. Saunders picked up his phone and began ringing the doctors surgery telephone number that came with the medical notes.

Miller was unsettled. He knew that he had a lot of menial, tidying up tasks to do, filing, checking and signing off final reports that his team had been working on. But the favour that Ollie had asked him about was bugging him, it was becoming a distraction, and so he decided to deal with it right away, so he could strike a line through that on the to-do list in his mind. He grabbed a pen and began writing down the details that Ollie had text to him. His first step was to google the man's name. He wrote GRAHAM ASHCROFT BURY COUNCIL into the search engine and scanned the first page of results. There was nothing of major interest in the first set of listings. The second page didn't yield any strong results either, just vague mismatches of first names and "council" business. It struck Miller as odd, if this guy was a senior member of town hall staff, his name ought to be coming up in dozens of Google results. He clicked the third page of results and decided that there was something wrong. Miller Googled Bury Town Hall and rang the number.

"Hello, you're through to Bury Metropolitan Borough Council, how may I help you today?" asked a very cheerful sounding lady.

"Hello, yes, can you put me through to Graham Ashcroft please?" asked Miller.

"Yes certainly," said the voice. "Do you know which department that is please?" she asked.

"Erm, no, sorry. I think it's like the big bosses office, something like that?"

"Do you mean Graham Ashworth, in the Chief Executive's department?" asked the friendly person.

"Oh, is that his name. Right, yeah, sorry. Can you

put me through please?" said Miller, as he scrubbed out Ashcroft on his piece of paper and scribbled Ashworth in its place.

"One moment please, may I ask who is calling?"

"Yeah, it's Alex Williams."

"Alex Williams, okay, hold the line please Mr Williams."

"Thanks a lot," Miller always used the nineteen eighties Manchester City goalkeeper's name when he was working under-cover, just because he couldn't be bothered thinking of any other names. The line was quiet for a while, almost a minute before the friendly voiced young lady spoke again.

"Hello Mr Williams, hi, I'll put you through now."

"Oh, brilliant, thanks a lot. Cheers."

Miller was buzzing, this was the end of the road for this stupid chore he was doing for Ollie. Job done in a couple of minutes, thought Miller as the phone rang through to Ashworth.

"Hello, legal?" said a pompous sounding voice at the end of the line.

"Hi, is that Graham Ashworth?" asked Miller.

"No, I'm afraid not. Graham is out of the office at the moment." Said the voice, sounding quite smug.

"Oh right, do you know when he'll be back in?" asked Miller.

"One moment," said the man, and Miller heard the ruffle sound of a hand covering the receiver, which lasted several seconds. Eventually the voice returned to the line.

"Er, hello, is it a matter that somebody else can help you with?"

"No." said Miller, firmly. "I want to talk directly to Graham Ashworth about it please."

"Hold on a moment, please."

Miller began to realise that something wasn't quite right. The muffle sound returned and eventually another voice came on the line.

"Hello, this is Graham Ashworth's line manager. He isn't available I'm afraid. Is there something I can help you with?" The new voice sounded a little harsher than the first, and equally as pompous.

"I need to speak to Graham. Is he off work?"

"I'm afraid I can't divulge that information. Now if you would just like to tell me what it is that you wish to enquire about, I am absolutely certain that myself and my colleagues will be more than capable of assisting you, Sir."

Miller put the phone down and scribbled a note on his piece of paper.

"Hmmmm," he said as he tried to rationalise why Graham's colleagues wouldn't just say if he was off work or not. If somebody is off sick, thought Miller, it wasn't a big data protection issue to mention it. Unless it was mental health, he considered.

"Ooh, sorry, Graham can't come to the phone right now, he's in the sick-bay, trying to lick a bee off his forehead at the moment." Miller was speaking in a sarcastic, patronising voice, as he accepted the fact that Ollie's little mission was not to be accomplished at the first attempt.

"Right!" said Miller loudly to himself as he put the Graham Ashworth piece of paper into the top drawer of his desk, and grabbed hold of the file at the bottom of his large pile. "Time to get cracking with all this shit." He began flicking through the file and looking for the post-it noted sections that required action from him.

Chapter 23

DI Saunders was buzzing, that much was clear to all of the team as they sat around the incident room waiting for the team brief. It was almost contagious when he was hyped, it made the rest of the SCIU department feel that little bit more enthusiastic.

"Okay guys, let's cut straight to the chase. What have we learnt from our night on the town? I'll start with you Jo, and we will go around in a circle, ending with me. I want a short, concise briefing on your investigations please. Go on Jo." Saunders sat down as Jo Rudovsky stood and came up to the front of the group, standing before the city centre map and the morose photographs of the dead homeless people.

"Thank you Sir. As instructed, we concentrated on talking to people in this area," Jo waved in a circular motion on the map to the west of the district, "we spoke to dozens of homeless people with all manner of personal issues, mostly addiction problems, alcohol, drugs, gamblers. Most of them were reluctant to talk to us, and I must say, we were reluctant to talk to some of them as well, there are some very disturbing sights to be seen when you look closely. Naturally, we weren't made very welcome, and we were verbally abused by most of the people we tried to engage with. It was quite a morale sapping night I'm afraid. In conclusion – of the handful of folk that *would* talk to us, we didn't speak to a single person who had encountered any home-made spirits on offer, and to be honest, the suggestion got a laugh from most of the people that we asked, Sir."

"Okay, thanks Jo. What about you Mike?" Saunders was absolutely desperate to mention his news, but it had to wait just now. DC Mike Worthington stood and pointed at the coach station area on the map.

"Me and Chapman patrolled around this area – all around Chorlton Street, China Town, the Village and down Portland Street into the Oxford Road area, then we doubled back up the canal, and round Ancoats to the northern quarter. It was an education to see the sheer numbers of homeless people that are out there. We encountered well over a hundred, we spoke to about twenty five people, maybe thirty. Same outcome as Jo's and Peter's enquiries I guess, they just thought we were taking the piss. One guy we talked to," he looked through his note-pad quickly, "ah, a guy called Simon Naylor, he said that it costs two pounds and ninety nine pence for four cans of Jack Lightning cider, and that's enough to get you off your tits for a good few hours. Furthermore, he said it only takes about five minutes begging on Market Street to get three quid – so there's absolutely no demand for home-made spirits really." Worthington shrugged as he walked back to his seat.

"I think it's fair to say, Sir," said Kenyon, "that people genuinely thought it was a mad idea, and all my instincts are telling me that we are definitely barking up the wrong tree with this line of enquiry."

"Agreed, Sir," said Rudovsky.

"Okay, thanks Peter, thanks everyone, so I guess it's my turn now," said Saunders. "As usual, I'm a hell of a lot better than you lot because, I have found out that the deaths were all deliberate, and that we are looking for a murderer who has poisoned these five people, and it is a person who is very likely to kill again. Now, before I expand on these details, I demand a round of applause, come on, up on your feet, all of you, worship me," Saunders gestured his team with both hands, encouraging them all to stand and start applauding their Detective Inspector. Miller was the first to stand and begin the ovation.

"Whooo - hoooo!" he shouted as the others reluctantly joined in.

"Yeah! That's right! Keep going, come on!" shouted Saunders, smiling and grinning at the team who were stood before him. "Come on, I want more. Worship me!" The group carried on with their awkward celebration for a little while longer, with Worthington doing what could only be described as a rain-dance around Saunders. It was stupid and ridiculous, but it was a good tonic, it made them all laugh and feel good after having such a miserable job to do the night before.

Once Saunders had asked them to stop rejoicing, and everybody had calmed down a little, they all returned to their seats and Saunders explained the situation as it was understood. It was obvious to everybody that Saunders had once again had a lucky, flukey result, but none of the SCIU team begrudged him of it. He was without doubt the most hard-working member of the department, and he did deserve these occasional lucky results. It was a great boost for everybody, as it meant that the cases that had been forced to one side could once again take priority.

"So I'm just left with the tidying up on this, I need to check CCTV from the area around each victim, I need to find video evidence linking the person to each crime scene, and then obviously I need to find out who it is, and pull the person in."

"Do you know if the street angel character is a man or a woman?" asked Miller.

"No, I couldn't get an answer on that, the dosser who told me about the angel started to realise that he'd grassed by accident, and he shut up as soon as he mentioned the street angel helping poorly folks out. I'm thinking it's a woman though. Gut instinct, I'm imagining a kindly old woman."

"You're going to be sat in some CCTV booth for a few days, next to some fat, farting security guard, who thinks he knows more about policing than the Chief Constable does," said Worthington. "Don't envy you much!" he added, with a look of despair on his face.

"Yeah, that's the downside. But I'll know the killer when I see her," said Saunders confidently.

"Or him." Said Chapman. "You'll be gutted if you miss a bloke walking around with an industrial bottle of turps at the murder scenes because you're looking for a woman."

"Fair point, you're right Bill. Open mind. Thank you." Saunders was grateful for the friendly advice from Chapman.

"Right!" Miller clapped his hands together as he stood up. "So does everybody know what they are working on now?"

"Yes, Sir." Said Saunders. "Bill and Mike are back on the Hyde bus station attack, and Jo and Peter are still looking for any evidence that could prove the canal killer theory."

"The Lancashire Dipper" case again? For fuck's sake," said Kenyon, under his breath.

"I'll swap you CCTV for that if you want?" said Saunders. Peter Kenyon looked down at the floor and shifted uncomfortably.

"No, I didn't think so. Get on with it, prove that there is a mass murderer prowling the banks of the canal and you'll win the Pride of Britain award."

"Right, thanks everyone, I'm nipping out on an interview, and then I'm going home. Don't work too hard!" shouted Miller as he strolled across the incident room floor towards his office. "And well done D.I. Saunders, great work."

*****

Ding Dong

"Oh, hello Andy. What an unexpected delight! Ollie, Andy's here." Pippa looked genuinely pleased to see Miller. "Where's Clare?" She asked, gazing beyond his shoulder.

"Oh, it's not a social visit. It's just something Ollie and I were talking about last night. I wanted to ask him something." Andy smiled as Pippa waved him into the house. "These are proper lovely houses, aren't they?" he said, remembering just how smart the Haughton Park development was.

"They're nice, but we miss the creeks and groans that the old house had. We think this one lacks character." Pippa was looking around at the newness of everything.

"Oh, hi Andy, alright?" said Ollie as he came down the top couple of stairs. "I was just working upstairs... on a bit of a squeaky bum deadline." He had an apologetic look on his face which Andy read as a "not-now-for-fucks-sake" look.

"Oh, right, well, I'll not keep you. I don't like Pippa's tea anyway," laughed Andy. The joke was ignored by Pippa, who was holding a glass of white wine. "I just wanted to see this house, try and get an idea about the chap's wife. Which house is it?" asked Andy, knowing full well which house it was as he'd just driven past it.

"Next door but-one, it's number nine. The wife is

called Suzanne. Are you popping round?" Ollie seemed glad that Andy was looking into it, but still had one hand on the banister and looked eager to get back up the stairs.

"No. Unfortunately, due to some of my past cases having such a high profile in the media, I'm instantly recognised as a copper most of the time."

"Ooh, get you!" Pippa laughed sarcastically, adding a snort at the end.

"I know, I know, it's embarrassing, but worse than that, it makes discreet enquiries difficult. Gone are the days when I could nosey about without mentioning police business, I'm afraid."

"Sure, sure." Ollie was stood, nodding, waiting for something to happen.

"Oh, and you gave me the wrong name. He's called Ashworth."

"What did I say?"

"Ashcroft. I spent the morning looking for a guy called Graham Ashcroft." Andy tried to make it into a sarcastic joke, but Ollie just shook his head.

"Ah, sorry. I thought it was Ashcroft. Simple mistake I guess." Ollie pushed his glasses up his nose, leaning towards the top of the stairs like a fidgety child.

"So, the car, it's on the drive over the road. Could it be possible that they've bought it off the neighbours?"

Ollie shrugged, "no idea." He stood on the stairs, just staring back at his friend.

"Right, well, I'll leave it then." He sounded slightly harsher than he had intended, but he was aggrieved none the less. An uncomfortable silence hung for a second or two.

"I'm sorry Andy, I'm, well, I'm sorry..." Ollie began walking down the stairs slowly, realising how rude and unpleasant he had been, albeit unintentionally.

"No, seriously, I was trying to do you a favour Ollie, one that's got jack-shit to do with me, or my job. But if you can't even be arsed to answer a few questions to help me out, there's not much hope is there? Like I said last night, phone the police if you have serious concerns, the number's one-oh-one. But I'm washing my hands of it, so I'll see-you two later.

Terrah now." Andy turned and left, closing the front door behind him.

"Oh, Ollie, I think you've really pissed him off!" Pippa stood with her back to the front door that Andy Miller had departed, her wine still in her hand.

"Well, that's going to have to wait. Busy." Ollie shot off up the stairs.

"God! You're a right dick-head sometimes Ol," shouted Pippa, scornfully as the office door closed upstairs.

"I'll sort it tomorrow love, I'm swimming against the tide here."

Pippa wasn't listening, she was looking out of the window, watching Miller speed off down the close.

"Oh, he's seriously pissed off with you Ollie." She muttered to herself.

*****

"Aw, now that was top. Just like my Granny used to make," said Andy as he finished his lamb chops. "Absolutely top drawer that love, thanks a lot."

"You're welcome love. I like to do a healthy meal every now and again. It's just too easy to bung a pizza in the oven most of the time." Clare took Andy's plate and placed it on the side by the sink. "You're doing the washing up though," she said as she returned to the table and stood before her husband.

"Sure thing, I'm happy to wash pots if it means I don't have to cook nowt!"

"Well that suits me. Now, do you want a beer, or a glass of wine?"

"Nowt, I'm alright actually. I'm in a bit of a mood if I'm honest."

"Oh?" Clare put her hands on her hips. "What's up?"

"Oh, it'll sound stupid. You know last night, when I was messing about with you, when you were asking what Ollie was talking about?"

"Yeah! You cheeky bugger!" She grinned as she grabbed the dish cloth and whipped it at him.

"Well, he asked me to do this favour for him, some neighbour has apparently vanished into thin air, and he wanted me to look into it."

"Right…" Clare looked a little confused, wondering where this was headed. She sat down at the dining table opposite her husband.

"Well, I tried to palm him off last night, but I gave in and said I'll have a quick nosey and see if I can find anything out. So anyway, I went round there on the way home tonight and he was being a right cock. Honestly, I've never known him to be so ignorant. I was trying to ask him questions about stuff that I needed to know about, you know, in order to help him out, and he practically said he was too busy to talk to me!"

"You're kidding! What a bloody cheek!" said Clare.

"I know, anyway, I told him to shove it. I'm seriously pissed off with him!" Andy stood and walked across to the sink and began rinsing the plates under the cold tap.

"That's not like Ollie. What did he say?"

"Nowt. He just stood on the stairs, he was practically rocking, waiting for me to piss off. It was weird. Even Pippa looked embarrassed."

"God, this sounds well weird."

"Well, I've told him I'm not having anything to do with it now, so he's shot himself in the foot." Andy ran the hot tap and squeezed the washing liquid into the sink.

"But?" Clare sensed that her husband was still stressed about something. "I know there's a but coming!"

"But, well, now I want to know what happened to the missing neighbour!"

*****

"Hi Andy, really sorry about before. Was about thirty seconds away from losing a big client. Not saying its okay but hope you understand. Pippa has made me aware of how rude I was by calling me a bell-end who doesn't deserve friends. Sorry. No harm meant. Ol."

"Is that it? It's shit. That's worse than saying

nothing, it's like you're trying to justify your behaviour, it doesn't look like an apology at all." Pippa threw Ollie's phone across the sofa.

"So, what shall I put?" asked Ollie, looking confused by this perspective that his wife was offering. He picked the phone up and re-read the message. Pippa looked as though she was thinking, so he left her a minute. After a while, he decided to ask again.

"Pippa?"

"Eh? What?" she snapped, turning her head abruptly.

"What shall I put?"

"God, are you still on about this bloody text to Andrew Miller? Just say sorry. Good grief Ollie, bore off!"

"Just sorry?" Ollie looked genuinely perplexed.

"Pass me the fucking phone Ollie." She held her hand out. Ollie handed it across. Pippa deleted the message that Ollie had written and wrote in caps SORRY, I'M A TIT before pressing the send button. "There, sorted." Pippa handed the phone back to her husband. Ollie read the sent message and smiled.

"If he doesn't reply within fifteen minutes, then you know that he is seriously pissed off with you."

*****

Andy was sat on the floor waiting for the start of C-Beebies bedtime story with his two and a half year old twins Leo and Molly. He felt a vibration against his leg and took his phone out of his pocket. He smirked at the message. Andy turned and showed his phone to Clare who was tidying up the various toys that littered the lounge floor.

"Well, at least he knows he was out of order."

"That's okay then, I'll just be a complete plonker at work tomorrow, but it'll be alright because I'll text the team saying soz. Na, I'm not replying to that text. He can sweat it out." Andy chucked the phone onto the settee behind him.

"Daddy, shush!" said Molly, holding her finger to her lips. Her eyes were wide open and she looked really annoyed at her father, which made him laugh and apologise quietly.

"Fair point Andy, but he's a good mate, and you haven't got many. So don't ruin your friendship over something that isn't such a big deal anyway." Clare had her back to her family as she put all of the toys that she'd collected into the toy bin down the side of the sofa.

"Mummy! Please be quiet!" said Leo. "It's bed time tory time!" His little voice was pleading and he looked just as outraged as Molly had done.

Clare held her hands up to apologise to her youngsters, and mouthed "sorry." Miller felt a tear build in his eyes and quickly wiped it away, smiling. He loved these people so much, and just being around them like this made him feel emotional all the time these days. He hugged his twins in close on either side of his chest and settled down to watch the story. His eyes were welled up and his smile was from ear to ear. He kissed each of his children's heads as a tear broke free.

"Bedtime story time!" he said excitedly.

"Yeah!" cheered the twins.

Chapter 24

On a case the previous year, Miller had been helped out enormously by a young police constable from F division, based at Horwich station. The officer was called Daniel Simmonds and his ingenuity and quick-thinking had enabled Miller, his boss DCS Dixon and a high-profile prisoner to escape unseen from an intense media frenzy that was unfolding outside the police station.

Miller had written to Simmonds' Sergeant to extend his gratitude to the young PC, and had remembered him as a copper to watch out for. Miller was keen to encourage him into joining the C.I.D, and had decided that the matter of Graham Ashworth's so called disappearance would be a good opportunity to test the lad out a little bit. He lifted the phone and pressed the zero, waiting for switchboard to answer.

"Oh, hiya can you do me a favour, I want to talk to the duty Sergeant at Horwich, please."

"No problem, connecting you now." Said the operator, and Miller's phone starting ringing.

"Duty Sergeant Horsfield." The voice was flat, sounding quite disinterested.

"Oh, hello, my name's DCI Miller, serious crimes investigation unit."

"Yes, Sir. How can I help you?" The Sergeant's voice perked up a little once he realised he was talking to a senior rank.

"I want a word with one of your officers, PC Simmonds. Is he on duty today?" Miller sounded very friendly and energetic, and it began to rub off on the Sergeant.

"Erm, Dan is on lates this week Sir, I'll just check if he's on duty today. Yes, he'll be in at two this afternoon Sir."

"Great, well, I want a favour off him, if he's up for it, so please will you ask him to give me a ring? I'll give you my mobile." Miller gave the Sergeant his contact details and thanked him for his help.

There was enough to be getting on with already, and Miller was annoyed with himself, and his downright inquisitive nature for not being able to forget about Ollie's stupid neighbour thing. But his instincts told him that things weren't right. Something *was* wrong, he'd got the sense of it as he'd driven around the Haughton Park development the previous afternoon, and looked at the man's house. The fact that the man's fifty grand car was on the driveway of the house opposite had again caused him a great deal of suspicion. The weird way that the man's work colleagues had handled his call added to the suspense. Like it or lump it, Miller knew that he'd have to get to the bottom of it, despite how much Ollie had pissed him off.

"Right. Let's do some proper work!" said Miller, as he began reading the reports that Saunders had left on his desk the previous night.

No sooner had he started, there was a tap at the door. Miller looked up, and saw through the glass that it was Jo Rudovsky, his DC who had become almost as famous as Miller had in the North West region, due to the heroic way that she had fought off armed robbers whilst off duty, sustaining life-threatening stab injuries in the process. CCTV footage of her standing her ground had been a national news story. The newspaper photograph of her in the hospital bed, hooked up to life support machines and the headline HERO were easy to remember for most people in the region. Her pretty, smiling, happy face on the photograph beside it had made her a very memorable "Pride of Manchester" and "Northern Hero" award winner.

"Hiya Jo, alright?" Miller put the report back in his in tray while waving his hand, encouraging her to sit down.

"Cheers Sir. You're not busy are you?" Jo took the seat, and swept the fringe of her short black hair forward with her fingers.

"I'm always busy Jo, you know that! I'm even busy with things that I shouldn't even be thinking about! But that's another story. What's up? Everything alright?" Miller could really do without this interruption, but Rudovsky would never have known, her boss seemed just as friendly and welcoming as always. Miller had really changed since Ellis had died. He had become a lot more of a people-person as far as his staff were concerned. It was clear to all of his team that it was because he had been so badly affected by the loss of his closest member of staff, Karen Ellis. He'd changed, and it had been a change for the better. He'd transformed from being a bit of a moody, can-it-wait kind of a boss, to a very encouraging and supportive one, who would really go out of his way for his staff.

"I'm fine Sir, thanks." She was smiling and looked a bit lost.

"How's Abby?" Miller was smiling sarcastically with a raised eyebrow.

"She's fine Sir, same as always." Rudovsky laughed, coyly raising a hand to her mouth.

"Same as always eh? So she's a mental bitch!" Miller laughed. Rudovsky snorted loudly. Her girlfriend Abby had given Miller a severe talking-to about unpaid overtime at a family get-together a few weeks earlier, and Miller had used every opportunity to take the piss ever since.

"I'm joking. She's a star. Right, come on - stop sulking, tell me what's up."

"I'm anxious that we're wasting time on this Lancashire dipper enquiry, Sir."

"Why?" Miller put his fingers up to his chin and used them to support his head as he leant forward. He stared at Rudovsky with an overly interested expression on his face.

"Well, I just feel, well Peter's proper on a downer with it and I'm getting the same sort of negative vibes. It's a shit case Sir, there's nothing to find. We're working for the media on it, not for the public." Rudovsky slumped slightly in her chair, the statement that she had just delivered to her boss had clearly been weighing her down. She looked a little more relaxed having got it off her chest, but the spark that she was known for was definitely missing.

"Did you come in here just to say that? Or are you asking me if you can work on something else?" Miller respected his officer for having the confidence to come and speak to him to directly about the case, and about how she felt.

The TV and newspapers had reported the suspicions of many people, that the canals and waterways of Greater

Manchester were being stalked by a serial killer. In the previous six years, over sixty dead bodies had been found in the canal, more than two thirds of them were so badly decomposed that no cause of death was ever explained. All but two of the bodies were male. Miller and his team had been given the thankless and unrewarding task of proving the theory of a serial killer dubbed "The Lancashire Dipper" wrong. The public, with the help of the newspapers and social media discussions, were convinced that there was a serial killer, and that it was a real, present danger. The police were forced into re-investigating the cases, in order to rule-out the theory. It just so happened that Jo and Peter had been handed the file.

"I'm not saying that I don't want to do it, Sir, not at all – all I'm saying is that there isn't a decent line of enquiry to go after. I'm pretty confident that most of the cases were treated quite lazily by the various C.I.D. units that dealt with them, but I understand that, naturally – a bloated, decomposed body bobbing about in a stinking canal isn't an inspiring job to attend and get excited about." Rudovsky looked uncharacteristically dejected.

"How can I help? I mean, I know what you are saying Jo, but…"

"I need you to stick a rocket up my arse with it Sir. I need motivating. It's just an admin job this, there's no real crime investigation work involved. I just feel like I'm wasting my life Sir. I wish I was dead." Jo grinned, and forced a laugh from Miller who wasn't anticipating the histrionic ending to Jo's complaint. She smiled, but Miller could see that she was being genuine about how depressing the whole "dipper" investigation was becoming. Miller knew that he would have to dig deep if he was about to inspire Jo, and get her enthused about the case, which was, as she had quite rightly pointed out, nothing more than an admin role. A fact checking exercise. A box ticking chore.

"Okay, listen. The official line is that there are no links between the cases, yeah?" Miller sat up and added a spring of enthusiasm into his voice.

"Yes, that's the official line Sir. I'm meant to either

prove that the official line is accurate, or prove that it's wrong." Rudovsky's twinkly brown eyes trailed down to the floor.

"And what do you think?"

"Peter reckons…"

"I'm not asking Peter. I'm asking you, Jo."

"Well, I was going to say, Peter has a different attitude to me, its creating tension between us. He thinks that every single body arrived in the canal through individual circumstances, and the only factor that links them is the canal itself."

"But,"

"But I'm not having it. I think that some – not all – but some of them must be linked. We're pulling in separate directions, Sir, and I love Peter, I love working with him. He's a great detective, and he always buys me coffee and that, but I'm really struggling with him on this one."

"Why do you think there is a link?"

"Mathematics, Sir. If you take a similar city with a similar sized canal network, say Birmingham – the number of bodies is a fraction of the numbers that we are talking about in our network. London, same story, and they have three times our population. Plus, the fact that all but two are men, and they are predominantly young men in their teens or twenties, it makes me think that it is as dodgy as hell, Sir."

"My thoughts precisely Jo. That's classified – don't say nowt to anyone. I want to be honest with you, I'm not up on the fence with this. I'm absolutely convinced there is a serial killer, or two, targeting pissed up young lads who have had too much to drink or too many drugs."

"Two, Sir?" asked Rudovsky, the fizz and sparkle suddenly returning to her generous, kindly eyes. Miller held up his hand to pause his colleague as he continued to speak.

"A coward who randomly kills vulnerable, defenceless people who least expect it. People who are pissed up, stoned, or feeling down and have found themselves in a lonely place, by the canal. I say keep going, and I'll have a word with Peter, and try and giddy him up a bit. But honestly Jo, if I thought that there was nothing to find – I wouldn't ask you guys to work on it. I wouldn't, would I? My opinion is that there isn't a killer, there's a pair of them who are working together, doing it for kicks."

"Why?" Rudovsky looked shocked, but also revved up by hearing this, Miller's exclusive opinion, she leant in towards his desk to hear what he had to say about it that little more closely.

"Confidence. If I was out and about at weekends, shoving people into the canal for the past six years, by now I'd be getting a bit paranoid that my face will have been described more than a few times by witnesses, that my head keeps turning up on CCTV and so on. I'd bet my car that it's a pair of them, most likely men in their thirties or forties, probably partners, a gay couple that get a great, sadistic buzz out of watching somebody drowning, panicking, you know, splashing about, struggling and ultimately dying. That's my honest opinion, and if I was in your frock, I'd be excited about trying to catch the killers and getting them locked up in Strangeways."

"Seriously?"

"Scouts honour. Let me talk to Peter, on the snide like, I won't say you've said anything. And I'll try and gee him up a bit. Alright?"

"That's brilliant Sir, thanks. Just what I needed."

"That's what I'm for!"

"I don't cope with negativity well. That's why I want to rise through the ranks quickly so I can work on my own." Rudovsky laughed and Miller saw her genuine, enthusiastic smile again.

"You're so full of stupid dreams and bullshit ambitions Jo, I love it!"

"And you saying that if you were in my frock is first class, grade one sexism Sir, so watch it!" Jo winked as she stood to leave. Miller laughed out loud. "Thanks again, Sir."

"Thank you, Jo. Go and get 'em mate."

*****

"Hi, is that DCI Miller?" the man sounded young and

slightly nervous.

"It is. Who's that?" asked Miller into his phone. He circled an error on the report that he was reading as he spoke into his mobile.

"Oh, sorry, it's constable Simmonds Sir, from Horwich police station."

"Ah, brilliant! Nice to hear from you. Bloody hell, that's a surprise. The Sergeant I spoke to said you weren't in until two this aft." Miller looked at his watch, it was just after ten.

"Yeah, he text me, told me you'd rung so I wanted to see what it was about, Sir."

"Well, ten out of ten for enthusiasm Simmonds, great start!" On hearing the young man's voice again, Miller remembered his face perfectly. He was rugged looking, well built with short blonde hair. Simmonds was a strong, athletic young copper who looked like he could play a bit of sport. He had a nice, cheeky attitude too, and Miller had been massively impressed by his use of initiative last time they had met. Most junior police officers fall apart when senior ranks are in their company, but Simmonds had definitely stepped up to the plate and made a great impression when it counted the most.

"I've got a bit of C.I.D. business that I want to talk to you about. How do you fancy coming over here to HQ to have a chat about it?" Miller stood up and walked across to the window, where he had a panoramic view of the city centre to the west and the Pennines to the east, with their gigantic white windmills that were spinning at quite a lazy speed today.

"Yeah, yeah, God that's amazing Sir. When?"

"When's best for you?"

"Now. I can be in town in, about thirty five, forty minutes, Sir. Is that too keen?"

"As long as it's not going to interfere with your day job. You can't be late for your shift. I'll need about half an hour with you. Does that work out comfortably?"

"Er…" Simmonds was clearly doing mental arithmetic, and that fact pleased Miller, it said a lot about the young copper when the desire would be to just say yes and to hell with it.

"Yeah, yeah, leaves me about forty five minutes either way, Sir."

"Nice one. Right, well I'll get the kettle on PC Simmonds! See you soon."

The call came through from reception thirty minutes later that Daniel Simmonds had arrived. Miller went down to greet him, and got a buzz from seeing how nervous and enthusiastic Simmonds was.

"Not been here since passing out, Sir." He said, as the two of them walked up the stairs in the huge glass built headquarters.

"Most officers who come back here are either getting sacked or promoted!" Miller smiled as he opened a door on the second floor and gestured Simmonds through into the SCIU office space.

"Thanks. Well, I hope it's not the sack!" Simmonds laughed and Miller patted his back.

"Not at all. I owe you a big thank you for your help last year. You played a bloody blinder there. I wrote to your Inspector, I hope they passed it on?"

"Yeah, thanks a lot. I photocopied it for me Mam! She was chuffed to bits."

Miller stopped walking and stepped into the kitchen area. "Coffee?"

"Please, just black, no sugar." Simmonds was looking around the office, surprised by how small this place was. He'd imagined that the famous SCIU department would be massive, a buzzing hive of energy and activity. It was tiny, there was only about ten desks in there, and only a couple of detectives in. They looked pretty bored too.

"Here you go." Miller handed Simmonds his drink.

"Thanks. Cheers. I mean, thanks very much, Sir."

"It's alright. You look a bit disappointed…"

"Yeah, no, I mean, it's a lot smaller than I thought. I imagined about fifty people working up here?" Simmonds was clearly surprised and it amused Miller.

"We are the elite mate! No, we have been hit with the same cuts as everyone else. We're at our absolute weakest since the department was formed, what, about eight or nine years ago."

"Ah, right."

"Anyway, come on, follow me through to my office." Miller strode away from the kitchen space and headed towards his glass walled office that overlooked the rest of the department. "Take a seat," he said as Simmonds walked through, desperately trying not to spill his drink.

"Thanks very much."

"Right!" said Miller, quite loudly as he sat down opposite PC Simmonds. It made the junior policeman jump a little bit. "I have a favour to ask."

Simmonds put his cup down on the desk that sat between the two men.

"Okay…"

"I want you to take this pork pie down to the serious fraud office for me." Miller pushed a white paper bag which had a pie sat on top of it across the table.

"What? You've…. Ah wait." Simmonds burst out laughing. "You nearly had me at it there," he said smiling. Miller laughed as he wrapped the pie up in the paper bag.

"I'm joking. Just a bit of CID banter. Now, in all seriousness, I do have a favour to ask. I can't ask any of my officers to do it as it's not official police business." Miller had a kind, encouraging look on his face. Simmonds was listening intently. "There is an unofficial concern that somebody has gone missing. It's causing a lot of confusion, as the person in question hasn't been reported missing. Now, I want you to go around to the house, as though it *is* official police business, in your uniform, and make some enquiries. How does that sound?" Miller sat back in his chair and studied Simmonds' expression. The young constable thought about what Miller had said for a little while before speaking.

"I'm a bit confused…"

"Sure. Well, the person that we suspect to be missing is a big deal in the local council over in Bury. He's a typical local government senior management type, thinks he's a different class, reckons his shit is all stripey and smells like air-wick."

Simmonds laughed.

"Now, if he isn't actually missing, and we go busting in there, we'll look like knobs, and he'll ring the Manchester Evening News to tell them how much we look like knobs. So we have to be really careful."

"But. What makes you think he's missing?"

Miller laughed. It was a stupid situation to be in. But he couldn't just explain to Simmonds that he was just a nosey parker and had a real problem with letting things go.

"Do you remember a few months ago, there was a big problem in the news about council house shortages, and a big posh estate in Bury was being rented out to homeless families? It caused quite a stir."

"No. I missed that." Simmonds began fidgeting, pulling a pen and notepad out of his jacket pocket.

"Right, well anyway, it was a big story, all these businessmen and accountants were holding demonstrations for the telly crews. One of the main organisers of all this is the guy who is supposedly missing."

"What's his name?"

Miller gave Simmonds all of the details, as the young PC made notes in his notepad, unaware of how much he was impressing the DCI with his questions and no-nonsense attitude. Miller told Simmonds about the weird response he had got from the council when he'd asked to speak to Graham Ashworth. Simmonds was most intrigued by the car detail. This was the thing that was bothering Miller the most too.

"Bloody hell. They're about fifty grand aren't they?" asked Simmonds.

"Yes, anywhere between forty and fifty depending on the spec. But it's not the kind of car you lend out for days at a time to a family of homeless council tenants, that you barely even know, is it?"

Miller was chuffed that Simmonds was also intrigued by all of this. Conscious of the time, and that the PC had to leave soon to get back to his own station across the city – Miller began summing up Simmonds' role. Between them, they planned that on Thursday, which was Simmonds' day off, he would come back to HQ in uniform, pick up a patrol car, and head off to Haughton Park, to ask Suzanne Ashworth if Graham Ashworth was around. The premise for the visit would be a fictitious road traffic incident the previous week in which Mr Ashworth's registration number had been mentioned.

"Seem's pretty straight forward." Simmonds smiled.

"The original theory that was reported to me was that Ashworth might be in jail. I broke the rules slightly and checked the system, and he was brought in for drunk and disorderly, breach of the peace, had a night in the cells at Bury and took a caution the next morning. This was around the time that he went missing. Other than that, he is squeaky clean, never been in a police car before."

"What was the caution all about?"

"He was kicking off with the new neighbours, screaming and shouting in the middle of the night, then turned on the attending officers."

"He sounds like a right bell-end, Sir."

Miller laughed at Simmonds' rather frank observation. "I know, exactly! He sounds like just the kind of bloke who could piss people off so much that he could go missing!" Miller smiled and Simmonds laughed again. "So, I want to find out what's happened. See what his wife says, and try your best to find out why the council were being so uptight about his absence. Make no mistake, I'm using this whole project as an opportunity to see if you're any good. So give it your best shot, and I'll look forward to reading your report on Friday."

"Thanks, Sir, I'm really up for it." Simmonds stood and outstretched his hand for Miller to shake. Miller gave him a firm handshake and a friendly smile.

"Listen, if anything goes tits up, get straight on to me. This is an under-cover operation at this stage, so I'm your only contact on this matter. Even my own officers are in the dark about it, for now."

"Not a problem, Sir. Thank you for the opportunity."

"The keys for a car will be held on reception for you, just flash your warrant card to them and they'll sort you out, tell you where it's parked."

"Great. Okay, well thanks again, Sir."

Chapter 25

On Thursday morning, PC Simmonds picked up the Astra patrol car as agreed, and felt an unexpected, giddy nervousness. He drove north out of the city centre, heading in the direction of Bury and the Haughton Park development. The anxiety that he was feeling reminded him of the same rush of nerves that he would experience as a teenager whilst bunking off school for the day, in a state of constant worry that somebody would see him and tell his mum and dad. Rationally, he knew that the chances of another officer seeing him, and noticing that he wasn't in an F division patrol car, and that this was his day off anyway were miniscule, but none the less - he felt alarmingly tense.

Simmonds had never heard of Haughton Park until DCI Miller had told him about the place. It was clear to him, as he drove onto the estate, why renting half of the houses out as social housing had been an unpopular decision for the home-owners on the impressive development.

"Nice car." Simmonds muttered to himself as he drove past a navy blue Jaguar XK parked up on a neighbouring driveway. "God, this place really is lush."

"Continue for four hundred yards, then take the left hand turning on to Fir Trees Grove and your destination will be right ahead." Simmonds turned off the sat-nav app on his phone and pulled the police car over at the side of the road. He opened his notepad and revised his brief. He stayed put for a minute or two, double-checking his questions and making sure that he knew precisely what he was doing. This type of an opportunity to impress the DCI of the best CID department in the north of England didn't come along very often, and Simmonds was absolutely determined to give it his best shot. He knew that he had to do even better than Miller was expecting, and this fact made him feel slightly excited and tense too.

"Right, okay, focus." Simmonds took a deep breath. He held the oxygen a few seconds too long before exhaling loudly. He hit the indicator and slowly pulled the police car off and drove it slowly for the final few metres of the journey.

As he turned into Fir Trees Grove, he saw that the white Range Rover Evoque was parked on its own driveway, at number nine. A very attractive young lady was stood beside it, talking to another woman. Simmonds parked the police car and stepped out, putting his helmet on as he locked up the car. He walked onto the drive and spoke to the ladies.

"Hello, I hope you can help me. I'm trying to find Mr Ashworth. Do you know if he's in?" Simmonds was smiling, and had a very friendly, easy-going nature.

"Hello. I'm Graham's wife, Suzanne." The lady was a stunner, thought Simmonds.

"Hello Suzanne. How do you do?"

"Is everything okay?" asked the other woman. On first impressions, Simmonds thought that she might be one of the social housing users.

"Everything's fine, thanks." He said, and looked back at Suzanne, and felt slightly embarrassed as he realised that he had been caught taking a rather greedy glance down her cleavage.

"Erm, you'd better come in." Suzanne looked slightly red faced, and Simmonds couldn't tell if it was due to his unexpected visit, or because he'd just been busted staring down her top. "I'll see you later Rachel, I'll pop over for a cup of tea later on, and you can tell me all about it love. Alright?" Suzanne placed her hand on her visitor's shoulder tenderly.

"Okay, no worries, see you later." Rachel leant in and kissed her neighbour on the cheek, then turned and walked casually across the road to the house opposite. Simmonds stood and watched her. The way she stood, the way she walked, she just didn't look right in this place. She looked poor, and most definitely out of her natural habitat, he thought. Suzanne prompted her unexpected police visitor to follow her into her house.

"Would you like a cup of tea?"

"Oh, great," he followed Suzanne down the drive towards the front door. "If you're making?"

"Sure, come on in. Close the door behind you." Suzanne breezed into the house, seemingly without a care in the world.

"Lovely place you've got here," said Simmonds as he followed Suzanne into the kitchen.

"It is, we're very lucky. Tea or coffee officer…"

"Dan, just call me Dan. I'll have a tea please, not so much milk."

"Sugar?"

"Just the one, thanks very much. It's always nice to get offered a brew! It doesn't happen often these days!" Simmonds was staring at Suzanne as she made the drinks. She looked very relaxed, and he too was starting to relax a little.

"Well, it seems that this house is becoming a regular place to visit for the police! Graham was arrested you know, taken off in the middle of the night, it was so embarrassing! And now I presume you need to finish off your business with him? The neighbours will certainly be gossiping, that's for sure!" Suzanne smiled, and stared directly at the PC. He was staring back, and it was quite clear to both of them that there was a certain chemistry in the air between them. Simmonds realised that his heart was beating quite fast, and he could feel that his face and ears were heating up. His radio crackled and another police officer asked the operator for an address check. Simmonds turned the volume down.

"Oh, I'm sorry. It's nothing to worry about, just a routine enquiry. Is Graham home?"

"No, I'm afraid not."

"Sorry, did you say… Is he your…"

"My husband, yes. But he's not around today I'm afraid." Suzanne strained the tea bag against the inside lip of the cup and walked towards Simmonds with it balanced on the teaspoon. "Can I just…" Suzanne was stood very close to the officer and he felt quite peculiar, until she pointed towards the cupboard that the policeman was stood next to. "It's the bin."

"Right, yes, sure, sorry." Simmonds moved and Suzanne opened up the door and a metal lid lifted up on the bin. She popped the tea bag into the bin and let the door close.

"Here you go," said Suzanne as she walked back to the kettle and passed Simmonds his drink.

"Brilliant, nice one. Thanks very much."

"So," said Suzanne, leaning back against the sink, facing Simmonds. "What do you want with my husband?" She had a playful, flirty look on her face and Simmonds could feel himself blushing further. He could seriously fancy this woman, he thought to himself as he tried really hard not to look again at her very low-cut t-shirt.

"Oh, er, well it's nothing much. There was an incident, an RTA that happened last week. Mr Ashworth's car was reported, by, er, one sec." Simmonds pulled out his notebook from his pocket. "Yes, his car turned up on CCTV just after an accident. We think he may have witnessed the incident, so we just need to ask him a few questions about it." Dan looked down again at his notes, and was pleased with how this was going. So far, so good, he thought.

"When was this?" asked Suzanne. She looked quite concerned.

"Erm, let's see. Last… it was the eighteenth so last Thursday." Simmonds glanced up from his notepad.

"A week ago today? Well it wasn't Graham, he wasn't driving. And it wasn't me either last week, I wasn't driving the car." Suzanne was confident, and Simmonds could tell that she was telling the truth.

"Oh, right. Okay," Simmonds looked a bit lost, and started writing down a few notes. This was a curve ball, and he hadn't anticipated it coming. Only he knew that there was no RTA, and that it was all just a nonsense to try and get a conversation with the husband. He needed to think quickly and stop mucking about flirting, he thought to himself. Pull yourself together man.

"Right, well, so - do you know who was driving?" He suddenly looked quite stressed and his care-free attitude had all but disappeared. A slightly harder edge had crept into his voice.

"Yes, it was Rachel, my neighbour. The lady I was talking to when you came in." Suzanne was not put off by Simmonds' sudden change in demeanour, she continued to talk, and behave in as care-free a way as she had done throughout the visit.

"Right, so, what is Rachel's surname, and address then please?"

"Her surname is, erm, God, I know this! Birdsworth! That's it. She lives at the house across the road, the one that you saw her walk in to."

"And, so your husband lets her drive the car too?"

"Absolutely, yes, she doesn't steal it!" Suzanne threw her head back and laughed loudly. It made Simmonds feel quite silly. He could feel all of this slipping away, he felt that he was making a massive balls up of everything, and it was all because he fancied Suzanne. Get yourself together you massive loser, he thought to himself.

"Well, I am going to have to talk to Mr Ashworth as well, as he is the registered keeper of the vehicle."

"That's not a problem. He's not here today though, but if you want to leave your card, leave a number he can contact you on, I'll see that he does."

"Oh, okay, well that works. I did try and talk to him at his workplace, but they were a bit..."

"A bit what?" Suzanne suddenly seemed a bit edgy. The playfulness was disappearing.

"A bit, unco-operative, shall we say?" Simmonds raised an eyebrow, hoping that Suzanne would offer up something that might be useful or interesting for taking back to DCI Miller.

"Oh, well, it's probably data protection or something." Suzanne's sudden anxiety seemed to have disappeared as quickly as it had appeared. "He's been fired."

Simmonds wasn't supposed to care, he wasn't supposed to know anything about the man, but he couldn't disguise his surprise at this detail, and the casual manner in which Suzanne revealed it.

"What, I thought..."

"What?" Suzanne shrugged.

"I thought that he was a manager there, high up like?"

"He was. But he's such an absolute loser, he went and got himself sacked, which is a really, really difficult thing to do when you're as high up the ladder as Graham was. He was earning over a hundred grand a year, and now he's earning nothing. And instead of looking for another job, he's gone off to Thailand to take his mind off things."

"Wow."

"Ha, yes, wow indeed, bloody hell."

"So, when did he go?"

"Oh, a few weeks ago, maybe a month. I don't care, I'm glad to see the back of him to tell you the truth Dan. He used to beat me you know. What a big hard man, beating up a five-foot-five, eight stone woman, who is scared of breaking a nail. He's a bastard, and I hope his plane crashes on the way home!" Suzanne had worked herself up, and Simmonds was feeling quite embarrassed.

"Right, well, so I'm sorry to hear about that. I suppose I'd better go across and speak to the lady across the road." Simmonds looked at his notebook. "Rachel Birdsworth. It sounds as though she will be best placed to help me."

Suzanne looked sad, as though she had more to say about her husband, more to get off her chest, but Simmonds certainly didn't want to become a shoulder to cry on. He had heard enough, in fact, more than enough to take back to Miller. The thought delighted him, things had turned around nicely and Simmonds was now thinking about nothing more than getting back to HQ and filing his report for DCI Miller. Suddenly, Suzanne, and all of her flirty attractiveness had become second-best. He had been in the house for less than ten minutes and he'd cracked the case. This was incredible. Miller was going to be over-the-moon, and Simmonds just wanted to get back there as soon as possible and cash in his chips.

"Well, listen, I'm really sorry to trouble you, and, well, it sounds as though you could do without him if he abuses you. You do know there is support out there for people who are trapped in abusive relationships, I could refer you for help…"

"No, I don't want to be put in a bed-sit in a different town. I've thought about it, Dan, but no. I'm okay. I'll roll with the punches, if you see what I mean." Suzanne tried to pull back her carefree, breezy attitude that Simmonds had first warmed too, but this depressing talk about her husband had seemingly upset her more than she wanted to let on.

"Well," Simmonds drained his cup. "I'll have to get on, I've got about five people I need to talk to about this bloody crash."

"Of course. Well, thanks, it's been nice to talk to you Dan. If you're ever in the area again, pop by, see if my awful husband survived his flight home!" Suzanne smiled but that flirty confidence had gone now, and Simmonds saw that she was really quite a lonely, vulnerable person behind the expensive make-up, the skimpy clothes and the sexy bravado.

"You know something, speaking off the record, not as a policeman, but as a normal person... you're worth so much more than that. Truly, you should get yourself away from him. He sounds like a really nasty piece of work from what you've said. Now I shouldn't say this, it's not my business. But you're a lovely young woman. No man has the right to hurt you. Look, I'd better be off. Nice to meet you."

"Thanks Dan. Thank you very much." Suzanne stepped across to where the policeman was standing and stood on her tip-toes and gave him a very light kiss on the cheek. "You're a lovely man, Dan. Thank you."

Simmonds waved to Suzanne as she stood at her door. He crossed the road to pay a visit to Rachel Birdsworth, who had apparently been driving the vehicle when it was seen near a fictitious road incident. Suzanne went inside her house after she saw him press the doorbell. There was no answer and PC Simmonds was reluctant to stay around, he had all of the information he required about the missing person – there was absolutely no need to add any delay. He walked down the sloping driveway, and across the road to his car.

Within seconds, the Astra police car was cruising off down the road, and Simmonds was laughing at how easy it had been to get the full story in less than a quarter of an hour.

"You absolute beauty!" He punched the air, and

squeezed his foot a little harder against the accelerator. "Back of the net!"

END OF PART TWO

PART THREE

Chapter 26

"Holy shit. Why didn't the policeman press the bell? What's going on? Seriously, Suzanne, something really shady is going on." Rachel was getting herself in a state.

"Don't be daft. He pressed the bell. I saw him. I watched him from my door."

"Right, come here." Rachel stormed out of Suzanne's house at quite a pace, and was heading across the road towards her own house, her neighbour was following orders, trailing behind her.

"Watch this." Rachel pressed the door-bell and the familiar ding-dong sound came from within the house. "See?"

"What?"

"There's no problem with my fucking door-bell. And I was stood in the kitchen, peeling spuds." Rachel opened her front door and let Suzanne see how close the kitchen was to the doorbell as she ding-donged it again. "So, he hasn't pressed it. I saw him come and stand at the door for about ten seconds before he shot off back into his police car. I was wondering what he was doing, I was trying to work out why he wasn't knocking on or pressing the bell. Then he darted off. See what I mean? He clearly doesn't want to speak to me, so what I want to know is, what exactly…"

"Hi mum! Alright?" Liam walked in, past his mother and their neighbour as they stood at the front door step. "Hi Suzanne!"

"Oh, shit is that the time love, God."

"Hi Liam,"

"No, I've been sent home. Study leave."

"You better not be wagging it Liam."

"I'm not mum, it's study leave. So, I'll just go and do a bit of revising upstairs," said Liam, winking as he spoke. "What's up with you two anyway, you look like you'se have followed through."

"Oh, nowt, just women stuff."

"Well you're not talking about shoes or handbags, I can tell by your faces."

"Cheeky little shit!" said Rachel, play-thumping her

son.

"Little, I'm like two foot taller than you mother. You little fart!" Rachel laughed at her son's wise-crack, and her mind was temporarily distracted from the terror that she was sensing about the policeman.

"Hey, you're not too big for a good hiding Liam."

"I am, aren't I mam?" Liam raised his fists to his mum in a jokey way and both Suzanne and Rachel laughed again at the cheeky teenager.

"Right, you – use your study time wisely, not on snapchat and all that twitter shite. I'm going over to Suzanne's for a brew. See ya in a bit."

"Alright, see yoh."

Rachel kissed her son on the cheek.

"You can have one as well Suzanne, come on, don't be shy. Let me take a photo while you do it, that can be my profile picture!"

"In your dreams!" shouted Rachel, as Suzanne smiled politely and headed away from the door.

Rachel followed her neighbour as Liam closed the door behind them. "Right, Suzanne, you need to be on the ball here." Rachel was chattering away as they walked across the road. "I need to know absolutely everything that's been said. Right?"

"Sure, it was quite straight forward really." Suzanne pushed down on the door handle of her own house and opened the front door. Rachel followed her into the house, pausing to have a quick look up and down the close, before closing the door.

Suzanne sat at the kitchen table and tried to recall every detail of the conversation with the policeman, as Rachel made them both a cup of tea.

"Did he seem particularly interested in what you were saying, or was he just going through the motions?"

"Hard to say. He was pretty taken with my boobs, he couldn't take his eyes off them. But he didn't seem massively enthusiastic about the car accident that he was talking about. He was quite a dish actually."

"So you were up to the part about phoning Graham's

work up?"

"Yes, so, I told him about Graham being sacked…"

"Did he seem surprised? Did the information make him seem like he gave a shit?"

"Erm, well, I guess so, he looked a bit, like, you know, shocked." Suzanne took a sip of her drink.

"Why would a copper give a shit about some total stranger saying that her husband got fired. It's bollocks this Suzanne. Shit. What if he's planted a bug?"

"A what?"

"A bloody listening device, you know, a bug to listen to what we are saying. Where was he sat?"

"Rachel, you're being a bit…"

"No I'm not Suzanne. Where was he sat when you were having the conversation?"

"He was stood up, there, next to the bin cupboard. I stood there." Suzanne pointed at the kitchen cupboards where she had made the drinks. She pointed at the spot where the policeman had stood. Rachel began feeling around, she opened the doors and pulled open the drawers.

"Rachel, for God's sake. You're being hysterical. He didn't open any bloody drawers, he just stood there and drank his tea while I told him all about what a horrid bastard Graham was. He couldn't wait to get away once I'd started!"

"Shit. You said was?"

"What? No, of course I didn't say was! I said I hope his plane crashes on the way back from his holiday!"

"Did he ask when he was coming back?"

"No…"

"Are you sure?"

"Yes, I'm not a bloody moron Rachel. I told him that he got sacked, and decided to piss off on holiday to cheer himself up. Exactly as we'd planned Rachel. Word for word. Please stop speaking to me like I'm a child, for God's sake!" Suzanne seemed to have blown her fuse as she reached the end of her statement.

"Okay. Sorry, sorry Suzanne. I can't help it though, worrying…"

"I know, but just simmer down. You're being

paranoid."

"I'm not, love. I'm really not." Rachel stood in front of Suzanne and took hold of her shoulders. She exhaled loudly, looked at the floor and started talking slowly, quietly. "You're in denial. Look, you need a reality check Suzanne. This copper came here to find out where Graham was. Why else would he avoid talking to the person who was driving the car? It's a bullshit story. He just wanted to know where Graham was. And when he realises that Graham isn't on an extended holiday in Thailand, he'll be back, you mark my words, and we'll be going in Styal Prison for the next ten years. We'd better have a word with Tania, and warn her that the shit is about to hit the fan."

*****

"How did you get on?" asked Miller as he saw Simmonds walking into the SCIU office with a huge smile on his face. "By the way you're wearing that big cheesey grin, I'm guessing it went well?"

"Oh hi, Sir, it's case closed!"

Miller laughed out loud and extended his arm, ushering the young PC into his office.

"Game, set and match. He's not missing at all, Sir, he's on his jollies, he's in Thailand, on an extended break to get over the stress of getting sacked from his job at the council."

It sounded like the well rehearsed statement that it was. Miller couldn't hide his pleasure at seeing the PC looking so pleased with himself.

"Cor blimey Simmonds! That's quite a lot of information!" Miller looked delighted.

"I know!" Simmonds laughed.

"So, he's been sacked. That would explain why they were being shy on the phone when I was asking to talk to him. What was he sacked for?" Miller looked intrigued. It wasn't the kind of job that people generally get sacked from.

"Oh, er, she didn't say. She just said that he's been a dick-head."

"Whereabouts in Thailand is he staying?"

"Oh, er, not sure."

"When did he fly out?"

"Not sure, erm, roughly a month ago, Sir."

"And he left the wife at home?"

"Yes, she said she's glad. She hates his guts by the sound of it, Sir."

"And you didn't ask what he was sacked for?"

"No, I...." Simmonds suddenly started to realise that this wasn't quite the FA Cup final last minute goal that he'd imagined it was. In fact, it seemed as though DCI Miller was pulling his story apart. He stood up a little straighter.

"When is he coming back?"

"Erm, I'm not sure, Sir."

"Did you ask why the neighbours are using the car?"

"Yes, well, I mean it came up, because it was the neighbour who was driving on the day of the made-up incident."

"And?"

"Well, she said that her neighbour was driving that day," Simmonds coughed, trying hard to get back some confidence in his voice. This was beginning to go tits-up and both of the men knew it. "I asked if the neighbour was insured and she said yes, she laughed, you know as if to say that's a dumb question. It was difficult, Sir, I was trying to win her trust, I didn't, I mean I couldn't interrogate her."

"I didn't ask you to... look, it's okay, don't worry, you've done..." Miller was struggling to hide his disappointment, regardless of how positive he was trying to be.

"Wait, Sir, it's hard this, a lot harder than it sounds. I was trying to win her trust, and it was working, she started telling me about how he knocks her about. She was close to tears, Sir. It wasn't appropriate to ask where he was staying, it wasn't like that, Sir. I didn't want to blow my cover. She was flirting one minute, then almost crying the next. She wasn't obstructive, she said her husband will phone me when he gets back." Simmonds looked crest-fallen. He began to experience a disappointing, sinking feeling, the first acceptance that he'd blown it. Miller felt for him.

"You've done alright. It sounds like it was tricky." Miller tried to be as enthusiastic as possible, but the young PC had only brought him a bit of a story. There was still plenty of intrigue. Miller had so many more questions, and he was unsure of how he could pursue them.

"It was tricky, Sir. The neighbour who uses the car was there when I arrived. Straight away, she was like "is everything okay?" I got the impression she was nervous, she seemed a bit shifty. But Suzanne, the wife, God, she was as cool as a cucumber, Sir."

"She's quite a looker isn't she?" Miller raised an eyebrow. "That's what I heard anyway."

Simmonds replied without hesitation. "Drop-dead, Sir. Footballers wife, she knows it as well. She's absolutely…" Simmonds remembered where he was, and who he was speaking to. He began to modify his word choice mid-sentence. "…she is what you would describe as highly attractive."

Miller laughed. "Yes, that's what I was led to believe. Apparently, her husband is a right old turd. Your first question should have been "what first attracted you to your millionaire husband?" Miller smiled, inviting Simmonds to laugh, but the younger man was too stressed, and annoyed with himself. It wasn't so much how he'd got on at the house, he was more annoyed with his delivery. He knew he could have presented his findings better, and it was really getting to him.

"Well, it's been nice seeing you again today. You've done enough to make me suspicious that it doesn't add up. I can feel it in my bones, there's something not right going on up there, and all I need to do is find out if any flights have taken anyone called Graham Ashworth to anywhere in the last few months, and if they haven't, I'll have enough reason to call this Suzanne's bluff."

"Well, for what it's worth, Sir, I've been invited back. When I'm in the area, she said pop in and see if her bastard husband has come back yet. She said that she hopes his plane crashes on the way home!"

"Interesting. Okay, I'll bear this in mind. I might be calling you again about this PC Simmonds."

Miller couldn't escape the fact that the young PC was gutted with his performance, mainly because of the ferocity of Miller's quick fire questions that had put him on the back-foot. But Miller had done it deliberately, to see how he would cope. "You've done pretty good today, cheer up. Good start!" Miller tapped his hand on Simmonds' shoulder. "Cheer up or I'll arrest you for sulking."

Simmonds smiled reluctantly. "Thanks Sir."

Chapter 27

"Aw Mum! Have you farted?" Britney looked disgusted as she walked behind her mother in the kitchen. She wafted her arm, and cleared herself a pathway through the smell.

"No I have not, you cheeky cow!"

"You have, it's rank! You need to see the doctors with that."

"I haven't trumped Britney, I swear down." Rachel looked around, and seemed confused. "Oh, I just opened a packet of ham. It's probably that."

Britney accepted the explanation with a nod and sat herself down at the kitchen island, the posh feature which had been so exciting when the family first moved in, but had now become the central dumping ground for random items, from a broken Sat-Nav to piles of clean underwear, hair brushes and discarded shopping bags.

"What's for tea?"

"I was doing some potato hash but I'll have to finish that later on. I've got to nip out. I'm just making some butties for now."

"Where are you going?" Britney's eyes were locked onto her phone, her tone made it sound as though she couldn't really care less.

"Got to nip out," said Rachel as she spread margarine on the bread slices as fast as she could.

"Suzanne's house by any chance?"

"Yes, love. Why?" Rachel stopped spreading the margarine and looked across at her daughter.

"Well, you are spending a hell of a lot of time with her recently mum. I thought you said she was a weirdo?"

"Never mind that. It's none of your business love. It's adult stuff." Rachel returned her attention to the bread.

"Oh, okay, thanks for patronising me." Britney's eyes flicked up from the phone for the first time since she'd entered the kitchen. She gave a long, hard stare at the back of her mother before returning her gaze to the phone.

"Don't be like that love. God, I wish you'd lighten up

a bit, you're turning into a right old nag bag." Rachel had a slightly angry tone to her voice.

"If I said something like that, you'd do your nut. But it's alright for you to say stuff like that. It stresses me out. If I answer questions going "oh, its none of your business, it's teenage stuff, you'd go crazy at me."

"What *is* the matter?" asked Rachel, putting down her butter-knife and turning around once again to face her sulky daughter. Britney's eyes were locked on the phone.

"Forget it."

"I'm going to Suzanne's, because I need to talk to her about something."

"But it's so important that we all have to have a butty for tea?" Britney still didn't look up from whatever it was that she was staring at on her phone. Rachel had to remind herself to count to ten. Her daughter was right, regardless of the cockiness and the attitude, Britney had a very valid point.

"Listen, love…"

"Why? So you can tell me a load of lies. I know why you're spending so much time with Suzanne. I know why you are so angry, and moody and snappy all the time. I know why you're stood there looking like a bag of bones. You think I'm thick mum, but I'm not." Britney's cocky, head-wobbling monologue was delivered without any eye contact being made, which angered Rachel even more as she stood there and listened to the abuse.

"Go on then, clever-clogs. What's the matter then? If you think you've got it all sussed out, tell me. Go on." Rachel was leaning against the island section in the kitchen, facing Britney. "Come on." She folded her arms across her chest. Britney just stared at the work surface. Rachel saw that a tear broke loose from her daughter's eye, which rolled quickly down her cheek, landing on her t-shirt. Another broke free and Britney dabbed at her face with her sleeve.

"What's up love? Come on, tell me." Rachel's voice had softened a great deal, as she walked around the island and put her arms across her daughters heaving shoulders.

"What's up?" asked Noel as he appeared in the

kitchen doorway. Britney began crying more, and Noel's interest was piqued further.

"Get away from me you little freak!" screeched Britney through her sorrow as Noel walked near, seemingly quite concerned about his older sister.

"Charming!" said Noel as he walked away, back towards the living room. "Can't be that bad if she is still being as abusive as ever!"

"Close the door please Noel, that's a good lad."

Noel closed the glass panelled door with a sarcastic look on his face and darted back into the living room where he was watching television with Shania.

"You okay, pet?" asked Rachel quietly.

"Yes, I'm... I'm fine. I just..."

"What, love? You're scaring me Britney, what's up?"

"I saw you kill him."

Rachel felt her whole body freeze up, from the tips of her toes to the top of her head, in one ruthless juddering wave of shock. She felt as though she had been spun around, and she couldn't stop. It was as if the whole room had started spinning in one direction, and she had begun spinning in the opposite way.

"Wha... you what?" she managed to say as the spinning got faster. She had to clutch tightly onto the work surface. Her legs were weak and she knew that she was heading towards a panic attack.

Breathe. Big breaths. Slow down. Big deep breaths. That's it. Deep breaths.

"I saw you run across the road, you chucked your fag away as you went, orange sparks flashed on the floor, then I saw him beating Suzanne up in the front bedroom, then I saw you come in the room and smash his head in." Britney's voice was very cold, she sounded very detached from the violence and graphic nature of what she was describing.

The spinning began to slow. A cold, freezing sensation hit Rachel's bowels, and it began working its way up into her tummy. Her heart was beating fast, and very hard against her chest. Rachel's mouth was wide open as she stared at the back of her daughter. The panic was subsiding, slowly but surely.

"I watched it, you, out of my window. I didn't know what to do when I saw you hit him. And he fell. And…" Britney started to cry again, this time with much more distress. "I was about to come… I saw you shut the curtains, and I was really scared mum, I wanted to help. I was getting my shoes on, and I was a bit drunk and I was really confused. Then I heard you come in. I was at the top of the stairs. I heard what you said to dad. Everything."

"Britney… why…"

"I wanted to tell you, I've been meaning to say something, but…"

"What, love? You should have come to me. If I'd have known…"

"Known what?"

"If I'd known what you were going through, I could have…"

"I thought I'd get over it. I thought it would get better, but I'm just in a daze all the time. I'm just scared, twenty four seven mum." Britney broke down completely, and let it all out, the tears, the snot and the big, heavy sobs of sadness and concern.

"I know Britney love, I am too." Rachel began sobbing as well. Noel appeared at the door and was staring through the glass, his cheeky grin was quickly replaced by a look of concern. He opened the door slowly and popped his head into the kitchen.

"What's up? You alright mum?"

"Yeah, yeah, it's fine Noel, we're fine." Rachel was wiping at her face as she spoke.

"You're not, summat's up. Why are you both scriking?"

"We've just been listening to a really sad song, that's all." Said Britney. "Now go away before I give you a Chinese burn, you little dick."

"I'm sick of this, I'm only seeing if you's are alright. When's tea mum, I'm starving?"

"In a minute love, just leave us alone for a bit Noel, please mate."

Noel did as he was told, and left his mum and sister in the kitchen. Rachel passed some kitchen roll to her daughter, and used a piece to dab at her own eyes.

"Come with me, over to Suzanne's. We can talk about it properly over there. Okay?"

"I don't really want to talk about it mum. I'm sorry for bringing it up."

"It's good that you have. It was an accident, love. I was trying to protect Suzanne, that was all."

"I know, I know all that. But I keep coming home every day thinking you'll be in prison and it's doing my head in. I can't sleep, I can't think at school. My heads in bits mum. All my mates hate me, they think I'm a stupid bitch." Britney looked as though she was about to set off again, her chin was quivering violently, and the snot continued to roll down towards her lip.

"Let me do these butties and we'll go across the road. You'll feel better when you know everything. Right?" Rachel's confidence was beginning to return, and the overpowering shock of Britney's announcement had begun to wane. "Everything's going to be alright. You'll see."

Britney knew her mum well enough to know when she was worried, and she knew her mum's voice well enough to know that she heard a very frail trace of doubt in what she was telling her, and it filled the young girl with a renewed sense of dread.

*****

"What's for tea Vera?" Kev was shouting into the kitchen from the back garden, where he'd been sat for most of the afternoon, enjoying the sunshine.

"Why do you call me Vera?" asked Tania, as she exhaled some smoke through her nostrils and stubbed out the cigarette butt in the ashtray.

"You what?" shouted Kev.

"I said, you fucking deaf bastard, why do you call me Vera?"

"Because it's funny." Kev laughed after he'd

answered, as though he'd reminded himself of how hilarious his joke was.

"How, how is it? Why is calling me Vera funny?" Tania pulled another cigarette from her pack, put it in her mouth and sparked her lighter. She took a big, greedy draw on it while Kev answered her question, shouting it from the back garden so that the entire community could hear as well.

"Vera, that's that miserable faced prison officer off Cell Block H, you know, you can remember Vinegar Tits can't you?" Kev started laughing again to himself.

Tania stood and went to the back door.

"So, now you've explained that, I still don't understand why you call me Vera, you bell-end."

"Well it wouldn't be very polite to say what's for tea Vinegar Tits, would it?" Kev slapped his leg as he laughed at his joke. Tania just looked at him with a look of pity and regret in her eyes. She flicked her cigarette and the ash flew off onto the patio.

"Oh, right. Nice one Kev. You're wasted sitting around here stinking of meat pies, you should get a job in comedy, you'll make millions mate. You'll be amazing - instead of just being a big fat bone idle boring twat here all day."

"No need for that Vera! Anyway, come on, you haven't answered my question. What's for tea?" Kev drained the last of the liquid from his lager can and scrunched it up in his hand.

"I'm going over to Suzanne's. You'll have to ring summat."

"Fucking hell, going over to stuck-up Suzanne's again? What the fuck do you lot get to talk about so much?" Kev stood and walked slowly towards Tania. "Pass us another can please love."

"Get your own, you lazy twat. Right, I'll see you in a bit. Don't wash those pots love, just leave them there for muggings to do. In fact, why don't you shove the hoover up my arse and turn it on, I'll vac the front room while I'm picking all your shit up."

"You what?"

"You heard."

"Yeah yeah yeah whatever Vera! Leave us a tenner for mine and Brett's tea will you?"

"I've already given Brett some money for his tea, and I gave you money before!"

"I've spent that."

"On cans?"

"Not just on cans."

"Well if you haven't got any money left, fuck ya. You can get a pizza out of the freezer and have that. See ya later."

"I'd love to know what you fucking slags are plotting!" shouted Kev, as his wife slammed the front door behind herself.

"I'm plotting to fuck off as far away from you as I can possibly get you big hanging mess." Said Tania as she strode confidently across Fir Trees Grove, and to the front door of Suzanne's house.

Ding Dong.

*****

"I thought you said we needed to talk?" Tania was being quite aggressive, and made no secret of her irritation when she saw Britney sat with Rachel in Suzanne's lounge.

"She knows," said Rachel. "I've only just found out."

"Knows what?" asked Tania, trying her best to look like a gangster, but her face was left hanging down on one side, making her look like she was a drag act suffering a stroke.

"She *knows!*" said Rachel, doing nothing to disguise her hatred of Tania.

"Oh, for fuck's sake!" said Tania, throwing her arms up in the air.

"Are you okay Britney?" asked Suzanne, wrapping her arm around the teenager.

"Jesus! Soon there'll be more people involved with this than there isn't!" Tania sat herself down on the settee and tutted loudly.

"Tell you what Tania, can you just shut up for a minute? You're pecking my head in." Rachel had suffered a massive shock in the past half an hour, she'd fought off a panic attack and she was emotionally drained. She was in absolutely no mood for Tania and her gob-shite opinions. Tania took the hint and sat right back, holding out the palms of her hands.

"Alright, alright, don't lose your shit."

Rachel and Britney explained the situation, and Britney went into detail about what she had witnessed, including afterwards, when her parents had gone back into the house, and Tania had crept over there too, trying to see what was happening. Suzanne became increasingly upset, as the details of the incident were re-told and re-lived by all who were involved, in one way or another.

The small group of people that were involved in the disappearance of Graham Ashworth had now grown by one fifth. There were now five people who knew about the situation. Rachel, Mick and Britney, Suzanne and Tania.

"Have you told anybody about it? A mate, or a boyfriend or anything?" asked Suzanne, kindly holding Britney's shoulder and talking softly.

"No, no, course not. I'm not a complete knob you know! I know that my mum is going to get sent down for murder, who am I going to tell that to?" said Britney, her eyes gave away her disgust at such a stupid question.

"Are you sure?" asked Tania, with her usual lack of charm and compassion.

"Course I'm sure. Are you sure?" Britney was staring straight at the woman, who she couldn't stand the sight of anyway, regardless of this event that had now connected their paths.

"Don't start with me, young lady!"

"Or else what? You'll paint me bright orange so I look like you?"

"Come on, now, you two. Leave it out." Suzanne was uncharacteristically forceful as she spoke.

"You should teach your kids some manners," said Tania in Rachel's direction.

"Tania, I'm not taking lectures from anybody about my kids love, least of all you." Rachel shook her head dismissively at the neighbour.

"What's that supposed to mean?"

"Well you're only allowed one to live with you."

"You fucking bitch!"

"What? It's no secret Tania. Your womb has caused more problems in Manchester than the fucking IRA bomb did."

"Right," said Britney, practically shouting. "Seriously. Shut up. All of you's." The three adults all looked at each other, and seemed slightly embarrassed as they realised how childish their behaviour had become during the past few minutes.

Britney was brought up to speed with the alibis and the agreed version of events so far. After almost thirty five minutes of the discussion, the conversation finally got round to the business that Tania had been called round about.

Rachel and Suzanne explained the policeman's visit. Once Tania had listened to both sides of the story, she knew pretty quickly which camp she was in.

"Rachel's spot on," she said. "Things are about to come on top, no mistake about it. And we had better all get our fucking stories straight."

"Where's Mick? At work?" asked Suzanne.

"Yeah, he's on late shift this week, he'll be in at about ten."

"Well, do we need to wait for him, or…"

"No. We need to figure out where we're up to. Let's try and suss out if this new development changes the story. If it does, we need to know what changes we're making, and we need to make it just as water-tight as the first story." Rachel's confidence was high, and she was treating this as though it was just a council tax arrears problem down at the Citizen's Advice.

"Why would the story be any different now?" asked Suzanne.

"Well, that's what we need to figure out for sure." Rachel was talking to everybody, but mainly Britney, who had inherited a great deal of information in a very small amount of time. "Our story is set up for a full on police bust, with one of us, or even all of us getting taken down to the police station under arrest. We need to know why that's not happened. Why hasn't this copper arrested us? Why is he sniffing about, pretending he wants to talk bollocks with Graham? I hate to say it, but it looks to me like the game is nearly up. And so, we need to concentrate, stay strong and of course, main job - stay one step ahead of the police."

"How?" asked Britney, looking scared, and vulnerable, for the first time that the adults in the room had seen since the cocky, confident teenager had entered.

"Don't worry about all that now love, we've already got all that sussed out. I'll tell you in a bit."

"So what's the plan now then, what's happening?" Tania exhaled loudly as she sat up, moving her large frame up towards the edge of Suzanne's settee. She had a look of arrogant disinterest on her face, but to the others, it seemed quite forced and badly executed. If she was trying to suggest that she was an old hand with murder and such like, she was coming across as a fake.

Rachel knew what a snide looked like, she had met with, mixed with and socialised with more fake, insincere people than she had with honest, down-to-earth, trustworthy folk. Tania was fitting the bill perfectly as a snide. In Rachel's view, the biggest threat to them all, to the entire predicament that they were in was this horrible Tania. She had the very least to fear, and the most to gain. As she sat there, cockily glancing around the group, pushing Maltesers into her mouth like she'd bought them, a thought occurred to Rachel Birdsworth. It scared her instantly, and also made her feel giddy with excitement. A cold sheen of sweat enveloped her forehead and her back, tingling her spine and forcing her to jerk slightly.

"What's up with her?" asked Tania, through a mouthful of chewed up chocolates, nodding at Rachel as she wiped her head with her sleeve.

I'm going to kill you, thought Rachel. And the tingling sensation started off again, the thrill and the fear was an intoxicating, paralysing mix. It was the only chance they had, and this inspirational realisation of the fact gave Rachel a renewed faith that Graham's death could remain a mystery. Only Tania would be able to ruin it. Now that Britney was involved, it was obvious to Rachel that Tania needed to be cut out of the picture.

"Tania, you've told your Kev about this, haven't you?" Rachel's question came from nowhere. It stunned the others, especially the person that it was aimed at.

"No. Don't be such a fucking idiot! You'd be in the Manchester Evening News by now if I had. Fucks sake Rachel. Why are you saying that?"

"I don't know. I've just got a funny feeling you've told him. And if you have, it would just make more sense if he was here, discussing this stuff with us." Rachel kneeled down on the thick, expensive looking grey rug, and locked her eyes with Tania's.

"Are you taking the piss? She's taking the piss, her!" said Tania to Suzanne and Britney, as she grabbed a few more Maltesers off the bowl on the coffee table. "She's talking a lot of fucking shit tonight, aren't we love?" Tania put the chocolates in her mouth and laughed dismissively. For Rachel, this angry reaction was the most sincere and candid behaviour that she'd witnessed from Tania, since the very first time they'd met. It made Rachel feel confident that Tania hadn't said anything to her husband.

"Alright, alright, chill out – no need to get stressed. It's a fair enough question!" Rachel was trying to be friendly as she spoke, adding a smile, which didn't seem sincere to anybody, least of all Tania.

"Tell you what though, if Kev was to find out about it, he'd want to be cut in on the money. And I want that money for myself – am I fuck sharing it with that prick!" Tania's brightly coloured face was turning a shade brighter as the red from her blood pressure fought the marmalade glow of her orange bronzer. Her eyes were popping out of her head and she looked like an absurd cartoon character from the nineteen seventies.

"Alright, it's fine. I'm just trying to figure out why

this copper has come knocking today, that's all. Keep your wig on Tania."

"It's alright, just don't want anyone having me down as a fucking grass! This is my chance to get rid of that twat once and for all. Swear down."

"Right, Suzanne – you really need to try and think about if there is anybody left that might be asking about Graham?"

Suzanne looked stumped. They'd been over this a thousand times. Nothing had changed. Graham had very few acquaintances, and those few that did have any interest in the man were convinced that he was in Thailand, as his Facebook posts and photographs of the beach, the horizon and the food were pretty conclusive evidence that he was indeed on the other side of the world. His family, who he had a very limited relationship with were all friends on Facebook, except his father who was living in a nursing home in Old Trafford, and Suzanne had kept up the weekly visits. Graham's father was in his nineties and suffering from several different conditions that were making his life quite uncomfortable as he reached the end. But Suzanne's visits were the highlight of his week, and she knew it.

"We're okay. We've got every angle covered," said Suzanne. "Honestly, Rachel, I truly believe that we have done enough. There is plenty of evidence around that Graham is still around us."

"Where did you put the body?" Britney's rather frank question created a stark silence. The adults looked at one another and then down at the floor. "Come on, don't tell me you've forgotten? I watched you all putting it in the car. It was like an episode of The Inbetweeners. God, I don't know how you haven't had the police here sooner."

"Britney, please..." Suzanne was reaching out again, but Britney moved away slightly.

"I rang nine, nine... that night. I couldn't press the last nine. But I wish I had done. You lot have got yourself in so much shit now. I don't know why I didn't just press it!"

"She's right!" said Tania. "I said this at the time, when I saw them trying to sneak his body out. I said to them, just phone the police, but nobody wanted to. So here we are."

"Wait, what the fuck has this got to do with you? Why are you here? It's got fuck all to do with you, you big orange tramp!"

"Britney!" shouted Rachel, genuinely furious with her daughter for the outburst.

"I'll tell you what it's got to do with me, you cheeky little bitch…." Snapped Tania, but Suzanne interrupted.

"She's black-mailing us," announced Suzanne, very calmly, with no emotion in her voice. "She's making me sell the house, and she wants half of the money, and for that price, we buy her silence."

"Well, I'll tell you what, I'd phone the police myself and go to jail rather than do that Suzanne! I wouldn't trust her to keep her trap shut. You're all fucking mad, the lot of you's. I'm going." Britney stood up, and the raw anger that she was displaying scared everybody, including her mother.

"No, Britney!" Rachel leapt up and grabbed her daughter by the arm as she headed for the door.

"Get off me!" shouted the teenager, and it came out very loud.

"No love, just come in here, calm down a bit!"

"Nah, you're all off your heads. I'm going to sort this out, it's getting out of hand." Britney turned and walked out of the lounge, and a couple of seconds later the front door closed loudly.

"Shit!" sobbed Rachel, her eyes were filling with tears. Suzanne stood there, looking at Rachel, the panic on her face was unmistakable.

"She needs a fucking smack, her." mumbled Tania.

Chapter 28

Britney had been sat on the wall outside the factory gates for over two hours, when her dad finally appeared amongst all the other back-shift workers, just after the bell went at 10pm.

She'd rehearsed what she was going to say a hundred times. She'd adapted it and altered it, and after so many variations, she was finally confident that she would be able to say what she wanted, without chickening out.

"Dad! Dad!" She shouted, as Mick marched out among the swarm of hi-vis wearing workers who were desperate to get home and open a beer, watch some television and have a late supper. Mick looked shocked to see his daughter there, and was concerned by how upset she appeared.

"Shit, that's our Britney. Right, take care lads, seeya tomoz." The workers that Mick was walking along with said their goodbyes quietly and carried on walking. Mick stopped dead.

"Alright love, what a nice surprise. That's made my day that has. Are you alright? What's up?"

Britney gripped her dad so tightly, he began to feel scared. "What's up love, y'alright?" He held her closely, and kissed the top of her head. Britney was shaking, and crying, and trying to hug the living daylights out of her dad. "Calm down now, love. Britney, what's up love. What's happened?" Mick had a vision of every worse-case scenario flash through his mind. Liam with a drugs overdose, Noel knocked off his bike, Shania choking on a gob-stopper, Rachel falling off a step-ladder. Britney getting pregnant. His heart was banging. "Come on love, tell me, what's up? You can tell yer dad."

It took a few minutes until Britney had settled down. Once she had, and had wiped away her tears, and reassured her dad that she was okay, the pair began to walk, slowly, in the direction of home.

"You having trouble with a lad love? Take my advice, they're all dicks. Be a lesbian or summat, get yourself a nice lass!"

Britney laughed. She hadn't thought it possible to laugh, or even smile. But her dad had made her laugh within a few minutes of seeing him.

"Come on, lets sit here a minute. I want you to tell me what's up."

Mick sat down on the bench in the brightly lit bus stop, and Britney sat down beside her father. It was quiet for a few moments. Mick didn't want to prompt her, he just sat and waited for Britney to talk.

"Me and mum have had a row." Britney's voice filled with emotion.

"What, a serious one?" asked Mick. He didn't seem too concerned.

"It's about that man across the road, who mum killed."

Mick Crossley made a completely involuntary sound. It was as though his stomach had punctured. It was the sound of pure shock. It took him a while to compose himself. Britney gave him the time.

"Wow! Fuck in hell Britney, that was unexpected!" Mick's heartbeat was thundering, and he wondered if Britney could hear it.

"I watched it. All of it. I just told mum today. And now I've found out about everything else, like Tania, and…"

"I thought you did. I wasn't sure. I couldn't say anything, but I heard you shut your bedroom door, the night…" Mick placed his head in his hands. He was staring at the pavement, shaking.

"I know, well, I was about to come downstairs and tell you what mum had just done, when she burst in through the front door."

A few moments passed. The father and daughter relived the surreal moment. It still seemed unreal.

"It's a mess, love. It's a total fucking nightmare this to be honest…"

"I know. This is why I've fell out with mum. A copper has been round today, to Suzanne's house, sniffing about."

"Eh?" The look of terror on her father's face scared

Britney. She'd never seen him looking scared. She hadn't even considered that it was possible for her father to be scared. She began to cry, but she tried her very best to be silent, so that her dad wouldn't know. Britney was also facing the floor, with her head buried in her arms.

"It's game over then," he said.

"What's game over?" asked Britney, struggling to conceal the upset in her voice.

"It's over, love. We're all going to jail. This was such a shit idea, God, how the fuck…"

Britney began sobbing, and her reaction made Mick cry too. They both sat on the bus stop bench crying, as the odd car and motorbike went past. Eventually, Britney spoke. "Right, so you and mum are getting sent down for this?"

"Probably, yeah, well, definitely yeah!"

"But if you didn't kill him, how long, I mean, what will you get?" Britney grabbed her dad's hand. It made him smile, and a tear plopped and landed on his hi-visibility jacket, glistening like a diamond under the bus shelter lights. Mick had to think about the question for quite a long time.

"I'm not sure. Your mum was on about it, something to do with assistance of a crime, or concealing crime. I don't know, its all them big words your mum comes out with. But what she meant was, even if you didn't do the actual crime, you're still up shit creek if you helped the person who did do it." Mick looked confused. He knew what he meant, he was just struggling to articulate his knowledge of evading the law to his fifteen year old daughter.

"I can't believe you have got this deep into it. If you'd have just rung the dibble when it happened, right, mum would have got away with it. She was helping her friend, she was protecting her friend. I'm telling you dad, you should have rung it in. It's your fucking fault this. You could have stopped it all dad. And now you're both going to jail. I can't believe it dad. I can't." Britney got up and stood before her father. She didn't recognise the man. Mick Crossley was bent double, crying and whimpering like an infant. "Look at you!" she shouted, although she didn't mean to. The tears were streaming down her face, and she wiped them aggressively.

"I thought you were mint. I did! My dad… no-one messes with my dad. My dad is hard, you don't mess with him. But look at you, you're nothing. You're like a big girl, crying and feeling sorry for yourself. You should feel ashamed of yourself mate. You're fucking pathetic."

Britney walked away, sobbing as she went. The sight of her dad looking so hopeless, so defeated really did offend her eyes.

"Britney, hee yar love, come back. Britney."

Britney walked away from her dad. She felt lost, stunned by the way her dad had reacted to her announcement, and disappointed by the lack of any fight in him. There was nothing there, not an ounce of anything. He was pathetic.

Britney had anticipated a lot more from him. The strong, dependable, cock-sure of himself man that she had always known, and loved, and respected. She had absolutely no idea who this feeble, hopeless, stupid man was. As she walked briskly away, to shouts of "come back love!" and "let's sort it out!" she knew that she was walking into a haze of darkness and uncertainty. All that she had come here for was reassurance, to be told that everything's going to be okay. That she was safe.

But today, she realised that her greatest fear was true. Neither of her parents had a clue what they were doing, and they were going to prison. The rest of the family, her brothers and little sister will be put in care. As Britney headed towards home, she couldn't stop the anger and frustration that was bubbling up within herself.

"Why didn't I press that last nine?" she asked herself, over and over, between long, sad, heavy sobs.

*****

"Who's that?" shouted Rachel from the landing when she heard the front door close.

"It's me." Said Mick, pulling his work-boots off at the matt. He sounded thoroughly pissed off.

"Have you seen our Britney?" asked Rachel quietly

as she walked down the stairs towards the front door, the sadness and desperation in her voice was unmistakable.

"Yeah, she came and met me after work. Said you'd had a row. She's really upset Rach, with both of us."

"Where is she?"

"I don't know love, she shot off, I kept shouting her back, but she was on one." Mick hung up his luminous yellow coat on the stand by the door. Rachel collapsed on the bottom step, crying and making a weird, sad noise.

"She told me, you know, about everything. I can't believe it." Mick started walking towards Rachel. Her head shot up and she placed a finger over her lip, and pointed up the stairs.

"What's for tea? I'm starving!" said Mick, realising that he needed to change the subject. He sounded like a wooden radio actor.

"I've not done you nowt. We'll have to have a walk down to the chippy." Rachel stood up and walked into the front room where Liam was sprawled out on the settee watching television. "Liam, keep an ear out for them two will you love? If either of them come downstairs you can clothesline them and sit on them 'til we get back. We'll be ten minutes, love, alright."

"Yeah, alright mum. In a bit dad!"

"Alright mate, see you in a bit, just going up the chippy to get some scran. Won't be long," said Mick, reaching his head round into the lounge. "Do you want out?" he mouthed silently, so that Noel and Shania wouldn't hear from upstairs. Liam placed his thumb up and smiled.

"Legend!" he whispered back to his dad.

"Right, see you in a bit. And don't forget what mum said, if either of them two come downstairs…"

"Alright, see ya in a bit, yeah?" Liam pressed the remote so that the TV started playing again.

Rachel held the front door open as Mick put his trainers on, then closed it quietly behind them both.

"The chippy is miles away Rach, a proper mooch!" said Mick as they got outside.

"We need to talk. Let's just get off this fucking

horrible close and then we can." Rachel had set off walking at quite a speed, and Mick was struggling to keep up.

"Slow down love, fuckin' hell, I've been on me feet all day." Mick usually liked to flop out on the settee with a beer after work. This exercise was a complete shock to the system and Mick was finding it hard to keep up. "Slow down Rach, or I'm not coming. Seriously love."

"Mick, I just want to run. Honestly, I'm so wound up, so stressed, I can't think of anything I want to do more than just run, proper run, get some of this stress out of my system."

"Well, tell you what, why don't you run down the chippy, and I'll see you at home when you get back?" Mick was still trailing behind Rachel, trying his best to stay with her, but she really was power walking and he was getting out of breath.

"Shut up Mick, whingeing. My heads about to pop, I'm going to have an aneurism, I can feel it."

"Right, well, I can't talk to you when you're zooming off like this, come on, lets go and sit on the park a minute. We can talk there."

Rachel crossed the road and headed into the small play area. She sat down on one of the swings and looked around. It was too close to the surrounding houses.

"Nah, not here," she said as she jumped up off the swing, just as Mick caught her up. "We'll be overheard. Let's just get off the estate and we'll sit on a bench or summat. But we need to talk Mick. Seriously, the shit is going to hit the pan."

"I know, Britney told me. Summat about a copper coming round today?" Mick was once again trying to keep up with Rachel as she stormed up the road that all of the various avenues, closes and walks that made up the Haughton Park development branched off from.

"Sshhh, you fucking knob!" said Rachel and put her finger up against her mouth. As the pair gradually found a mutually agreeable walking pace, Rachel told Mick the full story, about the policeman, the fake car crash story, the phoney visit where the policeman didn't press the doorbell.

Then she told Mick about Britney's extraordinary announcement at tea-time. And after all of this news - most of which Mick had gathered anyway from his brief conversation with Britney - Rachel told him all about the conversation at Suzanne's house, and how Britney had called them all idiots and stormed off.

"And now I don't know where she is, Mick." Rachel was more angry than upset. She could feel that her tight grip of control was slipping on what had seemed to be a pretty safe alibi regarding Graham's whereabouts.

"Well, for what it's worth," said Mick, "I think she went in a lot harder on me, from what you are saying..."

"Why, what?"

"Oh, she was saying all sorts to me, about me being pathetic and weak. She said I'm like a big girl. She's right though Rach. I am, I'm lost with all this shit. We're in too deep love. We've fucked up, and we need to forget all this plan A bullshit about pretending that Graham is abroad, and that everyone will just forget about him eventually. It's a fucking stupid idea."

"It's the only idea we've had, Mick. It's not stupid, it's all we had at the time. Don't start talking like that to me now."

"What do you mean?"

"Well I didn't hear you coming up with an alternative. So now things are getting on top, you're just going to say that it was a shit idea. Save your breath Mick, please, that type of shit-talk isn't helpful." Rachel was slowing her pace a little and Mick was finding it a bit easier to keep up with his partner as they left the estate and turned onto the main road.

"I don't know what is going to happen now that Britney is involved. But it's pretty obvious, we're going to be seeing that copper again. Question is, will the story stand up?"

"Why wouldn't it?"

"Because it's the police, they're not fucking stupid Mick."

"Well, number one, yeah, they don't have a body."

"Oh shit, yeah, that was another thing Britney said, she was asking where we put the body."

"You didn't tell her did you?" asked Mick, seemingly oblivious to the magnitude of what his partner was saying to him, that their fifteen year old daughter was asking where they had put the body. Adrenaline had taken over both of Mick and Rachel, and their minds were just set on the present moment, on trying to figure out what was going to happen next. Rachel pointed out a bus shelter a little further along the road. "Let's stop there for five minutes."

The couple sat in silence for a few moments, both going over things in their minds. Eventually, Rachel stood, walked all around the bus stop to see if anybody was coming, checking the bushes just behind. When she was satisfied that they had privacy, Rachel sat back down next to Mick.

"I had an idea, today, when we were all talking at Suzanne's."

"What?"

"The answer to our biggest fucking headache in all this!" Rachel started laughing, though it was quite clear that there was little humour involved. It was a sarcastic, bitter laugh. She took her cigarette packet out of her pocket and lit one up.

"You're talking in riddles love. What are you going on about?"

"I'm going to kill Tania. I'm going to make it look like that fat bastard Kev did it."

Rachel's comment was met with silence. Mick just sat there playing with the sole of his trainer. A minute passed.

"Did you not hear what I just said?"

"Yeah, I did. I'm just trying to work a few things out."

"Like what?"

"Like, how the fuck did we get here, me and you, expecting a visit from police over a murder that we're both involved in, and now you're planning another fucking murder? I thought this was meant to be a great new start for us lot. A new challenge."

"Well, it's not gone our way has it? Eh? Like every

thing else we ever try and do, it goes tits up. Except in our case, it goes even worse than tits up. But what are we going to do? Just fucking give up? Just kill ourselves and say life's not fair? Or are we going to fight back? Like we always do. Come on Mick, me and you. We're the best – we can do anything. We can sort this out." Rachel started crying as she came to the end of her rant. Her voice gave away the fact that she didn't believe in herself, or in what she was saying. She threw the cigarette dimp on the pavement and kicked it away.

In normal circumstances, this would be the natural time for Mick to step forward and take the pressure off. But he was spent. He had nothing to say, no hope to offer. Britney had been spot on earlier, when she'd shouted in his face that he was weak. He was, and he felt it too. For the first time in his life, Mick felt completely useless. He wanted to put an arm around Rachel's shoulders, but he couldn't.

"We're fucked love. No two ways about it."

Chapter 29

"Right love, you just try and calm down, right, and get yourself off to bed. I'll sort this. Leave it to me. I love you, you do know that don't you?"

"Course I do Gran. Thanks." Britney gave her grandmother a strong, hard cuddle. It felt like a massive burden had been lifted today, and the release of the pressure felt great. The secret that had been weighing Britney down for over a month was now finally out in the open. The secret that would flash-back in the middle of a joke at school, or when she was chilling out on Facebook, or while she was talking to her friends on the bus. Since it happened, the flashbacks had been happening pretty much none-stop.

The flashback of her mum smashing Graham round the head. The flashback of her mum sitting, collapsed and terrified at the front door. The flashback of her mum and dad and those retarded neighbours trying to fit the body in the back of the dead man's own car. The flashback of her mum's sad, scared, stressed-out face every day since it had happened.

Today had been a big day for Britney. She'd told her parents about it, and that had helped a bit. But now that she had told the entire story from start to finish to her gran, she felt that the biggest part of her troubles were gone. She was still agonising about the thought of her parents getting sent to jail, and the family being broken up – but that didn't seem so strangling and heavy and suffocating right now. It felt weird. She felt free, for the time being anyway.

"Right, get off me now love, you're hurting my ribs!" Maureen let go of her granddaughter and Britney's intense grip released.

"Night Gran, and thanks."

"It's alright darling. I'm so proud of you for telling me. You've shown what a big grown up girl you are. Go on, off to bed, and I'll see you in the morning, I'll take you to Subway for breakfast."

"Love you."

"Love you, now go on, off you pop love."

Maureen looked up at the wall-clock in the kitchen of

her small flat on the Gameshawe council estate. It was half past midnight, and she felt exhausted, both physically and emotionally. The information that Britney had given her tonight was beyond anything she could have ever imagined. Rachel killed a man, and her and Mick have disposed the body. Now the police are asking awkward questions. It was completely and utterly unbelievable.

Maureen had only one thing on her mind, and that was going over to Rachel's and finding out what the hell was going on. Finding out if any of this was even true. It was just so unlikely, even though it had come from her own granddaughter's mouth.

Maureen sat down and lit a ciggy in the front room. She finished the last of the tea that was in the pot in front of the gas fire. She really felt like she wanted to cry, but the tears wouldn't come. Her eyes were dry, she felt emotionally constipated, desperate to go, but there was nothing happening. As she put her cigarette to her lips, she realised that her hand was shaking violently.

"Bloody hell Rachel," she whispered. "Why haven't you come to me about this?" Maureen stared at her living room wall, and the pictures of Rachel, and the rest of the family through the years. "Why, love?"

Maureen sat there for another twenty minutes before creeping through to the spare bedroom to check on Britney. She was sound asleep, and her face looked soft and care-free. Maureen wanted to give her granddaughter a kiss on the forehead but worried that it might disturb her. She quietly turned the lamp off at Britney's bedside and crept out of the room, leaving the door open slightly so it wasn't completely dark. Maureen tip-toed all around the flat, switching off the kettle and toaster sockets at the wall, unplugging the television and turning off the lamps. She left the landing light on, in case Britney woke up.

It was just before one o' clock in the morning when Maureen quietly pulled her flat door closed, walked down the four flights of stairs and got into her car.

*****

Ding dong

"Who's that?" Rachel looked across at Mick. He checked the time on his phone.

"It's half one nearly!" said Mick. Neither of them wanted to go to the door. Britney had a key, and anyway, the door wasn't locked, so both parents knew it wasn't their daughter. It could only be bad news, they were both agreed on that, without saying a word.

"That'll be the fucking police." Said Mick.

Maureen appeared at the front room window, clasping her hands at the side of her face so she could see in.

"Fuckin'ell it's me mam!"

"Fuck's sake! I thought it was a fucking police raid then, Rach. What's your mam up to?"

Rachel had jumped up off the settee and was over by the front door. Maureen burst in as soon as it was opened, marching past her daughter and straight into the front room, where Mick was still sitting, and looking very confused.

"Mum, what's up? You alright?" Rachel was following her mother into the room when Maureen began speaking. Her words made Rachel sit down, as the stress and panic hit her bowels, and her legs felt like they could just give way right there.

"Don't say another word. Britney is safe, she's tucked up in bed at mine. I'll go back there in a minute. But before I go, I just want to know... is it true?"

Rachel nodded and Mick looked down at the floor.

"Good. I didn't want you to start any of that "is what true?" bull-crap with me. Okay. So it's true. That's quite something." Maureen sat down on the chair opposite her daughter and son-in-law. She blew out very loudly and looked down at her hands for a minute.

"Okay, okay, I just wanted to know if it was true. I knew Britney was telling the truth, but it was... it's pretty unbelievable! I can't believe it. But, anyway, not to worry." Maureen stood up and went over to the window. Rachel and Mick didn't look at her. They just kept their gaze focused on the floor. Maureen took in a big, long breath. Rachel was about to speak, but her mother cut in before her.

"I just don't know why you haven't spoken to me about this." At this point, for the first time, the emotions caught up with Maureen, and she felt her voice wobbling and a hot, angry tear burnt her eye. "You should have... I could..."

Maureen walked over to the settee and sat inbetween Rachel and Mick. They both put their arms around her, and all three had a good cry, huddled together. They stayed like that for a good five minutes, crying and sniffing and wiping snot and tears and whispering "sorry" and "I love you's." Eventually, all three of them were cried out.

Maureen stood, and grabbed a packet of hankies from her hand-bag. She handed the tissues out and they all felt stupid, wiping and blowing and rubbing their sadness away.

"Right. I'm going home, to check on our Britney. We'll sort summat, don't worry. It's going to be alright. Now, if you get taken in before I see you's again, take it for granted that I'll take the kids on, there's no question about that, right?"

Maureen's statement set Rachel off crying again.

"Shut up – don't get me going again, love. Right, seeya's. Love ya's." Maureen's voice quivered again, as she said it, as she headed quickly for the front door.

Chapter 30

FRIDAY MORNING

Rachel looked terrible.

"God, mum, you look like shit." Said Liam as he pulled his breakfast out of the toaster.

"Thanks a lot, son."

"Are you ill or summat?" he asked as he began to spread margarine on his toast.

"I've just got a lot of stuff going on, love. I'll be fine."

"Well I hope so mum, because you look like Michael Jackson's corpse." Rachel couldn't help but smile at Liam's stupid comment. She tapped him lightly round the back of the head.

"Little shit."

"Is it because of our Britney stressing you out?"

"No, no mate, is it heck. We've had a bit of a row, that's all, she's at that funny age."

"Has she run off?"

"Nah, she's at your gran's. It'll all be sorted soon. Don't worry, you're just like me, you, a right worrier. It's shite being a worrier son, so try not to let things get in your head, right?" Rachel tried to give her eldest a cuddle, but it was awkward as his main concern was trying to avoid dripping margarine on his mum, the floor or his clean school shirt.

"Love ya," said Rachel as he pulled away.

"Give over mum, I'm gonna be late." Liam managed to wriggle away from his mother and grabbed his bag off the kitchen island. "In a bit." He said as he headed out to the door.

"I said, I love ya." said Rachel.

"Love you too mum, see ya tonight."

Liam left for school and within a few minutes, Mick arrived home from dropping Shania at her primary school.

"God, you look like shit Rach."

"I've not slept. Couldn't. I even took some of your

sleeping tablets. I just couldn't get off."

"Me neither." Mick checked there was water in the kettle before turning it on.

"God, you're such a fucking blatant liar Michael Crossley! Shame on you!"

"What?" Mick looked shocked.

"You've been snoring like a bastard for the last five hours man!"

"Have I bollocks! Do you want a brew?"

"Nah, Liam's made me one. I feel really weird now, knowing that my mum knows. It's like, I don't know, it's as though it feels a bit better somehow, you know, now that she knows. Do you know what I mean?"

Mick was spinning the teaspoon around in his fingers, waiting for the kettle to boil. He looked quite happy, considering the daunting circumstances.

"Everything is going to be alright, I've got it sussed." Mick threw a tea-bag into his BEST DAD mug and splashed the hot water over it as soon as the kettle clicked off.

"What do you mean?" asked Rachel, her sunken, black ringed eyes came alive suddenly. She looked desperate to hear what Mick had to say.

"I'm going to go down the police station. I'm going to tell them I did it."

"What the fuck…"

"Rach, just shut up a minute. Let me tell you. I'm going to get five years tops, I'll be out in three. It'll cut everyone else out of the picture. It's the best way." Mick started stirring his tea-bag around in the cup.

"Mick…"

Mick placed his finger over his lip and stared kindly at Rachel. "It came to me, last night, walking back from the chippy. You saying that you're going to kill Tania. Our Britney saying I'm a nobody, that I'm a girl. It all just started plopping into place. Then your mam saying that about looking after the kids if we get sent down. It broke my heart that Rach. But, it's come to me now, what to do. It's time for me to man up. So, that's what's happening, right?" Mick put the hot, steaming tea-bag on top of a plate that was waiting to be washed up and poured his milk into the cup steadily, but his hands were shaking noticeably.

Rachel looked at her partner of the past eighteen years, they'd been together since they were at school together. She couldn't remember a moment that she hadn't loved him with all of her heart. But this announcement filled her heart with even more love for the man. Tears fell freely from her eyes.

"Fuck off," she said to the tears as she wiped them. "Where do they all come from?" she asked as she snorted up loudly. "You'd have thought that I'd have no tears left the amount of crying I've done, since…"

"So, what do you think? I want to move quickly love, if this copper is getting close to finding out what's happening, we need to get in there, wrong foot them, totally bamboozle them."

"Eh, wait Mick, fucking slow down babe. You're not asking me if you're getting a Chinese or a pizza. Slow down! We need to talk about it!" Rachel hadn't meant to raise her voice, but her temper and her emotions got the better of her. What had sounded like a perfect solution a few minutes earlier, now filled her with panic.

"Right, tell you what. Tell me which is better. You and me, and Suzanne getting sent down. Or just me?"

"Well…"

"It's a no-brainer, so stop trying to negotiate on it love. It solves everything, right? I say to the police that I seen him beating Suzanne up, I ran over there, smashed his fucking head in, Suzanne was lay on the floor, out cold. I took his body, put it in his car. And I'll plead manslaughter. I'll say I fucking panicked, I was pissed. It gets everyone off the hook. It's so fucking simple Rach, I can't believe we never came up with this before."

Rachel was staring at the kitchen clock as Mick talked. It did make perfect sense. It was a great idea, and she was impressed at just how much thought he'd put into it. He had a lot of confidence in his voice as he talked, and it gave a little bit of confidence to Rachel for the first time in ages.

"Our Britney is right love. Fucking hell, I've been

walking around in a sulk for weeks, feeling sorry for myself. This is perfect. You know it is. It'll get that Tania bastard of all our backs as well."

"Will it though?" Rachel's tears had stopped for now. She took a cigarette out of the packet and lit it, without taking her eyes from Mick who was stood by the sink with his brew in his hand. BEST DAD was all Rachel could see when he took a sip.

"What, if I go down to the police and confess?" Mick looked slightly confused. He hadn't envisaged any problems with this at all.

"She could just say that its bullshit Mick. It is bullshit." Rachel sucked hard on her cigarette and flicked her ash.

"What the fuck would she gain from that Rach? At the moment, she reckons she's getting half of the price of that house. The thick bastard hasn't even worked out that the owner is a dead body. How the hell can the owner put the house up for sale? God, she's a proper knob her. Thick as a bucket of shit."

"Alright, alright Mick. We know all this. What I'm asking you is how can you cut her out?"

"Simple. The first she's going to know about this, is when it comes on Granada fuckin' Reports that I've been arrested and charged, and I'll be banged up until it comes to court. Why would she go running down to the police station to say, "hang on, that's not how it was," and get herself implicated in it? Besides, right, even if she did do that, because she's a dud, the body's not going to have any DNA on it now, and there's jack shit evidence over the road, as you know. I've even put a new carpet in. I'll make all that a part of the story. I'll tell them that when I left, with Graham rolled up in the carpet, Suzanne was knocked out."

"So, smarty pants, how do you explain Suzanne thinking that Graham is in Thailand?"

"Well, alright, I admit that that's going to be a bit trickier. We need to get that watertight, but I've already got a few ideas about that."

"Go on, tell me one."

"Well, we'll say that after I'd gone with the body, you woke up on the settee in our house and saw that I wasn't about, so you went to the front for a fag, wondering where I was, but then you saw all the lights on over the road and went over to see what was going on, and Suzanne was out cold."

"So how is he in Thailand? How does Suzanne find out?"

"We'll have to figure that out. Suzanne stayed here a few days, was too upset and too scared to go back and face Graham. When she eventually did, he wasn't there. Just a note saying "soz I'm in Thailand.""

"What if the police don't believe it?"

"They won't care, will they? I go in there, tell them everything I just said to you, and they're buzzing, it's all neat and tidy, job done and everyone's happy! It's brilliant Rachel. I just want you to promise to come and visit me, that's all I'm arsed about."

Rachel got off her stool and walked across to Mick, and gave him a massive cuddle. They both cried for a moment, it was a mixture of joy, relief and also a sense of closure on this nightmare situation. Rachel was excited and devastated by the thought of Mick taking the blame, and doing the prison time. But she was completely devastated, because she would miss him first and foremost, and because his good name would be tarnished. But she was excited, because she could genuinely see some light at the end of the tunnel.

"What about the Facebook updates from Thailand that Suzanne's been putting on?"

"I'll say I did them."

"How did you get his password?"

"It was on a piece of paper in his glove box. Fucking hell Rach, we need to go over all these bits and pieces with Suzanne. It's simple babe. I'm doing it. I'm going for it."

"When?"

"I'm going to sort out a list of problems that we need to work out, like the Facebook updates, any weirdness with Suzanne, things she might have said to people, all that kind of stuff. We need to get everything absolutely nailed down, and then I'll go down to Bury cop shop and say I need to speak to an officer about an accidental death."

"But what about us, the family? How are we going to survive without you?"

"You'll be better off Rach, you know that. Single mum, four kids. You'll get more in benefits than you get in my wages. Plus you'll get all your fucking rent and council tax paid. You'll be loaded, you'll be miles better off! That's how fucking stupid this country is. You know the score, dealing with all the benefits stuff at the Citizen's Advice."

"Fuckin' hell Mick. I think this is the best idea you've ever had. And it's so romantic as well." Rachel's face had the first glimmers of happiness and hope on it for the first time since the situation with Graham occurred. It melted Mick's heart to see the first traces of the old Rachel returning.

"Cheers love. Come here you big snotty ball of tears and give us a kiss."

"I love you Mick, so much!"

"I know you do. And I love you too, you murdering bugger!"

Chapter 31

Mick was sitting on the settee, pondering whether to go into work for his final ever afternoon shift, or whether to just leave it at that. His mind was racing, a thousand thoughts were zapping through. When should he hand himself in? Would it do any harm to have one last weekend with the family? Should he say goodbye to the kids and explain everything first? Maybe just wait until the first prison visit? Will Rachel manage alright? What if Liam goes off the rails? What if Noel goes off the rails? What if Britney tells the police that it was her mum who did it? No, why would she? Would the family still be considered for re-housing after all this? Killing a neighbour is pretty anti-social after all.

Mick was getting dizzy with it all. But he was excited too, he felt like he was about to go on a holiday, or to a really big football match. He had butterflies, and a desire to just get his shoes on and get down to the police station and get on with it all. But there was stuff he needed to sort out first, and it was making him restless. He looked up again at the clock. Quarter past eleven. It felt as though an hour had passed, but it was less than five minutes. He looked back at his piece of paper, a confusing list of notes that a casual observer would never make any sense out of. It was Mick's list of loose ends that needed sorting out, half written and using lots of paranoid euphemisms and codes. The Facebook stuff from Graham was at the top of the agenda. There had been a total of four posts since the night that Graham had died. Mick thought that he could just get the password from Suzanne, then delete all of the posts, and then just rename the account John Smith before deactivating it. If he did it from a public internet access, McDonalds or Caffe Nero or somewhere, a place with CCTV, at least he could be seen as the person in control of Graham's Facebook, if the police wanted to check.

Ding Dong.

The doorbell made Mick jump. He'd been lost in his own little world, consumed by his busy thoughts. "God, I can't have a shit in peace." He muttered as he dragged himself up off the settee, mindful that he needed to get to the door quickly before the caller pressed the bell a second time.

"Oh, hiya," said Mick as he opened the door and saw his mother-in-law standing there, looking sad and scared. "Come in. Rachel's asleep, she's been awake all night you know. She's alright now though, she's sound asleep. Do you want a brew? You look like shit Maureen. Sit down in there." Mick gestured his mother-in-law through to the lounge.

"Cheers Mick, thanks a lot. I've not slept a wink, I've been crying all night. I feel like somebody has died."

"Well, they have. That's the problem."

"That's not funny Michael."

"I know, sorry."

"Anyway, I've thought of an idea. A way of sorting everything out."

Mick felt sad about how upset Maureen was. She was the salt-of-the-earth, and Mick adored his mother-in-law. It was upsetting to see her in such a state.

"What do you mean?" asked Mick, sitting next to her on the settee.

"I've been thinking about it. I've found a way of you staying out of prison, you and Rachel."

"Oh aye, tell us then," he said.

"I'm going to take the blame. I'll say I did it. It won't matter if I'm in prison, but it will if you and Rachel are. The kids need you. What's the point of me saying I'll look after them. I might as well take the blame for what's happened."

Mick's eyes were pouring with tears, but Maureen was none the wiser, he kept them hidden well. He was only found out when he had to speak.

"So, do you think that would work?" asked Maureen.

"God, I bloody love you, you daft old bugger!" said Mick as he cuddled Rachel's mum. "Have a fag if you want, I'll go and get you Rachel's ashtray."

Once Mick had wiped his face and blown his nose, and fetched his mother-in-law the ashtray, he sat down and told her all about the plan that he had come up with since he had last seen Maureen.

"Great minds think alike!" said Mick as he finished up explaining everything that he had already agreed with Rachel a couple of hours earlier. "What do you reckon?" he asked.

Maureen looked quite impressed, and Mick sensed that she felt a tiny bit of relief too, that she wasn't about to go into prison, even though it had been her own idea.

"Aren't you bothered though?"

"How do you mean?" asked Mick.

"Well, you didn't even kill anyone. Don't you mind the thought of going to jail?"

"I'd be going anyway, with Rach. It makes more sense this way. And it will get the blackmailing piece of shit from up there out of our hair as well."

Maureen started crying, mostly from relief that this nightmare situation that she had learnt about the previous evening looked as though it might not be quite as bad as it first sounded.

"God, I'll be glad to get it all put to rest to be honest Maureen. Our Rachel's been really ill with it. You've seen how much weight she's lost. It weren't as though she had a lot of spare flab to begin with!"

"I know, she told me she's had a bug though. I had no idea…"

"Well, listen, she's glad you know now. She told me this morning, said it feels a bit easier to cope with now that you know, and you're being so sound about everything."

"I've been praying all night long. That's why she feels better. God is comforting her."

"Look, go up and get in bed with her Maureen love. Go on, get yer head down for a bit."

"I might do actually! I hope I don't disturb her."

"Don't worry, she's had two of my sleeping tablets. She'll be out for a bit yet."

"Alright, well, I will. I'm feeling a bit more calm now, that's a cracking idea you've had there. Makes a lot of sense. I'm so proud of you, you know?"

"Yeah, thanks Maureen, I'm just glad we've come to some sort of sensible solution. It's been too much just waiting to see what's going to happen. At least this way, we all know what's happening. It's perfect. I'm feeling pretty buzzing to be honest with you. I've just got a lot of stuff to figure out, so, you go and get a nap, and I'll crack on."

Maureen stood up, leant down and gave her son-in-law a kiss on the forehead.

"God-bless you Mick. You're one-in-a-million love."

Chapter 32

"Good news Suzanne, got a brilliant plan. Can't talk here, Tania will see us and wonder what's going on. Meet you in McDonalds in Bury town centre at 4 to discuss. Is that okay? R xxx" Rachel pressed the send button on her phone and the text message disappeared off the screen.

"Right, I've sent her a message. Going to meet her at four in town." Rachel was still feeling sleepy, she'd managed three hours sleep. Mick had no choice but to wake her in order to get things moving along. Maureen was still upstairs, fast asleep with the big bed all to her self.

"Nice one Rach. Sorted. The sooner the better love. We need to make the first move, it's going to be a headache if we wait until the police come." Mick was tapping out a beat on his leg with a pen.

"Why though? Why can't we just wait it out?"

"Because of big fat Tania, you pellet."

"Oh aye yeah. Dickhead." Rachel made a gun with her hand and pretended to shoot herself in the face.

"Thick as two short planks, you!" said Mick, smiling.

"Alright, don't push it."

"Will you sort us out with loads of good stuff when I'm in prison?" asked Mick, trying to look as angelic as possible, still nervously tapping out a rhythm on himself.

"Yeah, course I will. I'll be down all the time. What sort of stuff will you want?"

"Don't know really. Soap, stuff like that. Razors. Toffees. Bars of chocolate. Loads of rolling baccy. Bring us a big massive bagful and I'll be running the wing in no time." Mick smiled to himself.

"Will you? Will you be the top dog?"

Mick burst out laughing, and Rachel joined in too. They were both feeling pretty good about this solution that Mick had come up with. But there was still a nervous doubt bubbling away. Mick just wanted to get on with it now and hand himself in. That way, he felt as though he'd be controlling the way the investigation was going to go, and

Tania would have no further part in the matter. Rachel's phone vibrated and a new message appeared.

"Oooh sounds ominous! Can't wait to find out what's cooking! See you at 4 and I'll get the McFlurry's this time! Suz xxx"

"Right, it's all sorted." Said Rachel, showing the text message to Mick. "We'll sort all these items out that are on your list, and then it's send you to prison time!" Rachel tried to make it into a joke, but her delivery failed to contain the all-important humour. Her joke stood awkwardly in the air for a moment before Mick saved Rachel's blushes.

"Just make sure we can get these three things sorted out." Mick showed Rachel the items that were causing him the most concern.

"No worries. Let me write them down. Right, so, if all this goes straight through without any trouble, when are you thinking of handing yourself in?"

"In the morning. So I want plenty good lovin' tonight!"

Mick had hoped that Rachel would laugh, or slap him, or call him a cheeky bugger. But she just seemed to go very pale, and those red, irritated eyes welled up with tears once again.

"Mick…"

"Shut up Rach. You know it's the best idea. It's going to be alright, I'm telling you now."

*****

Mick was hyped up. He couldn't remember ever feeling like this. He was relentless, wandering around the house like a restless caged animal roaming about its enclosure. He just couldn't sit, he'd tried to watch TV, he'd put on a DVD, tried playing the Playstation. He just couldn't settle. There was an urgency, right at the pit of his stomach, and it was bubbling more with each passing hour.

"Right love. That's me, I'm off. Bloody hell, are you still walking about the house? What are you like? Just try and calm down will you?" Rachel gave Mick a peck on the cheek.

"You're looking a bit more human!" Mick smiled, and was glad to see that Rachel appeared a bit more like her old self.

"Right, shut up, I'm going to miss my bus."

"Why don't you just get in Suzanne's car round the corner?"

"I don't want to chance it."

"Fair enough. Right, listen, as soon as you've got Graham's login e-mail address and password, text it me. Then I'll get to work sorting that out. Then, sort out that other stuff, make sure your stories are perfect, and we'll all be sorted."

"No worries, I'll be in touch. Okay?"

"Love you."

"Love you too Mick, more than Charlie Sheen loves cocaine and hookers!"

"Love you more than Gary Barlow loves not paying his tax!"

"Love you more than Deidre loved Ken, and Mike, and Samir."

"Love you more than... no I can't think of anymore. You win Rach. See you in a bit."

Rachel set off and Mick watched her power-walking off the close, at much the same speed that she'd had him trying to keep up with the previous night. As Rachel disappeared from view, Mick smiled to himself. It had been such a weird twenty-four hours. It was unbelievable how much had changed since he'd walked out of work the previous night. Now he felt slightly guilty that he had phoned in work and said that he wouldn't be in, because he had a tummy bug. But it amused him that he felt bad. He'd done his last shift. Shit, what were the lads going to say when they heard about this? Mick laughed at the thought of his mates, the factory's staff all stood around in little groups discussing the factory killer.

"They'll fucking love this! Best excuse for being off, ever!" said Mick, smiling from ear to ear.

*****

Rachel caught the bus with plenty of time to spare. The rattling old vehicle seemed to be taking longer than ever today, thought Rachel, as she vibrated and slowly juddered along the road, stopping and starting every two hundred yards for bus stops, traffic lights and school crossings. Rachel had never known the journey to take as long, as the bus seemingly crawled its way into the town centre.

Despite the slow speed of travel, Rachel realised that she was starting to feel happy. It was a ridiculous notion, and the realisation of it shocked her at first, and instantly made her feel guilty. Mick was about to get sent down for something that she had done, and her reaction was happiness. It was a bizarre situation, but Rachel could feel that the sense of hopelessness, the cloud of despair that had been hanging over her for the past month was finally disappearing. It was going somewhere else, and good fucking riddance to it as well, she thought.

Rachel took her phone out of her pocket and texted Mick.

"OMG, I just caught a reflection of myself smiling in the window. I haven't smiled since YKW. Love you so much Michael. I really do. Thank you. You are a hero and I will make this back up to you ten thousand times. Love you Mick, so much. R xxx"

She smiled again as she pressed the send button. Things were finally starting to look up. Mick might even get off with it. After all, it was nothing more than a good Samaritan situation, that had got completely out of hand, she considered. Drink, fear, and adrenaline were going to be Mick's only defence for his actions. Rachel had heard of other people getting off with similar crimes, although she couldn't think of the specifics of any particular cases to Google. But she was confident that it had happened in the past.

The bus pulled into Bury Interchange at twenty minutes to four. Rachel was careful to avoid the part of town where the Citizen's Advice Bureau office was based, she felt bad that she hadn't been in for weeks. The staff had been great with her when she'd phoned, but she still felt guilty for letting the team down. Even though the role was voluntary, she still took a great deal of pride in the position, and tried to treat it with the same amount of commitment that she would a paid position.

It was a relief to finally arrive at McDonalds. Rachel looked around the restaurant, but Suzanne hadn't arrived yet. She was disappointed. She was absolutely bursting to share this news. It was only ten to, thought Rachel as she got into the queue. She ordered two cappuccino's and went to find a seat for her and Suzanne. She chose a booth that was out of plain view of the windows, just for a bit of privacy – because Rachel thought that knowing her rotten luck, Tania would no doubt walk past and see them talking, and then come along and disrupt everything.

Rachel sat down, and looked around at all the customers that were happily smiling and laughing, without a care in the world. She began to feel an urgency building up within herself.

"Hurry up Suzanne," she said under her breath as she ripped the paper wrapper and sprinkled the sugar into her drink. She was shaking, but it was okay, it was excitement. She threw her paper wrapper on the table and stirred her drink with the wooden sticks.

*****

Suzanne was running a little behind schedule, and this unexpected knock at the door was likely to set her back even further, she thought.

"Oh bugger off." She muttered as she stood in the kitchen, choosing to ignore the caller. Suzanne knew that it wasn't Rachel at the door, as she had set off to town almost an hour earlier. Suzanne couldn't bear the prospect of Tania coming round and bombarding her for an hour, and she couldn't think who else it might be knocking, and pressing the doorbell.

The person knocked and pressed the bell again. It sounded quite official. It wasn't Tania anyway, Suzanne quickly realised that, as the person at the door hadn't tried the handle. Tania would have just walked in by now, reasoned Suzanne. She decided that it would be quicker and easier to just go and answer the door, and send whoever it was on their way. Then she could get on with her business, and get into town and find out what Rachel was so excited about.

"Bloody charity knockers. It's getting bloody ridiculous!" said Suzanne as she breezed across the hall to the front door and opened it wide.

"Hello?" she said. She was confused. She recognised the man stood before her, but she couldn't think who he was. "Now, where do I know you from?" she asked, employing her flirtiest, sexiest smile.

"Hello, erm, I don't think we've met before," said DCI Miller. "I'm a police officer. Is it okay to come in for a minute?"

That was where Suzanne knew the man's face from. He was a detective. Shit. He was on television from time to time, he'd been the main policeman in the Pop case the previous year. Oh crap! Thought Suzanne. Her legs felt rubbery and she felt a sudden, urgent need to fart as the shock of the moment hit her bowels. Suzanne felt light headed and she could tell that the blood had rushed to her face, just from the heat that was pumping through her cheeks.

"Oh, erm, well, I'm actually just on my way out. An appointment. Can it wait?" Suzanne felt as though she was about to faint. Her visitor's answer to that question would determine her immediate fate. Suzanne could feel the prison gates slamming shut in her face as DCI Miller spoke. His words made the rubbery sensation in her legs turn to jelly.

"Suzanne Ashworth, I am arresting you in connection with the disappearance of Graham Ashworth on or around the beginning of June. You do not have to say anything…"

Suzanne couldn't really hear the rest of what the man was saying after that, his words were just noises that were coming over in slow motion. It was like a chewed up video tape that just kept distorting and droning and making no sense. It was as though her head was being pushed under water. Before Suzanne could try and make any sense of the situation, she was sat in the back of the policeman's car, moving away from Haughton Park.

"There's… it's a mistake. There's been some kind of a mistake!" she said to the policeman, as he drove the car past the luxurious homes on either side of the road.

"It's alright, don't worry about it love, we'll sort it all out at the station." Said Miller, glancing up at his rear view mirror and trying to look as kindly and trustworthy as he possibly could.

Suzanne looked out of her window, she saw Noel. He was walking home from school, staring at her as the car drove past him and his friend. He waved. Suzanne wanted to wave back but she couldn't lift her hand. Not handcuffed. Not like this.

Tears of anguish began to trickle as Suzanne started chewing aggressively at her bottom lip.

This was it. Oh shit.

*****

"Hi Mick, just wondered, has Suzanne set off? Her drink's gone cold!!!! R xxx" Rachel pressed send. It said 16.33 on her phone clock. Suzanne wasn't normally late. But even if she was running a bit late, she could have had the good manners to text or ring. Rachel was feeling really irritable. The sound of people laughing, scraping chairs on the tiled floor, screaming toddlers and shouting infants were echoing off the walls. People were having great fun all around and it was making Rachel feel angry.

She put her phone into her jacket pocket, picked up her bag, and left her empty cup beside Suzanne's full cup on the table. She couldn't get outside fast enough. All the noise, the laughter, the staff shouting out orders, people talking shit all around her. It was driving Rachel mad. The noise was getting louder, filling her head. She could feel the start of a panic attack brewing. *Shit. Slow down, you know what's happening, just take control. That's it, slow, slow. Big, deep, slow breaths. Take a seat on the bench. That's it. Big slow breaths Fill those lungs up.*

Rachel's phoned pinged. She wanted to grab it and

see if it was Suzanne, to read a message that explained that she was stuck in traffic, or that she'd had a puncture, or that she was at the wrong McDonalds.

But she couldn't grab the phone just now, she had to concentrate, she had to carry on talking to herself about the panic attack which she was fighting off. The terror, the banging heart rate, the inability to breathe, the full on drama of dropping dead in front of all these people was fading, diminishing, lessening, ever so gradually.

Rachel was getting better at keeping control with her panic attacks. She was getting better at it each time. The key was to keep control, and to tell herself that she knew what it was, what was happening, and that everything was going to be okay. It used to be terrifying when she didn't know what was happening, when she had no idea if things were going to be okay, or not.

Eventually, after a few minutes of controlled thought, and self-reassurance, Rachel sensed that this one was past the worst. She was sat on the bench outside McDonalds, sweating and talking quietly to herself. Onlookers just assumed that she was a drug addict on a horrible come-down. She certainly looked the part.

When she finally felt strong enough to stand up, she set off towards the bus station, and had a look at the text message as she walked slowly and calmly.

It wasn't Suzanne.

It wasn't Mick.

"Text CLAIM now to 68777 and we'll get you your money from that accident."

"Mick you ignorant bastard why aren't you replying?" Said Rachel to herself as she stared at the phone. She pressed the phone icon on the text message, and the screen said "Dialling.... MICK."

"Answer the phone Mick! Please..." Rachel felt like crying, just out of sheer frustration.

"Welcome to the O2 messaging service, I'm sorry but the number..." Rachel hung up. She started scrolling through her contacts until she found Suzanne's number. She pressed the phone icon again. "Come on..." she said under her breath.

"This is the Vodafone messaging service…." Rachel hung up and quickened her pace as she headed towards Bury Interchange. Something was wrong, she could feel it in her water.

Rachel arrived home at half past five. She saw that Suzanne's car was on the drive opposite. She went inside her own house. Mick was giving the kids their tea. Britney was sat there, staring at her phone, sulking. Mick was laughing along with Maureen about total bollocks. Everything just seemed normal. The kids, they were just looking at her like everything was normal.

It was bizarre. Rachel just felt weird. Drunk almost.

Everything went in slow motion again. Mick looked up, and started making a long, drawn out drone noise. Rachel had to concentrate hard to work out what he was saying.

"Alright Rach, everything alright love?"

Mick looked scared, he rushed towards his partner.

Rachel had collapsed onto her knees. She was crying, sobbing uncontrollably. She started punching Mick as he went to her aid. She was throwing wild, hard punches at his chest and his arms as he tried to get near.

Liam and Noel were trying to get near and help. Shania was crying and hugging her Gran. Britney was sat on the settee, still holding her phone but now looking at the unimaginable drama of her mother screaming and crying, lashing out at her own family.

"It's too late Mick! You were too late!" she shrieked.

Chapter 33

"It's going to be alright. Trust me Rach. When have I ever let you down?" Mick hugged Rachel tightly, and kissed her cheek, and then her neck tenderly.

"Promise, Mick?"

"I promise." Mick let go of his partner. She should be his wife, by rights, he thought. But they'd never had the money to get married. Life had got in the way every time they'd talked about it. A bill, a blown head-gaskett followed by a birthday and then a new school blazer or a broken washing machine would always stall any plans. Still, they both knew that one day, when they could, they would get married. It was more a question of when, rather than whether.

"See-you then." Rachel was crying.

"Love you. I'm going to miss you every day." Mick's eyes were full of tears too.

Mick and Rachel had enjoyed and endured an eventful life together over the previous eighteen years. Most of the time, they'd been as happy, and content with their lot as they could be. Some of the time, they despaired at the difficulty and hopelessness of just trying to get by. Bringing up a young family with little money was hard going, but they had tried their best since they became parents in their teen years. The finer things in life had never been on the couple's aspiration list. The basic struggle of juggling bills and keeping on top of the day-to-day requirements of renting a council house, heating and lighting it, feeding and clothing their children and each other, while all the time trying to keep a happy, positive outlook was a full-time, all consuming, relentless commitment.

The house-fire had been the big turning point, for everybody in the family. Life suddenly went bad, for them all. Losing possessions hadn't taken too long to get over. But adapting to a life of six people living in the confines of a static caravan for such a long time had been a real test. Rows and fights could flair up for the most trivial of reasons. Just being so close together, having no space, it got on top of everybody.

Especially when somebody did an eggy fart.

Getting the house on Haughton Park was supposed to herald the new beginning. A clean slate. A chance to start a fresh, and get the whole family back to feeling some sense of security. At least, that was how Mick and Rachel had imagined it.

Standing here, at the entrance to Bury police station, Mick Crossley knew that he was doing the right thing. There was no question about it. It was the best solution to the mess.

"It looks more like a swimming baths than a police station, doesn't it?" He smiled. Rachel just looked down at her hands which were clasped together at her groin. "I've never really weighed it up before. But it doesn't look too scary. I'll treat myself to a chicken soup out of the vending machine."

"And some pickled onion Monster Munch!" said Rachel, without any hint of a smile. "You love them, don't you?"

"Yeah. Best crisps going. Right, any road, I'd best make a move. Seeya. Love you more than Boris Johnson loves being a dickhead." Mick leaned in and kissed Rachel again. It was a peck on her cheek, the bitter, sour taste of her tears made him feel sad. He turned, and looked again into the large glass fronted building. He actually couldn't wait to get in there now.

"I love you Mick!"

"Don't forget, I'm running this thing now. If you get brought in, you answer no comment to everything. No matter what Rach. Right?"

"Yeah, I know. No comment."

"That's my girl!" Mick kissed Rachel's forehead and turned to walk away. He must have had something in his eyes as he walked inside, he was wiping at them.

As she watched him disappear behind a wall inside the building, Rachel turned and started jogging away. Soon, her jog had developed into a run, and then into a sprint. Rachel was sprinting away as fast as she could. She wasn't heading anywhere in particular. She just needed to get away from there, as quickly as possible. It was all that she craved.

*****

"Hello." Said Mick, to the officer who was sitting behind the wooden counter, typing onto a computer keyboard.

"Hello. How can I help?" Asked the policeman, without looking up. He seemed quite bored, and Mick felt like he was a bit of a nuisance. Mick looked over his shoulder. There were a couple of sad looking teenagers sat near him. A drunk man looked as though he was trying to sleep on the seat opposite the counter, and a lady, possibly in her thirties was sat reading a leaflet in the middle of the waiting room.

"I said, how can I help?" the officer sounded quite snappy.

"I need to talk to someone." Said Mick, quietly.

"You are doing. How can I help?" asked the officer, who still hadn't looked up in Mick's direction at all.

"I've erm, well, I've killed someone." Mick was whispering, quite loud. The sad looking couple suddenly sat up a little straighter.

The policeman looked up from his screen, and focused his eyes on the man standing over him at the counter.

"You what?" he asked, confident that he had misheard the man at the desk.

"I said I've killed someone." Mick's desperate whisper wasn't at all quiet. " I'm just handing myself in." Mick looked nervous, and he felt a bit silly. It was a strange thing to be saying, and he realised this for the first time as the words came out of his mouth.

The lady with the leaflet looked quite scared, and put the brochure down on the metal seat beside her. The drunk man was completely oblivious.

"Are you taking the piss?" asked the officer, who was now standing, and facing Mick Crossley across the counter.

"No. Course not!" said Mick, feeling embarrassed by the policeman's response. "Why would I be?" he asked.

"Well, you know... we get people saying stuff like that all the time. Most of the time, they just want a warm bed for the night." The policeman still didn't seem too interested in Mick's revelation, and the cool, couldn't-care-less demeanour shocked Mick. This was not how he'd imagined that this was going to be at all.

"Well, I'm not... and I don't need a bed. I've got one at home. But I've come down to confess. I want to get it off my chest."

The policeman was just gazing at Mick, he'd been watching his mouth move up and down as he spoke.

"Okay. Just take a seat and I'll get an officer to come down and have a word with you. Shouldn't be too long, but it is tea-time so quite a few officers will be otherwise engaged until about seven. Just take a seat over there." The officer waved at the seating area and sat back down and restarted whatever task it was that he'd been distracted from. Mick just stood there a moment, wondering if this was a wind-up. He'd come in here to confess to a murder and he'd been asked to sit down in the waiting room. This wasn't how he'd imagined it would be at all.

Mick did as he was told, and took a seat. The sad looking couple seemed nervous as he walked across towards them. The lady re-started reading her pamphlet, desperately trying to avoid eye-contact.

It felt strange, realising that he could just walk out of here and the copper probably wouldn't even look up. Probably couldn't give a toss, thought Mick.

Eventually, after a fifteen minute wait, a lady police officer came to the glass door at the side of the counter and opened it.

"Is that him?" she asked of the policeman at the computer.

"Yes, that's him." Said the desk officer without looking up from his work.

"Excuse me, Sir, can you come this way please?" asked the lady officer.

Mick stood up and walked across to the door, feeling really silly in front of the other people in the waiting area. He was glad to get beyond the public area, and into the police station properly, where he was following the officer down a corridor. She stopped as she reached the doorway of an interview room and turned on the light inside.

"Power saving. We have to turn all the lights off and on when we leave rooms now. What energy we save, we pay out for on all the new bulbs we blow. Come in, take a seat." Said the officer. Mick was astounded by how friendly she was being. He was here to talk about a murder he'd committed. Mick thought that this was the most surreal experience of his life.

"Right, I'm police constable Kerry Townson, I need to take a few details down from you."

"Cheers." Said Mick.

Fifteen minutes later, PC Townson had finished taking down her notes and told Mick that she would have to go and check a few details out, and told Mick to sit there, asking him if he'd like a hot drink.

"No, I'm alright. Cheers." He said, looking down at the table top.

"Okay, I won't be long. See you in a bit."

PC Townson left the room, leaving the door wide open. Mick was amazed at how laid back the police seemed to be, especially as he was confessing to a murder. He'd always thought that murder was a pretty hardcore crime. He'd envisaged lots of officers pinning him down on the floor, tying his legs together, pushing his face into the floor and lots of shouting, calling him a murdering son of a bitch. He'd certainly not envisaged being offered a brew.

A few minutes turned into five, and then to ten. Time began to pass slowly and Mick was fidgety. His leg was bouncing up and down and he couldn't keep his hands still. His mind was wandering, wondering what Rachel was up to, wondering how she was feeling, wondering if she'd got home alright.

*****

Rachel arrived home loudly, which both shocked and pleased Maureen in equal measure. It was a relief to see her daughter.

"Any news on Suzanne? Anyone seen her?" she

puffed as she entered the living room. She had a sweaty, rosy glow about herself, and looked as though she'd run home.

"Hi love, how did you get on?"

"Hiya mum, okay. It was okay. Have you heard anything from Suzanne?" Rachel's face was filled with hope. Maureen knew that expression. She felt bad that she was about to change the optimistic look on her daughter's face.

"No. She's not been home. I've been keeping an eye out. Noel saw her though, when he was on his way home from school. She was in the back of a car, being driven away. Noel said he waved to her. She saw him, made eye-contact, but she didn't wave back."

"Arrested?" whispered Rachel.

"Looks like it, love, I'm sorry to say." Maureen nodded sympathetically.

"Well, it's just a lottery now. Mick's in there confessing. If Suzanne *is* in there, we just need to hope that's she's denying everything. If that happens, we'll be home and dry mum." Rachel looked old, haggered. She looked about twenty years older than she was. It upset Maureen greatly to see her in this state, but she suspected that things were going to get a lot worse before they would improve.

"Let's be positive then, eh? No point in worrying about it now, is there?"

"No mum, I know. I keep trying to tell myself that, but it's no good. I'm just frantic, I need to know what Suzanne has said. I need to know that the police believe Mick. Once I know all that, I can relax a bit. Start planning how to tell the kids."

Rachel's eyes had lost their twinkle. The kindness and positivity that usually gleamed from them was replaced with a void. An emptiness, a soul-less, sad, hollowness filled them now. She looked lost.

"Come here and give me a big cuddle love."

Rachel and Maureen squeezed one another tightly. They stayed like that for a minute at least. Both took enormous comfort from the embrace. After a while, Maureen spoke.

"I've told the kids you've got something important

to say to them. It might be best to do it sooner rather than later."

"Where are they?

"Scattered all around the house."

Rachel smiled, for her mum's sake.

"Noel's in the front room watching Brainiacs with Shania. Liam's upstairs, revising, or so he says. Britney's asleep in her room."

"Has she said anything to any of them, do you think?"

"No. I don't think so love. She's been really grown up about everything. I've been so impressed by her. She's been through a lot you know, her head's in bits."

"I know. I know. Right, I'll make her a brew and wake her up."

"I'll do it, love."

"No, please, let me, I need to be doing stuff. I can't sit still. I'm fine mum. I'll be fine."

"Alright. Fair enough love. Do you want one of these?" Maureen held out her cigarette packet.

"No. I don't even want a fag! That's how weird I feel."

"Right, well, I'll go and ask Liam to come down, and you make a brew for Britney and take it up. They all know something's up. Something bad. So, well, don't worry too much – they're all expecting bad news." Maureen set off to go upstairs.

"Cheers mum. You've been absolutely amazing about this. You really have."

Five minutes later, Rachel, Maureen and the four Crossley-Birdsworth children were all sat together in the living room. The TV had been switched off and Britney's phone had even been surrendered from her clutches. It was sat on the coffee table.

Rachel felt strange. This was so formal. She'd never had a formal relationship with her kids, except when it was parents evening at school, when she tried her best to talk slightly posh at the kids, which they'd tease her about for weeks after. With this family, everything had been very informal, and that was just how Mick and Rachel liked it. They thought of their kids as their little mates.

But, now, Rachel needed a little formality, just for a short while.

"Okay, I've got some very important things to talk about, right?" She was sat on the big pouffe, facing her kids. "And I just want you all to listen. There's going to be plenty of opportunity for asking questions and all that lot in a bit. But for now, I just want you to be quiet and hear me out." Rachel looked so sad, it scared the children. They looked as though they were all braced for something really awful.

The children all nodded. They all looked scared, but also a bit embarrassed, a bit sad, a bit confused. This was a very unusual situation, and they all had their own fears about what was about to be said. Was somebody dying? Had somebody died? Were they getting kicked out of the house?"

Each person that was sitting around the L shaped settee had their own little worry, their own notion of what the bad thing was likely to be.

"Your dad is in a lot of trouble…" The kids' eyes all flicked up at their mother. "With the police."

That was unexpected. That hadn't been anticipated by any of them. Least of all Britney. Her baffled reaction to this news was the most apparent of them all. Shania didn't really understand it too well and the boys just looked searchingly at one another, trying to figure out what on earth their mother was talking about. Their dad was as straight as they came. He wouldn't even buy a stolen flymo off a smackhead.

A noise erupted. It was a babble, four different voices all asking different incomprehensible questions at the very same time. Rachel put her hand in the air. It worked, and the children were silenced.

"Your dad…" Rachel could hear the emotion in her voice. "Is a very, very good man. He is doing something to protect you all. He is making a big sacrifice, for all of us in this room. He is going to go to prison, for a crime that I have done."

The babble erupted again. The hand gesture worked

again.

Rachel spent the next thirty minutes explaining what had happened over the road, what had happened since, and now, how Rachel and Mick had agreed to handle it. Rachel told the family that they were going to be the only people who would know this. And that it had to remain a secret, no matter what.

"Now, I could have made life a lot easier for me, and not told you all this," said Rachel, in conclusion to the sermon. "But I really want you all to know that your dad is an incredible man. And if your mates at school start calling you, start calling your dad a murderer, and all that, I want you to smile, feel proud, knowing that it wasn't him. But you must never, ever tell anyone. Not even your best friend. Right?"

The children nodded. They understood.

"Pinky promise?" asked Rachel. It made the youngest two smile. Liam nodded, as though immune to the old family joke while Britney just stared impassively at the floor.

"Why?" asked Britney. The question made no sense at all and Rachel looked confused. Why what? Why do a pinky promise? Why not tell your friends? Why what?

"Why what, love?"

"Why is dad taking the blame?"

"He's not taking… he's not, what I mean is…"

"He is taking the blame. Don't start talking a load of shit mum! You just told us all, you killed that bloke. Dad's going to jail for it. Sorry, but how's that not taking the blame?"

"Shut up Britney. Stop being such a bitch." Liam shoved his sister in the arm.

"Whoa! Stop!" said Rachel loudly. One level below a shout. "Don't start bickering. Not now. I'll bang your bleeding heads together! Right?"

"Why?" said Britney, cheekily.

"Because I said so. Right?"

Britney and Liam looked down at the floor, although both of them really wanted to blame the other.

"Listen to me. If your dad wasn't saying that it was him, then we would both be going to jail. Me for killing Graham, and your dad for helping me to hide the evidence. Now, your dad thought it would be best if he took all of the blame for everything."

"But, why mum," asked Noel. "Why did you kill him?" his sad, watery, eleven year old eyes were full of enquiry, and a yearning to fully understand all of this life changing information, that just seemed to be coming from nowhere.

"I've told you love. It was an accident. I was trying to help Suzanne. He was beating her up, really badly. He was spinning her around by her hair and punching her right in the face. I didn't go over there to kill him, love. I just wanted to stop him, I wanted to help Suzanne. It was a bad accident, that's all. None of this was ever meant to happen. Do you know what, if Suzanne had her curtains shut, it wouldn't have happened at all. If your dad wasn't watching Live at the Apollo, I wouldn't have been outside having a fag. It was all down to fate. And now, your dad wants to make it right."

*****

The PC returned to the interview room where Mick had been sat for the past thirty minutes.

"Hiya, right, sorry about the delay. I've had a quick check and what you're saying seems to check out. The computer is showing Graham Ashworth's disappearance as an ongoing live inquiry by the serious crimes team. I've given them a call, and one of their detectives is going to come over and speak to you."

"Right." Said Mick, relieved that the officer seemed to be taking it seriously. He'd half expected to be sent home, based on the initial, couldn't-give-a-shit reaction to his confession.

"So, what will happen next?" Mick looked happy. Things were starting to happen. The constable looked a bit confused, and raised an eyebrow at Mick's reaction.

"Well, I'm glad that's cheered you up!" she said, without a smile.

"Nah, it's not that. I have wanted to do this for weeks. Since it happened. I've only just got the courage."

"Ah, I see! I was starting to think that you were a bit retarded. Fair enough, you're grinning because you've made peace with yourself. I get it. Right, let's get you banged up in the cells until the detectives come. They said it'll be in the next few hours."

"So does that mean..." Mick's face was full of hope.

"Yes, it means that Michael Crossley, I am arresting you on suspicion of murder. You do not have to say anything but it may harm your defence if you do not mention when questioned something that you later rely on in court, anything you do say may be given in evidence."

Oh, thank fuck for that! Thought Mick, desperately wanting to do a celebratory air-grab, but thinking better of it.

So far, so good, he thought as a wry smile crossed his lips.

Chapter 34

Miller was having a night out with his wife Clare. Nothing much was planned, just a meal at the nearby White Horse in Worsley. It was a favourite haunt of both of the Miller's. Andy loved the food, especially the steak. Clare loved seeing the celebrities that popped in randomly, especially Manchester football legend Ryan Giggs, who lived just up the road from the pub.

"It's always a cracking atmosphere in here. I love it!" Clare was grinning from ear to ear. The place attracted a lot of highly attractive, minimally dressed young women, especially on a Friday evening.

"Do they really think that one of the United or City players is going to come in, and ask them for a date, and that's the rest of their lives sorted out?" asked Miller, looking across at the ladies, grumpily.

"Well, they've certainly kept your eyes busy Andy!" Clare was mocking her husband. She knew full well that he was acting grumpy and talking about the young women, just to buy him all this extra time to stare at them.

"Don't be so ridiculous! Jesus, you're putting me off my onion rings!" Miller waved his arm in dramatic fashion, and the over-dramatic gesture made Clare laugh out loud, throwing her head back at her husband's dreadful acting.

"What?"

"You. God, you're funny. You used to look at me like that, once-upon-a-time."

"Like what?"

"The way you've just been looking at those young women."

"Clare, seriously love. Have you got a bit of lettuce in your eye? I haven't looked at them in any way that you're on about. I was just saying, they look like slags. What footballer wants to meet a woman who looks like a daft little slag? If anyone is going to get pulled by a Premier League football player in here tonight, it'll be somebody who's a bit more sophisticated. Someone who dresses sexy, confident, without letting too much flesh escape. Elegant, understated, slightly coy. Someone who absolutely oozes red hot sexuality, but says nothing about it – just keeps it smouldering. In fact, I'd better hope that you're still here when I get back from the gents…" Miller stood and smiled at his wife, licked his finger and pointed it at her, making a "tsssss" sound. "…because you're smoking hot tonight Clare Miller!"

"Ooh, very good! Excellent recovery there, you cheesy bastard!" Clare threw her napkin at him as he walked past the table. He caught it and threw it back.

"Back in a minute."

Clare smiled as her husband walked down the steps and took his phone out of his pocket. She knew that he probably didn't need the loo, he just wanted to check his phone, check his texts and e-mails. It wasn't ideal that he was doing it during a night out – but as far as Clare was concerned, it was a damn sight better than him doing it over the table. Words had been said in the past about that, and Clare's opinions were extremely well known to her husband. The fact that he slid off every thirty minutes for a toilet break was the unspoken, unmentioned compromise.

"You could at least wait until you're round the corner, you dip-stick." She said as she raised her large glass of Pinot Grigio to her lips.

Clare had been right. Miller wasn't using the lavatory. He was just checking his phone for any updates from work. He'd had a text from Saunders, he'd felt it vibrate on his hip. It was one of those random, unexpected messages which completely filled his head with intrigue and enthusiasm. The worst possible kind of message to receive when on a night out with the wife.

"Sir, got a weird one for you. RE that miss–per case up in Bury. Some neighbour of hers has walked into Bury nick and confessed to killing the miss-per. Suspect is called Michael Crossley. No previous. Not exactly sure what's going on with this, but I've instructed them to lock him up. Time of arrest 20:50. Thought you'd want to know. Cheers. Saunders."

Miller was stood in the middle of the noisy, busy gents toilets, staring at his phone, seemingly oblivious to the venue and the activities taking place all around him. Men were urinating to his left, and washing their hands, bantering and joking loudly to his right by the hand driers. The text message made absolutely no sense at all to Miller. Saunders wasn't even aware that he had brought Suzanne Ashworth in today, considered Miller. He wrote a quick reply.

"That's really odd. Get me a bit more info please Keith, previous address, work background, family, friends. Whatever you can find on him. Smells fishy this. Cheers." Miller put the phone back into his pocket and breezed out of the toilets, wafting the stench of pine cleaner, stale urine and wet farts behind him as he walked quickly back towards his table.

"Everything alright?" asked Clare. She had a twinkle in her eye.

"You what?" asked Miller, unsure of what his wife was talking about.

"Is everything alright? When you went to the loo, you were joking and smiling. Now you've just come out of there looking all glum and worried. What's happened?"

"Eh? Nowt. What you going on about?" Miller picked up his pint and took a greedy sip.

"Come on Andy. You know, that I know, that you went in there to check your phone."

"I didn't. I went for a pee. I was bursting."

"Well, look, your hands are bone dry. You always wash your hands when you've been for a wee. If you'd have dried them on the hand blower, you'd still be in there, and wouldn't be out for another half an hour. You've not dried them on your jeans, because you'd have still been wiping them when you came out of the toilet. That's what you always do." Clare smiled at her husband, who had a sheepish look on his face. She was glad to see that Miller absolutely knew that his wife had the upper hand. He was busted.

"You're right. Okay, look, I'm sorry. But like I've said before – you should be a detective. You're very good. Very thorough." Miller looked slightly embarrassed. He did want to switch off from work. He really did want to spend a night out with his wife and completely relax. But it wasn't that simple, not in his job. It's a cliché, it's a yawn creator, but it was true.

"I'm sorry. Honest."

"Well what's going on?" Clare started playing with her hair. "Is it a big case? I mean it's Friday night Andy. You were supposed to have done your years of pissing about with work at weekends. I thought that no weekends was supposed to be the best thing about your rank?"

"I thought you didn't want to hear any more of my work stories?" asked Andy, picking up his steak knife and getting ready to attack the last third of his medium to rare rump.

"Not if they're boring ones. I only like the juicy ones!" Clare smiled. She didn't want to ruin the mood. She admired her husband's dedication to his work. It was the main reason that he was so good at his job. He never really switched off from it, and she was lying to herself if she thought that he could.

"Well, you'll love this one actually. Right up your street!" Miller looked excited to spill some gossip.

"Ooh, that sounds good. I'll just nip to the ladies, and you can recharge our drinks. Back in a tick."

Miller stopped carving his beef, and placed the cutlery down. He drained the last of his beer as he walked to the bar.

A few minutes later, Miller returned to the table with a fresh pint of beer, and a new glass of wine for his wife.

"Thank you love." Said Clare.

"Cheers," said Miller, holding up his glass. The couple clinked glasses before Clare pressed her husband for his story.

"Do you remember I was telling you about Ollie, and his missing neighbour?" Miller took a sip of his drink and wiped the froth from his top lip.

"Ooh yes," Clare's face lit up. "I was meaning to ask you about that as well!"

"Well, even though Ollie really pissed me off, I still ended up looking into it. Despite myself!"

Clare laughed. She was playing with her hair. "And is he missing, the neighbour, or not?"

"He bloody is! And I've just brought his wife in for

questioning this afternoon."

"Oh?" Clare looked really intrigued and rested her chin on her hands.

"Yeah, she lives a few doors away from Ollie and Pippa. Her husband disappeared about a month ago. She says he's in Thailand."

"And presumably, he's not?" Clare was hooked already. Mainly because of the Ollie and Pippa connection. It made it all seem so much more real.

"Nah, he's not been abroad since last year. Anyway, I've put her in a cell for the night. Hopefully, she'll cry all night and confess everything first thing in the morning!"

"You bastard!"

"I know. But, I thought that would be that. However, I just got a text off Keith, that's what I was reading in the bog, he says a neighbour has just walked into Bury police station about half an hour ago, and confessed to killing him."

"What? That's a bit of a coincidence isn't it?" Clare thought it all sounded a bit naff.

"Exactly!"

"Wow. That sounds like a pretty interesting one! It's certainly better than your last story about the guy with the melted welly stuck to his arsehole."

Miller put some steak into his mouth and nodded enthusiastically. Clare seemed to have another thought. Her smile lost its momentum.

"Wait. Does that mean you're going down to the police station to interview this neighbour?" Clare looked a bit annoyed. She should have seen this coming.

Miller was chewing away at his steak, pointing at his jowls as Clare stared across the table at him sternly. Eventually, he swallowed his food, and patted his mouth with the screwed up napkin.

"I'm going to speak to him at some point in the next twenty four hours." Miller lifted his glass and took another gulp at his ale.

"Ah, I get it! You're going to take me home, loiter around in the kitchen until I say I'm going to bed, then you're going to get in your car and drive to Bury nick. That's what I reckon!" Clare had got herself worked up, and she was angry because it was all her own doing. If she'd have just stayed quiet, talked about something else, it wouldn't be a problem.

"I'm not having an argument about it." Miller spoke quietly.

"Neither am I!" said Clare, snappily. The couple that were sitting on the table at the side of them both glanced over at the same time.

"It doesn't affect our night out. We're still having a lovely night out, just me and you."

"We were! And then…"

"Then, what? Come on Clare, turn that frown upside down." Miller grinned at her and pointed at her mouth.

Clare didn't smile. She was too pissed off. She locked eyes with Miller, returning his friendly affection with a cold, angry glare.

"Oh, what's the point. Come on, I want to go home." Clare drained the full glass of wine and stood up. Miller didn't know what to say. He took a hearty sip of his beer and stood up too.

"I've still got a bit of steak there…"

Clare had set off, and had walked gracefully down the three steps towards the bar area, and then the door. Miller wanted to grab the rest of his steak and shove it in his mouth, but he thought better of it.

"Fuck's sake," he said under his breath as he reached the jostling queue at the bar, hoping to hurry the staff into getting his bill.

"Can I …" shouted Miller as he caught the waitress's eye.

"Hee yar mate, pipe down. There's a fucking queue here!" A bald headed man in his early thirties was just ahead of Miller in the queue. He looked as though he'd had a few already, and was a bit put out by Miller's queue jumping attempt, voicing his concerns in a typically bombastic Mancunian fashion. There is no such thing as a stiff upper lip in Greater Manchester.

Miller knew how to diffuse the situation.

"Soz mate, but my wife's just stormed off. I'm not trying to be a twat."

"Fair enough then, hee yar, jump in front of me, here."

"Nice one!"

"You're right mate, we've all been there. Due on is she?" shouted the man, laughing at his vulgar joke. Miller just smiled politely.

"Nah, I've really pissed her off. I need to go outside and act like I'm sorry!"

Miller's new found friend nodded sympathetically. "We've all been there, like I say," he shout-said. "Hee yar!" he turned back around and shouted at the bar staff who were busy serving other customers. "Hee yar! Hurry up, this bloke needs to get off, he's in deep-shit with his missus! Hurry up!"

Despite Miller wanting to die from embarrassment, he was grateful to the baldy piss-head for attracting the staff's prompt attention.

Two minutes later, he was done, and walking briskly around the back of the pub to the car park. Clare wasn't there.

"Great. Fucking great. Absolutely fucking marvellous." Miller pointed at the back of the car with his key-fob and the central locking sounded as it released the door locks. He got in and slammed the door.

"You fucking started it woman!" he said quietly, thoroughly miserable that a quiet, chilled night out had been wrecked, once again. Miller drove the car out of the car park and headed up Worsley Road, knowing that Clare would be walking home, and she'd have got just around the bend past the garden centre. He slowed the car a little as he approached the bend and saw his wife, walking slowly, sulkily. He drove past slowly and pulled the car over to the kerb just ahead of her.

"Surprise!" said Miller as Clare opened the door.

"Oh, I thought you'd have gone straight to the police station, leaving me to walk home on my own." Clare was still annoyed, the walk and the fresh air had done nothing to calm her down. Her shoes were killing her at the front and back of her feet too, which wasn't helping matters. She clicked her seatbelt into the slot and the car started pulling away.

"Stop going on, let it be."

"Oh, you're a star you Andy!" Clare exhaled loudly.

"Don't be like that. You're over-reacting." Miller squeezed the accelerator a little harder.

"I'm over-reacting?" shrieked Clare.

"Yeah, you're being a right diva. Proper drama queen. It's not like you at all love." Miller was driving quickly, his good mood was completely ruined now.

"You are a genius, you. You're trying to deliberately antagonise me even further now, so you can cause a massive argument, and swan off to work with a clear conscience, convincing yourself that it's all my doing. Brilliant. Absolutely brilliant Andy! You're a star."

"You're wrong love. I want to drop you off at home, and then I'm going to go back to the pub and finish my tea. And then I'm going to tell the bloke at the bar that, yes, he's probably right!"

Clare didn't know what Miller was saying, and she had no interest either. She was absolutely fuming, and just stayed silent, looking out of the window for the remainder of the journey home.

Miller kept his thoughts to himself. His thoughts were about Graham Ashworth, and the neighbour with the murder confession. Only a couple of minutes had passed before the car was parked up on the street, outside their home.

"Look, I'm sorry. Okay?"

"Whatever!" said Clare as she unbuckled her seatbelt. "Are you coming in, or going out?"

"Are you going to carry on being a misery-guts? You're like something out of a horror film." Miller was staring dead ahead at the silver VW Golf in front.

"Come on Andy. We were having a night out, and all you're planning is to whisk me off home so you can go back to work. It's a bit shit, isn't it?" Clare was glaring at her husband.

"Look, Clare. You've just had a big hissy fit in the pub, in front of people we know. And I haven't even done any-thing wrong!" Miller laughed sarcastically.

"Right! Fine! To answer your question Andy, yes, I am going to carry on being a misery guts, so fuck you very much." Clare opened the car door, stepped out and slammed it as hard as she could, before walking quite slowly and methodically up the steep drive in her high heels. It really angered Miller, and he wanted to beep the horn and shout obscenities back. But past experience had taught him time and time again that when a woman is being like that, the quietest man was always the wisest man. "Blessed are the meek, for they shall inherit the earth." Said Miller as he watched his wife disappear into the house.

Before he drove the car away, he waited a few minutes. He wrote Clare a text message, apologising for his work interfering with their private life again, but after writing it, and staring at it for a while, Miller deleted it slowly, letter by letter, knowing that he didn't really mean it. Miller was pretty confident that it was Clare who was in the wrong this time. He'd not even said anything about going to Bury. She'd said it, she'd worked it all out, and she was the one who was pissed off with the findings of her own opinion.

"Husband of the year award looks fucked, again." He said as he drove the car off to the bottom of the street. He did a three point turn and drove back past his house to see if Clare was pining for him at the living-room window. She wasn't.

"Okay, game on. Let's see what became of Graham Ashworth!" Miller turned right onto the East Lancashire Road and pressed his foot hard against the accelerator as he headed in the direction of Bury.

Chapter 35

Thanks to the bittersweet fortune of his wife's bad mood, Miller had managed to get himself over to Bury police station just after ten pm. Every part of his detective psyche was in hyper-drive, burning with questions and fizzing with scenarios. This kind of coincidence didn't just happen. A neighbour randomly presenting himself to the police station, to confess to a murder, just a couple of hours after the missing man's wife was brought in. It was all pretty far out, a very peculiar state of affairs, and it had Miller buzzing. He found it completely tantalising to have a case like this, in comparison to the vast majority of his normal workload.

Once inside the police station, he was dismayed to learn that the officer who'd booked Michael Crossley in, had gone off-shift - literally moments before Miller had arrived. He'd wanted to ask a few questions of the arresting officer, before he would come face to face with Crossley himself. But, it wasn't to be.

Miller was handed the custody report from the Sergeant. He stood in the custody suite, and read through it, seemingly oblivious to the loud, senseless ranting of a middle-aged drunk man who had just been brought in for drinking and driving. The custody suite was noisy and angry, shouting police officers and even louder Sergeant's booming voices were echoing around the place, competing with the gibberish nonsense from the drunk man, the din from the inmates on the adjacent custody blocks and the brain rattling sound of cell doors being slammed shut.

Somehow, Miller remained ignorant to it all as he stood and read the report which PC Kerry Townson had completed prior to her clocking off.

"Okay, fetch him down to an interview room for me please, I'd like to have a chat with him if that's okay?" asked Miller of the Custody Sergeant, who was hovering beside the DCI.

"Yes Sir, take yourself down to interview room four, just on the left there, and I'll get him brought down. I'll tell you, he's a weird one. There he is, look." The Sergeant pointed to the CCTV monitor bank by the side of the two men, and pointed out Michael Crossley. He was sat on his mattress, looking quite relaxed and contented, like a man that didn't have a care in the world.

"God, you're right. He certainly looks like he's at peace with himself, doesn't he?" asked Miller. The Sergeant smiled and nodded.

"Agreed Sir. He looks like he's sunbathing by the riverside to me!"

Miller laughed loudly, which annoyed the drunk man who was still gesticulating at the top of his voice.

"Oh ye can fuck off as well you ugly bastard!" He shouted. Miller ignored him and kept his attention on the CCTV feed from Crossley's cell.

"I'll have him brought down to you in a few minutes, Sir." said the Sergeant.

"Thanks, I really appreciate it. I've not been in a custody suite on a Friday night for years! It really takes me back!" said Miller, cheerfully.

"Oh, this is nothing, Sir. Pop back at two in the morning if you want!"

"Erm, I'll get back to you on that, if that's okay?" Miller smiled at the Sergeant as he walked past. "Thanks for all your help, it's appreciated."

A short while later, Miller was in the interview room, talking to Michael Crossley.

"So, Michael, you've wrecked my Friday night! You've made my wife shout at me in a crowded pub!"

"I'm sorry." said Mick, sombrely. He looked and sounded quite genuine. Miller was only trying to break the ice, start things off on a friendly footing. He didn't come across too many young blokes that were this polite, he thought. A normal response in this situation would be a shrug or a "so-what?" expression. Mick had made a good impression on the DCI already.

"Oh, don't worry about it too much. I'll sleep at a mate's." Miller wanted the interviewee to laugh, but he didn't. Mick was leaning forward, just staring at the table top, looking quite focused. The duty solicitor, a smart, fresh-faced man of Asian heritage was sat upright beside him, making notes on his A4 notepad.

"So. You've presented yourself here tonight, saying that you've killed a man." Miller's voice was sympathetic. He wanted to win Mick's trust straight away.

"Yes, I had to come in and tell you. I've been living a life of hell since it happened. I don't think I've slept. I can't go on like this." There was little emotion present in Mick's voice, but he sounded genuine. There were lots of time-wasters that presented themselves with murder claims. Miller knew exactly what to look for, and he felt quite confident about things so far.

"Do you know the name of the man that you killed?"

"Yeah, course I do. He's a … he was a neighbour. Graham Ashworth. Lived in the house opposite mine, well, the house where I'm living at the, sorry. The house I was living at until tonight." The man looked broken, he'd struggled to say that the house was in the past, thought Miller. But there was also a noticeable sense of relief present, he had a glaring sense of contentment about him. Miller couldn't put his finger on it, but he was certainly intrigued by all of this. It was definitely more interesting than watching Gogglebox on the television with his wife, anyway. And that's probably what they'd be doing now if he was at home, he considered.

"Was it your intention to kill this man?" asked Miller.

"No. No, was it heckers like."

"Okay, well, I've read through the statement that you gave to the constable when you arrived, so I do have an understanding of what you've said. Now, before we go on, I want you to bear in mind that killing somebody accidentally, is not seen as murder in the courts. What that means is, even if you did kill this man, it doesn't automatically make you a murderer in the eyes of the law."

"DCI Miller, my client does not require legal advice from yourself. That is my function, if you don't mind?" The solicitor looked quite annoyed by Miller's comments.

"Understood. But in my experience, you guys just

tell your clients to say no comment to every question. If your client said no comment to every question when making his confession, then we're all in for a long night."

"All I'm saying, is that I will dispense the legal advice."

"Fine. Have you advised your client about this matter yet?"

"Not yet, no." said the young legal expert.

"Well cross it off your to-do list, I've just done it for you." Miller winked at the solicitor and held his thumb up.

Mick was fidgeting with his hands on the table top, not really listening to what the policeman and the legal representative were going on about.

"Right, Michael, bear in mind what I have said. I'm trying to tell you that you can be completely honest – it won't make any difference at court if you tell half truths, or full truths. Okay?" Miller was smiling gently, supportively. He had a nice, kind face that Mick trusted already.

"Sure, I understand."

"Okay, take your time and just tell me what happened, what led up to you killing this man." Miller was sat with his hands clasped together on the table top. The gambit about manslaughter had worked, it had convinced Mick that Miller was on his side.

Mick took a drink of his water and stared down at the table top as he began.

"It all started when we moved in, this guy over the road, he was just taking the piss out of us. The first night we moved in, he was trying to start a fight with another neighbour a few doors up. My missus woke me up and told me. She said it's kicking off and I had to go and settle everyone down. What it was, the council put all these rules in, they said one sign of trouble in these new houses and you'll be booted out, no messing like." Mick glanced up at the detective. Miller looked interested in what he was saying.

"Go on," said Miller, softly.

"So, my missus, Rachel, she's proper paranoid, I mean, it's our first night and it's kicking off…"

"But you weren't involved at this stage?"

"No. Absolutely jack shit to do with us. We were in bed, I was fast asleep."

"Sorry, I don't mean to butt in. But why *did* you get involved?" Miller looked genuinely interested.

"It's Rach. My missus. She takes stuff on herself, she's always trying to sort stuff out, she's good like that. She saw that this guy was about to get his head punched in, and she wanted to stop it."

"So she woke you up and sent you to sort it?" Miller smiled widely, knowingly. It was a man-to-man "what are wives like?" expression, which made Mick smile. The smile pleased Miller, he was working subtlety on building Mick's trust and all of the signs were positive.

"Exactly. Well, she went first, knowing I'd follow, to protect her like." Miller could see that this man loved the woman he was talking about. His face changed when he spoke about her, and he seemed to adopt a smile in his voice. His eyes gained a certain moistness.

"Sounds like she's the boss?"

"I let her think so," said Mick, smiling. That love was back, it poured out when he talked about her. Miller liked this, he was going to be an easy read this one, he thought.

"Sorry, I won't interrupt again. It's very unprofessional. Carry on Michael."

"Right, so, I went out and the guy, Graham, the bloke I killed, he's toe to toe with this other neighbour who'd just moved in that day as well. It was pretty obvious that Graham was trying to get Kev, that's the other neighbour, he was trying to get him to give him a crack. So me and Rach split it all up, told this Kev and his wife to go inside and shut up before they get kicked out. So they went inside, and next minute, this Graham starts giving me shit. He's calling me a scrounger and a scumbag. Rachel told me to go inside, she started nipping my arm so I knew she was being serious - so we went in the house and a few minutes later, the police came. It was all a set-up you see. Graham had wanted the police to come along when it was kicking off, and his plan had failed. He just looked like a knob. So, then he started giving the police a load of shit, and they chucked him in the back of the van! He was calling them allsorts, so they took him off. He was an absolute nightmare, I'm not joking. Weird, weird bloke."

Miller was writing down notes as he listened. He was interested that Mick had shown absolutely no remorse for his crime, and it was particularly notice-able when describing the man he killed. If, as he'd said, he was here to confess because he felt awful about taking this man's life, it wasn't very obvious – if anything he was contradicting himself by calling the victim a weird bloke. Miller's instincts told him that something was wrong with this man's story. Something was definitely wrong.

"So this was what - a month before Graham was killed?"

"Roughly, yeah. I'd say it was about a month."

"So, if it was the night you moved in. What was the date of that incident?"

Mick looked up at the ceiling and thought about the question. Eventually, after a good think, he answered.

"It was a Saturday, eighteenth of May, because I got paid on the fifteenth, and it was just after pay day."

Miller continued making his notes.

"Tell me what happened on the night that Graham died."

*****

Suzanne Ashworth was sat inside a police cell. She had absolutely no idea how long she had been there for. It might have been four hours, or it could well have been fourteen. There was no clock in there, there wasn't even a sky-light or a window with bars over it. She had no idea if it was still daylight outside, or if it had been dark and was now a new day. Suzanne had been asleep a couple of times, but the smelly, thin plastic mattress they gave her wasn't very comfortable. It was getting noisier and noisier as the time went on. The kind of noise that other prisoners were making suggested that it was after closing time at the pubs. Drunken, nasty, nonsensical screams and shouts, kicks and slaps against the steel cell doors echoed and reverberated around the place. It was a scary place to be if you weren't familiar with the police cells at weekend. Suzanne couldn't understand why she'd been left in the cell for so long. If the police wanted to interview her about Graham, that was completely understandable. But what was the idea of just chucking her in a cell and fobbing her off every time she pressed the assistance button? That's all that had been going through Suzanne's head.

It had been a very long time since Suzanne Ashworth had been locked up in a police cell. Almost ten years in fact. But today, tonight or whenever it was, possibly even this morning, she felt as though nothing about the cell had changed in all that time. Even the paintwork looked as damp and flakey as she remembered it. The names scratched into the door fascinated her. She spent a long time reading the names and the pathetic comments that had been painstakingly scratched into the paintwork, most probably by fingernails. Well what else could it be? Wondered Suzanne as she imagined the people who had written such refined remarks as "fuck off twats." She tried to smile as she wondered why that had been the best that the graffiti creator could think of on the night. But she couldn't smile. There was nothing to smile about, not even stupid, pointless graffiti written over many hours by a brainless moron.

Suzanne knew that she had a lot of explaining to do, and she was starting to doubt that plan A was going to cut it. Suzanne had always had a plan B lined up, just in case. It was her secret of course, none of the others had been enlightened with the details of plan B.

But, based on the rather unorthodox manner in which the police were treating her, Suzanne suspected that this "let her stew in her own sweat" tactic was a pretty clear indication that the police had enough to bring her in, enough to suspect her of something, but very little else after that. No substance. If the best they had was a tactic of letting her sweat until she was ready to confess, she considered, then the police had made a very significant error of judgement.

As the cell alarms continued to beep, and the police

officers carried on clanging the cell door shutters and the prisoners persisted on banging and howling and crying and screaming, Suzanne forced herself to drift off once again into a hazy, difficult half-sleep.

*****

Mick was visibly trembling. He took a deep breath, before starting to tell DCI Miller about the circumstances surrounding Graham Ashworth's death.

"Well, I do this job on the side at weekends, washing up and chopping up veg and stuff for a restaurant in town. I got home about midnight, it was a Friday because I was watching Live at the Apollo that Rachel had recorded for me. So anyway, I'd had a pint at work, finishing off, and then a few cans of beer at home. I was getting into my red wine and feeling pretty chilled out. Everyone was in bed, and I'm just sat in the living room, loving the peace and quiet, just buzzing off the comedians on telly, giving my nose a good pick and all that, you know what I mean. Next thing, I hear all this shouting. Not in the house though, it was outside. So, I paused the telly and listened. I could still hear it, and I heard a scream so I shot up, went to the door to see what was going on. It wasn't that type of place, you see. Back on the estate, that kind of thing was normal. But it was really weird to hear it on the posh street. When I got to the front door, I could see Graham in the upstairs window over the road, battering the shit out of his missus. He was shouting at her, she was screaming and crying for help, stuff was getting smashed and that. He was proper hitting her. Honestly, I mean battering the living daylights out of her, punching her, ramming her into walls. It made me feel sick. I thought fucking hell, I just didn't know what to do. My heart was pounding, and I could hear her screaming and pleading with him to stop. I went back inside, got my trainers on, and ran over. The front door was locked so I went round the back, ran upstairs and he was booting her in the face." Mick stopped for a second, took a drink of water and wiped his mouth with his sleeve before continuing. "I picked up this object, I don't know what it was, a metal thing, like summat off an old fireplace or summat. It was just lying there, holding a door open. So I lifted it and rammed it against his head, here." Mick pointed at his temple. "Just to get him to stop kicking her head in. He fell down to the floor, and I went over to Suzanne. I thought she was dead. Graham was making this gurgling noise, but then he just stopped. He started juddering, shaking like, and then he stopped doing that. He was just lay there staring up at the ceiling. It was proper scary, I mean, I've never been that scared before. I just fucked off out of there, I couldn't believe what was going on, I couldn't believe none of it." Mick was looking down at the table. "As far as I was concerned, they was both dead. He'd killed her, I'd killed him. That was what I thought, and I just shot off out of there, wondering how the fuck I'd just gone from monging out on my settee to killing a bloke in about two minutes flat."

The tone of Mick's voice whilst retelling his story concerned Miller. For such a traumatic, scary, spontaneous situation which he was describing, with such an horrific outcome, Miller thought that Mick's timbre was just too monotonous. Miller got the sense that Mick was fibbing about all this. It all just sounded too flat and rehearsed. Something was missing from the story. Something that would put a bit of meat on the bones.

Despite his suspicion that Mick was talking shit, Miller continued to play his supportive character to the best of his ability.

"That sounds absolutely horrific! I don't know what I would have done in that situation." he said, calmly and compassionately.

Mick could have had no idea that Miller's suspicions were aroused, the detective looked just as kind and warm, and totally interested in what had happened. He looked like he wanted to help. But Miller's suspicions were most certainly aroused, he could smell a rat. A dead, festering rat.

"It was. Honestly, I shit you not, it was the worst night of my life. I staggered home, I felt like I was going to collapse in the street, my legs were buckling under me. I got in the house, and noticed I was totally covered in blood. I didn't know how, I'd not really been rolling around with the guy. So I got in the shower and I started panicking, I was like, shall I phone the police, or just leave it. Then I was worrying about my finger prints on the metal thing, then I started thinking about prints on the front door handle, then the gate handle, the back door, on the banister, and God knows what else I'd touched."

"Where was your wife while all this was happening?"

"She was upstairs, asleep, in bed."

"Did she not wake up, you coming in and having a shower?"

"Nah, once she's asleep she's asleep. She has sleeping tablets."

"Which ones?" asked Miller. He just wanted to see Mick's reaction to basic, straight forward questions. It would help him to pick out any peculiarities in his face or voice when talking about real things, and lying.

"Which what?" Mick's eyes flicked up from the table top and met Miller's.

"Which sleeping tablets does she have?" Miller was good at playing the good cop. He was like the kindly teacher at school that all the kids wanted to please.

"Oh, er, the Boots ones. Sleep easy." He'd looked up at the ceiling again as he considered the question. Miller was happy with that.

"So what happened next?"

"I got dressed, put my trackies on, and went back. I can't remember everything perfect, it's like in sections of memory. I'd had a few beers you see, and I was absolutely shitting myself."

"Just tell me what you can remember, please Michael. Take your time, mate."

"Well, I went back across to the house, just to see if everything was as I'd remembered it. I took a baseball bat from the garage, just in case."

"In case…"

"In case that Graham had got up, and was ready to stab me or summat. I just didn't have a clue what was what."

Miller was absolutely bursting to ask questions, such

as why didn't Mick just phone the police. But he didn't want to interrupt the flow. He was making mental notes of points that he wanted to bring up later on.

"Go on."

"So I went in there, crept upstairs. I couldn't hear anything at all. It was just all silent, and really creepy. That was when I knew for sure that Graham was dead. I'd never seen a dead body before – but it was pretty obvious that he was dead, he'd gone a really funny colour, like that cheap ham from Tesco. It was freaky, totally blew me away, realising that he was really dead, and I'd done it."

Mick's index finger had started tapping on the table-top. Tap, tap, tap. His eyes looked up again and met Miller's. He looked quite genuine, thought Miller, but his tone of voice was just monotonous, and Miller thought that he sounded quite robotic. He nodded at Mick, encouraging him to continue with his story.

"Suzanne didn't look dead though, she looked as if she was asleep. I went over to her and she was breathing really heavily, she absolutely stunk of booze, spirits. It was rotten, the smell was hanging. She sounded like she was snoring, and trying to say something, but she was totally out of it - I didn't know if it was the booze or the kicks in the head. Her face and head was all swollen up, and I just started panicking, I didn't have a clue what I was meant to do. I didn't think to phone the police, or the ambulance, just didn't think to. A few days later, after everything had happened, after I'd started calming down a bit, that was all that was going through my mind. I thought fucking hell, if I'd just rung nine nine nine, I'd have been sorted. I could have explained and everything. Got Suzanne off to hospital, checked out properly. But anyway, whether it was the beer or the adrenaline or what, I don't know, I just panicked. I put the bed sheet all round Graham's head to stop all the blood getting everywhere, I tied it really tight, then I grabbed Graham's arms and pulled his body down the stairs. I found his car keys, went out and opened up the back of the car, dropped the seats as silently as I could. Then I went back in, picked Graham up, threw him over my shoulder and chucked his body into the back of the car and locked it up. I was proper paranoid, looking over the street, checking no lights were on. I was trying to be as quiet as possible, but every single little noise sounded proper loud."

Miller was just nodding, but his friendly smile seemed to have slipped. Mick noticed it, as he got a glance of Miller's face, and did a double-take. Miller looked slightly solemn, his supportive air seemed to have vanished momentarily. Mick's finger was still tapping out a rapid beat on the table. And it seemed to be getting faster. He was fidgety, his shoulders seemed to be moving around. It was as though somebody had paused the interview and brought some music into the booth. It was as though Mick was dancing in his seat. Or he was agitated.

"Carry on," said Miller, nodding.

"So, right, I'd got Graham in the back of the car, I was pretty happy that no-one was watching, no-one had seen anything. So, I went back upstairs, I was shaking by now, proper shaking, I couldn't have pressed nine nine nine by this point, honestly, that's how bad my hands were shaking. I'd have just dropped the phone on the floor. I couldn't think straight. I realised I was just stood, in Suzanne's house, staring up the stairs, shaking."

"Do you want to pause now, take a breath of fresh air?" asked Mick's solicitor.

"No, no, I'm nearly done."

"You seem quite unwell, reliving this traumatic moment," said the duty solicitor, his tone of voice sounded quite insistent that his client took a break.

"No. I've got to... this has been eating at me for the last month. I need to get it all off my chest."

"For the tape, my client is refusing advice of a break."

"Thank you," said Miller, looking quite irritated by the solicitor's random interruption. Miller's attention returned to Mick Crossley.

"So, I snapped out of it, I suddenly came to a bit, I could feel myself sobering up. I went upstairs to where Suzanne was lay out on the floor, I managed to pull her up onto the bed first, then I got her over my shoulder and carried her over to my house, I put her on the settee in the front room. She was trying to argue and that, proper confused she was. So I went in the kitchen and got her a drink of water, and I slipped her two of Rachel's sleeping tablets, I told her they were pain-killers. She was sobbing, I couldn't tell what she was saying, and I was thinking I need to get her to the hospital pretty quick. My mind was racing, I was like, should

I wake Rachel up and get her sit with her?" Mick took another thirsty gulp at his transparent plastic cup of

water, draining the cup. "But then I was like, no – she'll want to know where I was going, wanting to know what's happening. So, I stayed there a few minutes, waited for Suzanne to calm down, I was patting her back, gently stroking her head where there was no big lumps. I stayed like that about five minutes, ten minutes. All the time, I'm shaking like a shitting dog, I'm thinking any second now, the police are going to bang on the door and it's all over. But it was silent, there was nothing going on outside, just silence. By the time Suzanne was calmed down a bit and snoring, I put her in the recovery position in case she puked up, and I waited a few more minutes to check she was alright."

"Go on," said Miller, after a few seconds of silence from Mick.

"So, that was when I…"

"Come on Mick, you're doing great. Honestly mate, keep going." Miller was really beginning to look pissed off, but the friendliness in his voice was unmistakable. The stirring tone of the comment really lifted Mick's spirits, he had begun to feel as though he'd been losing Miller's interest, and it was making it difficult to keep focused.

"Right, yeah," said Mick, continuing to tap his index finger rapidly against the tabletop as he spoke. "So I went back in the house, looked everywhere for a knife, a sharp knife. I needed to get that carpet out of there, it was absolutely covered in blood. I mean, seriously, it was like a bottle of vimto had been poured on it. Anyway, I sorted that, cut round the bed and just a rolled it all up and put it in the back of Graham's car, right on top of Graham. And then, I just jumped in the front, drove off and that was that."

"That was what?" asked Miller, intrigued by the psychological importance of Mick's finger tapping. It told him that the things that were being said were actually true, that he'd actually been involved in all this. But the truth had only started to be spoken about after the event. The finger tapping only began when Crossley began talking about tidying up, moving the body.

Miller watched the finger continue to tap tap tap away and wondered why he'd not done that all the way through the story.

"I set off, went and got rid of Graham's body."

"Hmmm, now that's interesting!" said Miller, with another lift of energy to his voice. "Where is the body?" he asked. "Talk me through this bit slowly please."

"I pulled out of the estate, and I was thinking of places to put a body. Absolutely mental, I know, like something off the telly. I'm driving this guy's car. Absolutely mint car, a Range Rover Evoque, top spec. I'd never driven anything like it in my life. I looked at the dash, it said I was going ninety five miles per hour – honestly, it felt like sixty. Anyway I'm in this weird, half pissed, half buzzing, half terrified frame of mind. I realise I'd driven up to Haslingden, and I started panicking, thinking fuck, what if the police pull me. I'm over the limit, I've got the car owners body in the back of the car. I'm like…" Mick put the cup to his mouth, but there was no water in it. His finger was still tapping out a rhythm on the table.

"I'll get you a drink in a sec, just want to hear this bit first, please," said Miller, his arms were folded across his chest. He was nodding.

"So next thing, I'm driving along this section of road, over the tops, driving down into Accrington, a place I'd never even been to before. It was just the first place that was signed, and I was getting more urgent about dumping the body. It was the most beautiful sunrise I've ever seen that day, that morning, and the view up there, on that road, it made me cry. It was so beautiful." Mick's voice broke, and he was filling up. His finger was tapping faster. This was all true, thought

Miller. But only from the moment that he went in and saw the body. This guy had been a robot until then. Miller could tell something was up with this story, and he was becoming more and more intrigued by the minute.

Miller could see unequivocally that this bit of the story really happened. Most of what this guy had said about killing Graham Ashworth was total nonsense, thought Miller - but right now, Mick Crossley was talking about something that really happened. It spooked Miller to think that everything he'd just heard in the last hour was a lie, or a fabrication of what had actually happened. He was amazed that this man's story about murder, saving a beaten up woman, carrying her drunken, beaten body across the road in the dead of night, and loading a dead body in a car, before driving off into the night was all told in a droning, well revised, doubly rehearsed monotone.

But he nodded politely and patiently waited until Mick Crossley had confessed the rest of his bullshit story.

"I know this is hard, but you're doing really great, honestly Michael, you're really doing well." Miller leant across and touched Mick's hand softly, offering a quick, encouraging tap. Miller looked up at the solicitor and as their eyes locked, Miller could see that the young Asian looking man was hearing the exact same lies and nonsense. He didn't believe what his client Mick Crossley was saying either.

"Where's the body, Michael? Where did you put it?"

"It's in Accrington. I rolled it all up in the carpet, with loads of rocks, and taped it all up with some parcel tape that I..." Mick Crossley's face went a deathly shade. He stopped talking as he realised that he'd just come very close to making a mistake. Miller noticed it and pounced.

"That you what?" asked Miller.

"That I got from home."

That's a cock up, thought Miller. That detail is going to be useful, he thought as he kept his eyes trained on Mick.

"Okay, where is the body? Accrington is a big place. I need to know the exact place that you dumped it?"

"Yeah, I know where, I mean exactly where." This was the part that Mick was most excited about, this was the part where he would convince Miller that he did do this, that he was responsible. His finger was beating at such a rate, there was a visible blur, and the rhythm was getting faster yet.

"It's in the cut. I chucked it off the bridge near KFC and the Fire Station."

"What, you threw the body, wrapped in carpet and loaded with rocks off a bridge into the canal?"

"Yeah." Mick was tapping furiously now.

"I'm sure I read that Graham Ashworth was

described as fourteen, fifteen stone. You must have had your weetabix that day!" said Miller. There was no humour in the comment at all. Miller looked at his watch. It was after eleven o'clock now. This guy had talked for a lot longer than Miller had anticipated, and he was glad that he did. Miller was pretty sure he had a good portion of the truth there. He wanted the rest of it now.

"So, if I go to the canal near the KFC in Accrington, I'm going to find a man's body wrapped up in carpet and parcel tape, in the water beneath the bridge? With rocks inside there to weigh it down?"

"Yeah, honest."

"And, let me clarify something. You arrived at the bridge in the victim's car, rolled out this piece of blood soaked carpet on the floor, just as the sun was coming up, and then you dragged a fifteen stone body out of the car, then laid the dead man out, grabbed some rocks, rolled it all up in the carpet, then you wrapped parcel tape all around it, lifted this quite considerable parcel up, what, over a hundred kilograms, and then chucked over a wall into the canal?" Miller had one eyebrow raised, quite sarcastically.

"Yep. Well, it was a barrier, like, it's on a dual carriageway. It was a struggle, I'm not going to lie. But it had to be done, I was shitting myself. " Mick was completely ignoring the detective's deliberate expression of disbelief.

"All on your own, without the help of anybody else?"

"I've told you everything, now. That's my confession." Mick's shoulders dropped, and Miller realised for the first time that they'd been tensed all the way through this. He was done.

Miller looked down at the table and paused for a while. After a pause that seemed to last minutes, he exhaled loudly.

"Have you ever heard the expression "a crock of shit?" asked Miller. His smile was back, but it didn't contain any warmth anymore. DCI Miller looked scornful.

"Yes?" said Mick. His eyes had returned to the table-top.

"Do you know what it means?"

"I... well, yeah..."

"Let me explain. It derives from ancient Rome. It goes back about two thousand years, so it's a proper old fashioned saying. The crock was a big bowl, made out of pot. The Romans used to have a shite in it - it was all they had for a toilet back in the day. When it was full, it was full to the top with everyone's shit. It was absolutely horrendous, it stunk, and it really was about as bad as things got when the Roman's had a crock of shit. Nowadays, we say that something or somebody is full of shit. But it all means the same thing, the expression "a crock of shit" dates back to Roman times."

"That's extremely fascinating, I must say. And if you could just get to the punch-line now please, Mr Miller?" said the solicitor, looking quite bored with the detective's comment. Mick Crossley was just looking at the detective with a glazed, confused expression across his face.

"What about "twaddle" have you ever heard of that?" asked Miller.

"No. Well, I don't know. Might have..." said Mick, wondering why Miller was turning on him, wondering what possible reason he could have to doubt the story.

"What about a load of old codswallop?" asked Miller. His face had changed. The kind, friendly expression was gone completely. There was absolutely no hint that it had ever existed.

"What?" Mick was visibly stunned. His mouth was hanging open.

"You're fibbing to me. I can just tell."

"What?" Mick's face was panic-stricken.

"I've come in here on my night off, I've tried being alright with you, and you're just talking a load of shit to me. What's your game mate? Really, what's going on with you?"

"What?" Mick was completely blown away, this was unexpected in the extreme, and he was not prepared for it. The next statement from Miller would confound his confusion further.

Miller needed to throw a few curve ball's. He wanted to see Mick's reaction, he wanted to see a genuine reaction.

"Graham Ashworth isn't dead. I know that for a fact. So, I'm thinking, why is this bloke coming in here and admitting to murdering a man who is alive and well?"

The solicitor who was sitting next to Mick sat up slightly and cleared his throat. He too was thrown by this unexpected announcement from the DCI.

"He is dead. I should know... I killed him!" Mick had a pleading look in his eyes.

Miller held his hand up to his chin, and had adopted his very best pondering look.

"Are you shagging Suzanne Ashworth? Is that what's going on here?"

"What?" Mick's face turned pale. He had no idea what was going on here.

"Fucking hell Michael! What? Why do you keep saying what? Have you seen Pulp Fiction Michael, the bit where Samuel L Jackson say's "say what again! Say what one more time mother fucker!" well, you just remind me of that guy..."

"Can we stop now please. I'm making a formal request for a break." The solicitor stood up, and in doing so exhibited a great deal of authority in the room.

"Yes, that's fine, we're done. I'll get Michael sent back to his cell. I'm going to see Suzanne Ashworth. She's in custody you see. I'm going to go and tell her what you've just been saying. Maybe then I'll find out what the hell is going on here, with this absolute crock of shit!"

Chapter 36

"Right, up we get!" bellowed a female officer through the hatch before clanging up the shutter. Suzanne's eyes blinked open and she stared at the mouldy, dirty ceiling. It didn't take her long to focus and remember where she was. There was another loud, intimidating noise as the heavy metal bolts on the door were released at great volume and the police officer swung open the heavy cell door.

"You're being interviewed soon. Do you wish to have a solicitor present?"

"No. Not at this stage."

"Okay, here's some coffee and some toast. You can have five minutes in the exercise yard if you wish?" The officer looked the same age, maybe a tiny bit older than Suzanne. She talked like an android. Her work had clearly drained her soul of any humanity, thought Suzanne.

"Thanks." She said. "What time is it?"

"It's six fifteen." Said the officer.

"Jesus. I came in here in the afternoon, what, about four o'clock. Time flies when you're having fun." Suzanne didn't want a laugh, but a smile would have done. It might have just confirmed that the woman who stood before her with the drink and the small plastic plate of toast was real. But there was no smile.

"I'll be back in five minutes." The door slammed shut, causing another prisoner to start kicking off in the next cell along.

"Can you fuck off banging the doors you inconsiderate bastards?" screamed one furious resident further down the block.

"Cheers," said Suzanne as she stood and walked the couple of steps to the tray that had been left on the floor.

"Excuse me," she shouted, "I asked for a tall skinny mocka frappuchino. This simply won't do!" The tone of the remark didn't contain any hint of humour. Suzanne took a swig of the lukewarm milky coffee in the plastic cup. "Eeurgh."

"Shut up you stupid cow!" shouted another prisoner,

and a wave of noise started up once again.

"Ha ha ha! Get me a fuckin' skinny mockachino!" shouted another inmate whilst banging her hand against the door. "I want one! Wooo hoooo!"

Suzanne nibbled at the toast, but it was so cold and dry that she wondered if it had been left over from the previous day's breakfast shift. She drank the rest of the coffee in one, head-back motion and made a loud rasping noise after she swallowed it. She went over to the toilet in the corner of the cell and had a wee, holding her fingers up in a V formation at the CCTV camera that was observing silently above her head.

The five minutes passed quickly, and Suzanne's cell door was opened again and she was allowed to put her shoes on, which had been left outside the cell overnight. She was led out into the small, high walled exercise yard, which she walked around continuously for a little over ten minutes.

Soon afterwards, she was back inside the police station, walking through the maze of brightly lit corridors with her uniformed companion. The cold, arms-length way that she was being treated by this darlek officer made her feel that the police knew something. But her mind wasn't set just yet, she would need to see how the land was laid in the interview room first. Suzanne was shown through into a well lit room where the policeman that had arrested her the previous day was sat, reading his paperwork.

"Good morning!" said DCI Miller, very cheerfully. He looked worn-out. He's been working on this since they'd last met, thought the detainee.

"Morning," said Suzanne, fluttering her eyelashes in a very exaggerated fashion. She stood with the female officer at the table.

"So you don't want any legal representation?" asked Miller.

"Not at this stage, thank you." Suzanne sat down and looked flirtatiously at Miller. "Please excuse my breath. I haven't had the opportunity to brush my teeth." Suzanne smiled widely, allowing Miller a great look at the detainee's teeth, should he wish to inspect them.

"Don't worry about that. Okay, I'll hit the record button on here then, and we'll get going." Miller touched the red button on the device on the trolley that was parked beside the table.

"Okay the time is six thirty five on the morning of Saturday the ninth of July. My name is DCI Andrew Miller of Manchester central police station. I am interviewing Mrs Suzanne Ashworth aged twenty eight years in relation to the disappearance of her husband. During this interview I will talk to you about the disappearance of your husband, Mr Graham Ashworth of last known address nine Fir Tress Grove, Bury, Lancashire."

"It's Greater Manchester."

"I beg your pardon?" asked Miller, looking up from his notes.

"Bury. It's in Greater Manchester. Has been all my life time." Suzanne smiled.

"Okay, for the benefit of the tape, Bury is in Greater Manchester. It ceased being in Lancashire when the county boundaries were revised in nineteen seventy-four. Okay?" Miller winked, and smiled.

Suzanne grinned. "That's better!" she said.

"Okay, great. I will also ask you about anything else which may become relevant during the interview, in order to properly establish the facts and issues surrounding this enquiry. Do you understand why you are here?" Miller sounded quite monotone as he read out the formal introductions.

Suzanne nodded.

"Can you please say yes or no, for the benefit of the recording? Do you understand why you are here?"

"Yes."

"Do you understand your rights?"

"Yes."

"Do you wish to have a legal representative present with you during the interview?"

"No. I'll be out of here by the time they arrive!" Suzanne smiled seductively and looked down at her chest, then back at Miller.

"Okay. You have been arrested in connection with the disappearance of Graham Ashworth. Where is he?"

"You mean you don't know?" asked Suzanne, smiling flirtatiously again.

"Okay, I think you're in a rather silly mood this morning. Please just answer my questions." Miller didn't look at her, he just kept his eyes down on his paperwork.

"Sorry, am I annoying you?" Suzanne touched her breast gently, and pretended to brush something off the figure hugging t-shirt.

Miller blushed ever so slightly and looked up at the female detention officer who was stood by the door. He coughed quietly. Suzanne hadn't stopped staring at him once.

"Did you say your name was DCI Miller?"

Miller ignored the question. He just kept his attention on the list of notes on the desk.

"I thought I recognised you. You're the famous copper off the telly, the one who was looking for Pop, weren't you?" Suzanne looked excited, and animated. Miller accepted that she was in a playful mood, so he decided that it would be wise to change tact. This wasn't going to be as straight-forward as he'd hoped.

"I have been on telly loads of times, but nobody ever remembers my appearance on The Krypton Factor. I won the Grand Final of that, in nineteen-ninety-eight." Miller looked extremely pleased with himself.

"What did you win?" Suzanne didn't seem too impressed.

"Nothing, just a paperweight thing with a green letter K inside it. The prize is the kudos, but nobody really cares after two weeks."

"Nah, I can't remember you on that. I never watched it though. It was boring."

"Well, I'm sorry, but it wasn't boring was it? You could say it was cheesey, or a bit naff. But it wasn't boring at all."

"I thought it was. I was only a little girl then though. I loved Gladiators. That was miles better than the Krypton Factor. In fact, my brother used to call it the crap ton factor!"

Suzanne giggled and held her hand up to her mouth.

"So, here we are, I've got you in to talk about your missing husband, and you're trivialising matters, and deliberately devaluing my proudest moment. That makes my special police instincts worry that you're guilty." Miller nodded sombrely at Suzanne, who was still grinning.

"Guilty of what?"

"Not answering my question."

"Sorry. I'm just excited. What was your question?"

"Where's Graham?"

"You know where he is."

"I don't."

"I know you don't! That's why you've banged me up all night, and got me up at the crack of dawn to try and scare the life out of me! Well too bad Mr detective! You see, I know that you don't know where he is, and that you want to try and trick me into all kinds of amazing confessions. Well too bad." Suzanne smiled, and Miller did too. He let his smile hang a few seconds longer than was necessary as he searched Suzanne's face.

"So, are you refusing to tell me where Graham is?"

"No. I feel that I've been extremely open about it. He's in Thailand."

"Ah, so he's in Thailand. This is where we get into difficulties. You see Suzanne, there is no way that Graham is in Thailand. He's not there and we both know it. So I'm sat here wondering why you're telling people that." Miller had a sarcastic grin on his face.

"I'm sat here wondering why you're bothered!"

"Come on Suzanne. I'm trying to locate Graham, that's why I'm bothered. And I know he's not in Thailand. I'll bet my cat on it."

"Well, listen, as far as I'm aware, he is. Now is that all? I've got a hair appointment at twelve."

"You've not been in here for a while, have you Suzanne?"

"Can't remember."

"Well I can confirm that you haven't. You were last arrested in two thousand and seven. It makes me think that you've either turned over a new leaf, or you've just been good at not getting caught. Which is it?"

"Which is what?"

"Come on Suzanne. Stop being a silly sausage. Where's Graham?"

"In Thailand."

"How long has he been in Thailand?"

"Ages. About, urm, four or five weeks."

"He hasn't left the country."

"Don't know then. As far as I know, he is in Thailand. Now will that be all, Mr detective?"

"Okay. Let me put the question to you another way. Graham has not left the UK since October last year. I checked with the Borders Agency, and all UK passenger flight and sailing data. All three systems are saying that your husband is not overseas. All three systems confirm that Graham Ashworth has not checked in at a British airport or a British seaport at any time since October last year. He hasn't crossed the channel by train either. His passport number has not been used to book any tickets or seats on any international crossings at all, since your holiday last autumn."

"He might have gone on a jet-ski then. He's good at driving them you know."

Miller laughed out loud. Suzanne looked pleased with herself and laughed too.

"You're quite funny you. Good looking, funny, flirty. Extremely bright and intelligent. I bet Graham loved the bones of you didn't he?"

"You're talking about him in the past tense. Has something happened? Is he dead?"

"I don't know. That's what you're in here to talk about. He's certainly not in Thailand, like you keep suggesting. So we've got a real dilemma here, haven't we Suzanne?"

"They're winding you up!" Suzanne laughed, and put her hand to her mouth again. She wasn't taking this at all seriously, and it was beginning to concern the DCI.

"Who is winding me up?" asked Miller. He played along, managing to look vaguely amused by Suzanne's silliness, while trying hard to disguise his frustration.

"The Border Agents. Truthfully. He's gone abroad and I hope he never comes back! I absolutely hate the bastard."

"I can't see why. He's got you off the streets, off the game. A nice big house, and you're looking well. You don't look like you're using anymore?"

"He's in Thailand." Said Suzanne, and it sounded as though she'd snapped a little bit.

"Why did he visit Accident and Emergency on Monday the twentieth of May?" Miller had thrown an ace on the table. Suzanne Ashworth juddered visibly. It made Miller smile. There was a pause.

"Oh, er. I'd completely forgotten about that." She said. Miller opened both of his hands, in an effort to encourage the suspect to carry on talking. Good, thought Miller. Found her button at last. Geronimo.

"He'd fallen down the stairs. Tripped up at the top and tumbled all the way down." Suzanne looked troubled. Her cockiness had been dealt a hard blow, but Miller could see that her brain was whirring and she was working on trying to bounce back. A sense of being in control was what kept suspects animated in these interviews. The moment that the control is pulled back a little, that's when things start happening. Miller could see that he had clearly made a dent in his antagonist's armour.

"Okay, you win." Miller checked his wristwatch, and exhaled quietly. "Interview suspended at six forty four am." He leant forward and pressed the stop button on the digital recorder, and made a note of the details that flashed up on the screen.

"Officer, can you take Mrs Ashworth back to her cell please?"

"Hey! Just a minute! What about my hair appointment?" Suzanne looked genuinely pissed off. This hadn't gone how she'd planned it.

"You're entitled to one phone call. But they won't be open yet. See you in a bit."

"Well you'll have to either charge me or release me

by four pm Mr clever dick. I've seen twenty four hours in police custody on Channel Four. I know how this all works you know!" Suzanne had an air of arrogance about her, as she smiled sarcastically at the senior policeman, despite her frustration.

"I doubt it. I'll be charging you and you'll be on remand before this weekend is through lass. So you can forget about getting your hair cut. It'll be short back and sides where you're going princess." Miller winked, and in doing so demonstrated a much more controlled arrogance. "See you in a bit. And you might want to reconsider your position about getting some legal assistance."

"I'm fine, thanks." Suzanne was now clearly annoyed and the hot flush that Miller had witnessed at her front door the previous day returned. But she was determined to try and keep the bravado going. She smiled sweetly as Miller held open the door and gestured the prisoner and her chaperone out into the corridor.

"Keep talking shite if you like Suzanne Ashworth, but you know it and I know it. You're up to your expensive fake eyelashes in shit and no amount of silliness is going to amend that fact."

"Is that so?" asked Suzanne, her tone of voice suggested that she couldn't care less what Miller had to say.

"It is. Sorry to piss on your chips, but I spent most of last night in Bury police station, hearing the whole story from your neighbour."

"What? Which one?" Suzanne looked scared. Finally, Miller had pierced her armour and had drawn first blood.

"That's for me to know, and for you to find out!" Miller tapped his nose and laughed as Suzanne Ashworth was led away, looking considerably less confident.

Chapter 37

After interviewing Crossley, Miller had contacted Lancashire County Police about the canal story. Because the supposed site of the body was outside the Greater Manchester zone, Miller had to involve the neighbouring constabulary and hand this aspect of the investigation over to them. He'd requested that an officer keep guard of the location until first light, when a full search of the site could be carried out by forensic investigators and the marine investigations team.

A police officer needed to be in location as soon as possible, explained Miller. It was highly unlikely, thought Miller, but still a necessary precaution in case somebody came along to try and remove the evidence. Miller hadn't considered that arresting Suzanne Ashworth would result in Michael Crossley wandering in and confessing to the murder. Who knows what could happen at the location.

Shortly after ten am, Lancashire officers had contacted Miller to confirm that they had discovered an item that Crossley had described exactly. The grisly find which closed the canal, the tow-path and the northbound section of the A6185 was a bloated, rotting, stinking body wrapped inside a large piece of water-soaked carpet. Complete with heavy rocks inside, the neatly folded parcel was wrapped up delicately like a giant fajita wrap, though with a much less appetising filling.

"Could one man have lifted that over the barrier?" asked Miller of his opposite number, DCI Gibson who was stood at the canal-side with the forensic scientists, twenty five miles away in Accrington.

"Nah. No chance." Said DCI Gibson. "It's a two-man job, at least. And there's a lot of time and care been taken on the packing, too."

"He said he did it there. Pulled up on the bridge, pulled the carpet out of the car, pulled the body out, placed some rocks in, rolled it all up and chucked it in."

"Bollocks. That's absolute bollocks. There's been at least three, four rolls of duct tape wrapped round this to hold it altogether. It's taken a while to pack this up so well."

"Right, cheers. That's good stuff."

"And, you can't pull up on this bridge. It's a dual carriageway. Cars are travelling sixty, seventy miles an hour."

"It was at dawn on a Saturday morning, apparently."

"Fair comment. Still wasn't done here though, no way. A panda car, taxi driver, a hospital worker, someone coming home from a night out would have passed by. It's the main link road from the town to the motorway. Nah, it's not plausible - even if you gave them a very fast pull-over, jump out, chuck it in and race off again window of thirty seconds before another car would have driven past. I'll tell you now, there is no way on earth that they've packed that up here. It's total bollocks."

"You said they, two or three times. You're absolutely convinced that it wasn't my suspect on his own?"

"You'll see yourself on the photos. There's no way one person has done that. I reckon two would struggle to be honest. You might be looking for three, maybe four people."

"Cheers. That's brilliant. I've got loads of ammo to hit him with now."

"Okay, no problem, but my advice is simple, tell your Manchester crooks to stay off our patch! We take a pride in our county and we don't want your lot thinking they can come and dump their unwanted bodies here!" Gibson had a sarcastic slant on his voice, and Miller recognised that it was a bit of teasing banter, more than a direct instruction.

"Okay, I'll send the word around." Miller laughed at Gibson's chuckle. "Thanks DCI Gibson. I really appreciate your help with all this."

"I bet you do, you've not had to come and smell this fucking body, have you not?"

*****

Miller looked through his phone book. Scrolling through until he read SAUNDERS and pressed the call icon, even though he knew that his number two wasn't in work today.

"Hi Keith, how's it going?"

"Oh, hi Sir. How lovely to hear from you on a Saturday." Saunders tone was sarcastic.

"Are you not on duty?" Miller's tone was insincere.

"No. Why, what's up?"

"Oh, it doesn't matter – I didn't realise that you weren't in. Who is?"

"It doesn't matter. Go on, what's up?"

"Oh, I just need somebody picking up. It's this case I was telling you about the other day. The missing neighbour."

"Oh aye?" Saunders was interested, Miller could tell by the sound of his voice.

"Yeah, we've got a body. I just want the neighbour from over the road bringing in. She's called Rachel Birdsworth. Lives at number sixteen Fir Trees Grove, Haughton Park.

"Right, I'll go and pick her up then. I'm just at the Trafford Centre, I'm after some new jeans."

"Well go and get this Rachel, arrest her on suspicion of murder, and drop her off at Bury police station, then you can go back, can't you?"

"Sir."

*****

Suzanne Ashworth was in a much grumpier, much more focused mood as she was returned to the interview room. That playfulness, the flirting and general mocking of Miller seemed to be completely forgotten. It was as though a different person had walked in. The five extra hours in the cell, mulling over Miller's bombshell announcement had clearly helped her slip into a much more serious frame of mind.

"Hello again," smiled Miller. He looked absolutely shattered, thought Suzanne.

"Hi," she said, her eyes were looking down at the table-top now. That effervescent confidence was all but gone. Miller read the signs, and he was led to the conclusion that Suzanne knew that she was busted. But he was to find that his instinct was wrong this time.

"So, do you have anything further to add to our rather silly chat earlier?" asked Miller.

"I don't know. I am screwed whatever happens, aren't I?" Suzanne had her eyes fixed on the grey table top. She ran her fingers through her hair, which was starting to show the first signs of grease coming through at the roots.

The comment intrigued Miller. This wasn't the straight forward reply that he'd anticipated.

"We're getting ahead of ourselves. Let's try and pick it up where we left off. Is that okay?" asked Miller. He was being kind, gentle. He seemed to have forgiven her cocky, daft behaviour earlier.

Suzanne shrugged, and remained focused on the table top.

"Where is Graham?"

"I don't know."

"Why was he sacked from his job?"

"Drinking."

"What do you mean?"

"He developed a bit of a drink problem. He'd start sending e-mails to colleagues when he was pissed. Threatening e-mails. He threatened some councillors on an e-mail. He got a warning for it, then, a few weeks later, he wrote to the Chief Constable, threatening to go to the papers about how he'd been treated when he'd been arrested. At the same time, the guy who owns the Haughton Park development wrote to the council and demanded that he gets a bollocking for behaving like a twat. It was the last straw and the council sacked him. Well, they made it sound a bit better than that, he took early retirement, with immediate effect."

"With full pension and redundancy package?"

"Yep. That's how it works. You know the score."

"When was that?"

"I don't know. A month, six weeks ago."

"When did you last hear from him?"

"On Friday the third of June."

"That's very specific."

"I was severely beaten up by him on that date. I

know nothing about this, I want to add, right?"

"I beg your pardon?"

"I was pissed. Totally, totally pissed. Apparently, I was beaten unconscious by my husband. But what I'm trying to say is, I have absolutely no memory of this incident. I know that it probably did happen, because I was covered in bangs and bruises the next day. And in the days leading up to it, he'd been hitting me here and there, taking out his frustration on me."

"What was the frustration about?"

"Getting sacked. He was livid. Thought it was everybody's fault but his. God, he was infuriating – he would go on and on and on. I wanted to wrap a wok around his head, I really did."

"Tell me about the night you were beaten up. The last time you saw him."

"I'd been drinking, a lot. I was seriously planning on leaving him. But I can't remember anything of that night. Not a thing. Honestly."

"But how do you know that it was your husband if you have no recollection of anything?"

"Because he did it regularly. He's a wife beater. He can't have a fight with another bloke, he has to beat his pretty little wife up to feel strong."

"And that had been going on for a while?" asked Miller, wearing a sympathetic frown as he listened.

"It had been going on from before we were together."

"Is that how you met?" asked Miller, "when you were on the game?"

Suzanne nodded. She took a few seconds to answer. "He was aggressive, he liked to pull hair and punch, liked to bite the girls. None of them wanted to know. He had a reputation…"

"And you used to put up with it?" asked Miller.

"He couldn't find any other girls that would take him. They'd all tell him to fuck off, they called him a creep. His nick-name was noodle-dick. I felt a bit sorry for him, he was such a loser. I told him, I said, if he wants to be nasty, he has to pay more. He agreed, just said "how much?" so I said "three hundred," just off the top of my head like. He smiled and said it's a deal. He'd pick me up, check us in at some Holiday Inn or whatever and then start pushing me about. He liked to role-play that he was raping me. He'd get pretty violent to be honest, but I told him, he can't bruise my face, or I'll get him shot in the knees. He respected that. Anyway, as time went on, I was his once, twice sometimes three times a week girl."

"At three hundred quid a time?" asked Miller, whistling a tune to show how surprised he was at the cost.

"He's loaded. I mean, properly loaded. His parents were loaded. It's how it all works in that world isn't it? They're born into cash, then their rich dad sorts out a job through his rich mates, and they're on big money from the start. It's all kept in the same little pot, isn't it?"

"And you had no problem with him beating you up?" Miller never ceased to be amazed by the stuff prostitutes would put up with.

"It's no worse than what my dad used to do to me." Suzanne was staring at her hands on the table-top. She thought they looked naked without her rings.

"So how did you end up becoming Graham's wife, if you knew that he was an abusive man who slept with prostitutes?" asked Miller, forgetting his professional obligations for a moment, and becoming more wrapped up in the human-interest angle.

"He asked me to stop being a prostitute. It was obvious that he was in love with me. He said that he would employ me himself, and that I'd get paid two grand a week. He said if I agreed to it, he'd pay my pimp off and he'd send me to rehab and get me off my habit."

Miller looked genuinely astonished at what Suzanne told him. "What was your habit?" he asked.

"Smack, and booze, and the occasional binge on pills. I was a fucking wreck. He saved my life, he really did." Suzanne looked at Miller. She was biting on her bottom lip in between talking.

"So you went to rehab?"

"Yeah, Penrith. Near Carlisle. I was in there for

nearly six months. Not cheap. He spent a trolley full of money on that. He visited me twice a week. He'd bring the most crazy bouquets of flowers, a bottle of perfume, new pyjamas and stuff. He treated me like a Goddess, he'd arrange with the staff to take me out for meals and things. He looked after me so well. After I'd been discharged from my rehab, he put me up in a flat in Manchester. He got me these boobs, these teeth. Honestly, I was treated like a WAG for a while. But he pretty quickly got obsessed. He was paranoid that I was going back on the street, worried none stop that I was using again. He rented a flat on the street opposite mine, and he just sat in there watching me, keeping tabs on me. I kept pleading with him to relax but he just couldn't."

"And so, you moved in with him?"

"Well, it wasn't… I mean, nobody in my life had ever given a fuck about me before. I was flattered. Honestly, the only people who ever showed any affection were after one thing. I kind of admired Graham's honesty about it. But, well… it wasn't just about what Graham did for me financially, he made me feel special. I'd always felt so worthless and inadequate. Graham made me feel really good. I wasn't with him just for the money. He made me feel good about myself. He got me off drugs and drink. He gave me a fresh start." Suzanne was crying, and she wiped her tears away, and sniffed loudly.

"Was he hitting you at this point?" asked Miller, totally absorbed in Suzanne's story.

"Not at this point. He was the ultimate gentleman. He was a very, very pathetic man, he had absolutely no confidence with women, unless he was paying them. If he saw it as a business transaction, he was cold, dead behind the eyes and in full control. If it was an emotional transaction, he couldn't deal with it. That's why he could only get sex if he paid. He was a very damaged man."

"Now three, possibly four times you've referred to Graham in the past tense. You tried being a little smart Alice about the past tense earlier this morning, when I used it. But now *you're* using it. Why is that?" asked Miller, completely throwing Suzanne out of her sad, indulgent story about life with Graham.

"Well, I, well something has obviously come to light. Why else would I be here? You obviously suspect that I've got something to do with Graham's…"

"Graham's what?"

"For fuck's sake. Graham's death." Suzanne's lips started trembling. Miller focused on her mouth. The quiver looked fast, it looked like a genuine tremble of anguish and grief. Miller had several years experience of watching amateur actors and actresses in these situations. He recognised every phoney emotion, every crocodile tear, he'd seen every wail of fake grief. He could have handed out more Oscars than Bob Hope through the years, but he felt that this was genuine heartache that he was witnessing from Suzanne, and it surprised him greatly.

"Do you want to stop for five?" asked Miller, softly. Suzanne's face was streaming with tears. She waved her hand, as if to say that she wished to carry on. Miller handed her two tissues from the box on the trolley that held the voice recorder.

"No. I'm fine. It's just so sad…" she said, and again, her emotions got the better of her. Miller waited a few more moments before he asked his next question.

"For the benefit of the tape, are you saying that you know that Graham Ashworth is dead?"

"Yes. I know. I don't know where his remains are. All I know is that he was beating me up. My neighbour Rachel Birdsworth saw him, from across the road. She ran over to help me. I swear to God, I have no recollection of any of this. Apparently, in a bid to get Graham to stop beating me, Rachel accidentally killed him."

*****

Mick Crossley was sat in his cell. He looked even more relaxed now, thought Miller, than he had done the previous night. Miller was observing the prisoner on the CCTV feed. He looked placid, tranquil, even though Miller had told him to his face that he didn't believe his story. This man was happy as a pig in shit, and was clearly very confident that his story was good enough to be believed, thought the detective. Once more, Miller was struck by how unusual his demeanour was. But at least he now had a good reason to explain why.

"Can you get Crossley out and get him down to an interview room for me please Sergeant?" asked the DCI of his uniformed colleague at the custody desk.

"Certainly. I'll have him brought down to interview room three, Sir."

Once again, Mick Crossley was polite, and courteous as he entered the booth. He nodded in a friendly, almost apologetic way. The last time these men had spoken, Miller had promised to find out what Mick's crock of shit was all about. Mick had a look of faint concern about him, he seemed a little cautious around the DCI, scared almost.

"Hello again Michael."

"Hi, alright?" he said. He nodded at his duty solicitor too, a different one from the smart young man who had been with him the previous evening. This one looked much less ambitious. He had a big, round, grumpy face, and a lot of greasy, swept back hair. He was well into his forties and had a rather considerable gut on him, which forced him to sit with his knees spread widely.

"Right, well, a lot's happened since we last spoke, so, if it's okay, we'll get cracking...." Said Miller to both men.

"My client and I need a few minutes, if that's okay," said the new brief, and Miller realised immediately that he had hot, rotten breath, caused by a dodgy filling, he supposed. Miller waved the breath away from him and felt in his pants for some chewing gum.

"Here," he said, offering the pack to the solicitor. "Your breath is horrendous mate – you need to see a dentist pronto."

The harshness, along with the unexpected, direct delivery of his comment made Mick Crossley laugh out loud. "Ha ha ha oh my God, as if you just said that out loud!"

"For fucks sake!" said the solicitor, his face had gone bright red.

Miller waved his breath away again. "I'm serious

mate. That's absolutely unbearable!" Miller stood and walked out of the room, trying not to gag.

A few minutes passed before the interview room door opened and the duty solicitor invited Miller back in.

"There was no need for that behaviour," he muttered as Miller passed him.

"There's no need for bad breath in this day and age. Seriously mate, there is no need. If you've noticed people leaning back a lot when you're talking to them, that's why."

Once again Mick Crossley laughed out loud. Miller was surprised that a man who was facing such serious charges could be in such a jovial mood.

"I really don't think I've ever met somebody who is so rude." Snapped the solicitor, his face was filled with contempt for Miller and his heartless remarks.

Miller shrugged and began talking through his formal introductions to this second interview with Mick Crossley. He'd had too many frustrating days and nights at the hands of solicitors to care about their personal feelings. Miller thought they were the scum of the earth, and he held the criminals that they were there to advise in greater esteem.

"Right then, this has been a hell of a story. You coming in here last night, confessing to a murder, then the body was discovered this morning – exactly where you said it was, in exactly the state that you described it, down to the colour of carpet that was used to wrap it up. All in all, a very neat and tidy operation. I honestly can't remember a missing person case escalating to a murder enquiry, and the case being solved in such a record time." Miller looked at his watch. It was just after 12pm. "All said and done... this whole scenario has been booked in and checked out in under thirty six hours! Quite incredible." Miller was smiling, and nodding encouragingly at Mick Crossley, who couldn't really help but smile back politely.

"Except... there's a problem Michael. So nobody is phoning the Guinness Book of Records just yet."

"Mr Miller, my client has given his full confession. You have already said that you are satisfied with this, and you are saying that the information he has provided has checked out." Miller had annoyed the brief, and now he wanted to be annoying back. Miller waved his arm again, wafting the breath away. Mick didn't laugh this time. He was concerned by whatever it was that Miller was getting at.

"Graham Ashworth was a fat man. He weighed almost fifteen stones. Now, if I go out of here and get fifteen stones in weight, I seriously doubt you'll manage to lift it up. But if I got fifteen stones, and then added another five, six stones from the rocks that were snuggled up with Graham, we're talking in excess of twenty stones. You can't lift that, in the shape of a giant cigar Michael. Can you?"

Mick didn't seem phased by the question. "It was me. I was on one, had to get rid of it. I was pumped with adrenaline!" he said.

"You were so pumped on adrenaline that you developed super powers?" Miller laughed, forcing his head back and showing off his well looked after, dazzling white teeth. "What happened next, did you pick your car up and fly home with it? Miller was laughing uncontrollably, but Mick's mood was changing rapidly, right before his eyes. That agitated state that he had gotten into the previous night when tapping his finger against the table seemed to be returning. He looked alert, his shoulders had tensed up, and he was sitting up straighter.

"Hey, listen, right…" he said.

"No, you listen to me. I'm going to find out who the others were. There were three or four people responsible for this, and I'm going to arrest and charge all of them. It's obvious who you're protecting, pal, so shut up with all the silliness now. I'm a DCI me, Michael. Not a DIC. Now, are you going to use this opportunity to tell me who the others were?"

"No comment." Said Mick. A nervous twitch made him twist his torso round suddenly. The affable, pleasant expression on his face had dropped and was replaced with a look of confusion and anger. There was a pinch of attitude in there too.

Miller was only just getting going. "Okay. So let's say I buy your story – let's say that you did indeed have your spinach that morning, and you managed to wrap the body, and the stones, and lift the twenty stone package up over the four foot high barrier…."

Mick looked intrigued, hopeful almost. He was concentrating on Miller's mouth as the detective spoke.

"…I still can't place you in the driving seat of Graham Ashworth's Range Rover. And we both know why, don't we Michael?" Miller leant back and studied Mick Crossley's face. It was a familiar sight for Miller, observing a liar who was desperately trying to poker-face and hide the sinking, panic sensation that was bubbling up, overwhelming and drowning them from the inside.

"No comment."

"No comment? Ooh, got you running scared have we Michael?"

"No comment."

"You can't drive mate. Can you?"

"No comment."

"You're saying you drove Ashworth's car, but you can't even drive!"

"No comment!" Mick's voice was becoming angrier, and snappier each time that he spoke. His eyes were developing an undeniable anger, a bad-attitude stare.

Miller was playing with him, just toying with him like a kitten with a ball of wool, and he was enjoying himself very much.

"Okay, you do the no comment reply as much as you want. That's what Rachel is saying as well, in her interview room." Miller smirked at Mick Crossley's double-take expression. "What, you're surprised?" Miller shook his head. "You should see your face! It's a picture! You really are a star you Michael. I'm astonished that you thought you could just walk in here and 'fess up for your missus, and we'd buy it. It's cute, I'll give you that. Very cute indeed! My missus is going to love this story tonight when I get home and tell her!"

*****

Rachel Birdsworth was following her partner's advice

to the letter. She no-commented everything that she'd been asked since her arrest just an hour after Graham Ashworth's water-logged corpse was discovered.

"Why are you prepared to let the man that you love, take the punishment for a crime that you've clearly committed?"

"No comment." Said Rachel, her head hung down, her was hair obscuring much of her face.

"Do you hate him? Is that it? You've found a great opportunity to kick him out for ten years! Get him out of your face! Is that why you're letting him take the punishment?"

"No comment."

"When you two morons were cooking up your stupid little story, did you not think that the weight of the corpse's packaging would make it obvious that there were other people involved."

"No comment."

"Who are the other people involved in the disposal?"

"No comment."

"Are they related to you?"

"No comment."

"Are your teenage children involved?"

Rachel's eyes shot up from looking down the table and met with the DCI's. Boom, thought Miller, Got ya.

Rachel's stare was lazer guided. Her eyes burned through Miller's.

"No comment."

"We have reason to believe that three to four people were party to the disposal of Graham Ashworth's body. You, your fellah Mick, your son Liam and your daughter Britney. What do you think about that?"

"It's wrong."

"Oh, I thought you were saying no comment." Miller smiled. He'd won the first round. He'd beaten her and she knew it. "So, it's wrong is it? Your kids aren't involved in the murder?"

"No."

"Ah! You are. Michael is. But the kids definitely are not!" Miller smiled again. Rachel would just love to reach over the table and stick her finger-nails right in his eyeballs - the smug bastard, she thought. Come on Rach, sort your head out. He's got you biting. Remember what Mick said. No comment, no matter what. Come on. Sort it out. Rachel was giving herself a pep talk in her mind. She was gutted that Miller had gotten the better of her. It was a dirty trick though, bringing the kids into it. Dirty trick.

Rachel inhaled deeply and counted to five before exhaling loudly.

"No comment."

"Where did you put the body in the car? I've looked in the back of an Evoque. There's not much room in the boot for a body as big as Graham Ashworth's. Not with the carpet, that we've just found out is the same brand and batch as the carpet in the rest of the Ashworth residence."

"No comment."

"It got me wondering if the body was too big for the boot, and that one of the seats had to be collapsed and the body had to be put in the boot, and on the back-seat in an L-shape formation. I'll bet his head was on the backseat, and his arse and legs were in the boot. Or did you put his face in the boot and put his legs on the backseat?"

"No comment."

"Either way, one of you's had the dead body over your lap. How disturbing is that?"

"No comment."

No reaction either, thought Miller. She wasn't in the back with the corpse, she didn't bat an eye-lid at that grotesque suggestion.

"You were driving, weren't you?" suggested Miller. He felt that the jigsaw pieces were starting to fit together now. The kids weren't there. He never thought that they were. He just wanted to provoke a reaction. The one that he got.

"No comment."

"Michael told me that he was driving."

"No comment."

"But he can't bloody-well drive, can he?" Miller started laughing.

Fight, thought Rachel. Don't fucking argue back. Just stay focused.

"No comment."

"You were driving. You murdered him, and you drove the body. That poor bastard Michael has got nothing at all to do with this, you horrible, evil woman!"

"FUCK OFF!" shouted Rachel, the words jumped out of her, covering the DCI with spray.

"Two-nil." Said Miller, cheerfully. "Interview suspended at fourteen thirty five hours." Miller pressed STOP on the recorder. "Take her back to her cell please Constable."

Chapter 38

"Are you still pissed off with me?" Miller was talking on his hands free system in the car as he made his way north up to Accrington.

"No Andy." But it was obvious in the tone of Clare's voice that she was screaming blue murder. "It's fine."

"Well, I'm sure you'll want to know all about it anyway, it's a proper weird set-up. We found Ollie's neighbours body this morning."

"Oh God!" said Clare, completely forgetting that she was in a mood with her husband for prioritising his work-life over and above his home-life. Or at least, that was how it sounded in her head. "That's so grim."

"I know. He's been in the canal for a month. I'm just on my way over there now."

"Where? In Accrington?"

"Yes, and hopefully, I'll be able to get back to Bury nick to charge them with murder. Then I'll buy you some flowers and a soppy card about how sorry I am, and a nice bottle of Prosecco. How does that sound?"

"It sounds alright. But knowing you, it won't happen, you'll still be there until midnight and you'll have to get a bunch of flowers at the all night garage on your way home." Clare sounded distant. It was as though she was watching television and her mind was more interested in that than the conversation she was having.

"Are the kids okay?"

"Yes, they're fine. Look, Andy, I'll see you later love, alright."

"Yeah, alright. Love you Clare."

"See you later." Clare pressed the call-end button and looked out of the living-room window.

A little over twenty minutes later, Miller was at the crime scene in Accrington. He had driven from Haughton Park to the site where Graham Ashworth's body had been discovered, using the most direct route possible. He drove north of Bury, taking the motorway and dual carriageway all the way up to the junction for Accrington. It was the third town that was available along the route, and most interestingly to Miller, this would be the last town before the road would split into two options. Decision time for Graham Ashworth's killer. Blackburn or Preston to the west, Burnley and Colne to the east. More time, more distance and more chance of being caught. Miller knew that all of these factors would result in creating more panic and more stress for the people involved in the crime. Mistake time, Miller called it, because history told him that it was when people always messed up. He just needed to try and find out how.

Miller had spent the journey to the old brick manufacturing town trying to imagine doing it at dawn on a Saturday with a dead body on the back-seat. Even at a fast rate of driving, the journey was already twenty five minutes. The options for driving east or west would panic the people in the car. They were forced to come into Accrington. Graham Ashworth's final resting place was decided through sheer panic - by an overwhelming need to dispose of the body, considered Miller.

Miller was stood on the bridge, looking down into the murky water below, while the police officers and forensics staff were packing up their kit. He was trying to figure out how Rachel and Mick had ended up at the canal. If they'd been forced off the road because of the upcoming motorway junction, how did they arrive here, at the canal?

Miller was bothering his nails as he stood, looking across the horizon of the old northern mill town that had sadly become just another victim of high unemployment and urban decay.

Two things were troubling him. Firstly, he could see with his own eyes that Mick Crossley did not wrap the body here. It was not possible, just as DCI Gibson had explained earlier. Several factors said that it wasn't possible. Not only was this bridge on a dual carriageway, with no hard shoulder to park up - there simply wasn't the space to lay a carpet down, pull a body out of a car, wrap it all up and then start wrapping tape all around the object. It wasn't done here, and that was the first thing that Miller was bothered about. If not here, then where? And why say it was here?

What difference does it make? Would the real place tell a different story? Miller's mind was racing.

And then it occurred to him. The sat nav in Graham's car would have shown up a waterway on the map. Miller took his phone out of his pocket and opened the Google Maps app. Within seconds, the screen loaded up, showing Miller's precise location, his marker was situated on a white road graphic with a blue waterway criss-crossing beneath.

"They drove here, to the canal because they saw it on the fucking sat nav. Why else would they choose the most exposed location in the town?" Miller was talking to himself, zooming out of his location on the phone screen. Miller saw that there were ten, twelve, maybe fifteen bridges that crossed the canal in Accrington. But this one was the first that they'd come to as they drove through the town. They'd chosen the worst one, it seemed to Miller as he switched the maps app off and put his phone back into his pocket. He turned around and looked at the dual carriageway. The traffic was relentless. It was clear to Miller that even at dawn on a weekend, this place would have a steady stream of traffic coming out of the town towards the motorway, and vice versa on the opposite side of the carriageway.

Miller cursed his O.C.D as it occurred to him that he wanted to come back and witness this location's early morning Saturday traffic for himself.

"Fuck that." He muttered to himself, unconvincingly, annoyed that if he'd known, he could have done it earlier that morning. Maybe he could watch CCTV footage of the road at that time? He pulled out his pocket book and scribbled "Council – CCTV road over canal?"

Miller started walking down the hill, back towards where his car was parked on the KFC car park. He hadn't noticed it as he walked towards the crime scene, but there was no mistaking the Asda store on the opposite side of the road, as he made his way down the hill. Miller took out his notebook and made a few notes before continuing back towards his car, feeling pleased with himself for resisting the fried chicken smell that had started to make his mouth water. There were more pressing matters.

*****

Miller was feeling really tired now. It had been quite a while since he'd worked an all-nighter, and he'd forgotten how drowsy, almost drunk the fatigue could make him feel. He wondered if he was getting too old now. He used to get a buzz out of this peculiar, detached sensation. Now he was becoming quite disturbed by his weariness.

As he entered the Asda supermarket, he headed straight towards the customer toilets and began rinsing his face with cold water, trying to freshen himself up as best that he could. A few minutes later, the Manchester DCI was walking through the aisles of the Lancashire supermarket, looking for something. His heart rate was quickening and he realised that he was becoming quite excited.

The building had a huge sign on the roof. It said OPEN 24 HOURS. When he'd spotted it, Miller had realised with an excitable jolt that this supermarket was the only shop that Graham's killer and his or her helpers would have encountered on the journey between the murder scene and the canal.

He was excited, but was also feeling rather despondent. Although he had only just become aware of its existence, a lot rested on this visit to this supermarket. Miller had a deep sense that this place wouldn't bear any fruit, due to the period of time that had elapsed. But, he clung to his hopes. If the killer had bought anything here and paid by card transaction, it would be evidence that would stick.

Michael Crossley had very nearly said too much about the parcel tape that had been used to wrap the carpet up. The local officer, DCI Gibson had described it as duct tape. He'd said that three or four rolls were used. Who has three or four rolls of duct tape just lay around the house? Wondered Miller as he was walking faster around the superstore. He stopped dead in his tracks as he reached the aisle that he'd been searching for, hoping that they had in this store. At the top of the books, comics and magazines section was a small, blink-and-you'd-miss-it D.I.Y section. On the left hand side was a small selection of motor accessories. Oil, windscreen wash, shampoo and wax was surrounded by car air-fresheners and wiper blades, floor mats and car-care kits. Opposite these items was the section that Miller had been hoping to find. Home improvement.

There was a small selection of basic items, from cheap tools and paint-brushes to wallpaper paste and polyfilla. There, right at the bottom of the display, next to masking tape and sellotape was the duct tape that he'd been hoping was stocked.

"You fucking beauty." He muttered to himself as an elderly male customer turned round and tutted in his direction.

"Sorry," said Miller as he took his phone out of his pocket and scrolled through his e-mails. He found the correspondence from DCI Gibson, with the photographs of Graham Ashworth's body and the wrapping. He zoomed in on the duct tape that had been cut away from the carpet in the photograph. It was silver. The only colour that was on sale at this store.

Miller was buzzing. He knew that the CCTV in this store would show the person buying the duct tape. He knew the date, and approximate time of the purchase. His only concern was whether the footage would still be available. He seriously doubted that it would be.

"Hi," said Miller as he reached the customer service desk. He was speaking to a lady with a bright green blouse on and a rosette that said "happy to help."

"I hope you can help. I'm a police officer with Greater Manchester police, I'm taking part in an investigation…"

"Oh, is it about the body in the canal?" asked the middle-aged lady behind the counter.

"Yes, it is. News travels fast…"

"It's terrible. It's a little girl isn't it?" The woman had a sad, but morbidly excited expression on her face.

"It's not a little girl. Is that what people are saying?"

"Yes. Apparently, so I've been told, it was…"

"Nah, it's a man's body. It's been in there for over a month. I'm just trying to find out if the duct tape that was used to wrap the body was bought here?"

"Ooh good God! How grisly!" said the woman, now feeling excited, like she was now a part of the enquiry. "Is that the one you're on about?" she asked, taking the package off Miller. She scanned the barcode and pressed product inventory on the screen. A list of all sales of that item in the past three months appeared on the screen.

"We don't sell many of these, let me see. We've sold sixty units in this inventory period."

"What's an inventory period?" asked Miller.

"Quarterly, it goes in three monthly cycles."

"Okay, can you see all the sales in that period?"

"Yes. You can come round here if you want love." The lady opened the small door at her side and allowed Miller through.

"Thanks a lot," said Miller, standing next to her and scanning the computer screen. "Can you see any bulk purchases? Two, three, four rolls sold at the same time?"

"To be honest, most sales are single. Here we are. Five rolls were sold at half past three in the morning, where are we, on the fourth of June."

"Bingo. That's it. That's the killer!" Miller smiled and the customer services assistant made a weird, excited noise as it occurred to her that she'd just done something really important. This was a story for her mates in the canteen at brew time, that was for sure.

"My goodness!" she said, as Miller patted her back.

"How far back does your CCTV footage go?"

"To all of the aisles."

"No, I mean, how long is it saved for?"

"Oh, ha ha, I see. Sorry, silly me, I thought you meant…"

"Is it a week, a month, how long do you save it up for before it's deleted?"

"Ooh, now you're asking. I don't know. Let me get somebody who *will* know." She grabbed the microphone at the side of the desk and pressed a button on its base. Suddenly, the lady's voice was booming all around the store.

"Staff call, can a member of our senior leadership

team please come to the customer service kiosk immediately please."

Within seconds, a bossy-looking ginger-haired lady came over. She was wearing a suspicious, "what's-wrong-now-you-useless-bastards" smile.

"This is our store manager, Hazel. This is a policeman from Manchester, he's here about the body in the canal. It's a man, not a little girl."

Hazel's face corrected itself, and she began looking at Miller with a little less of an "oh-for-fucks-sake" expression.

"How do you do?" she asked.

"I'm fine thanks. We're just looking at this purchase here." Miller pointed at the computer screen. "It's of significant interest to the murder enquiry. I'm just wondering if you still have CCTV footage from that date?"

Hazel was thinking hard. Miller could see that she was doing sums in her head.

"It was thirty five days ago." Said Miller, in a bid to speed things up.

Hazel was still doing sums in her head and Miller was anticipating the almighty, disappointing no that was due any second.

"Might have." She said.

Miller couldn't disguise his delight. He was beaming from ear to ear. "Really?"

"It might go back that far. It just records and records until it reaches the end of the hard-drive, then it starts again, writing over itself. I can't remember how many days it is, but we had it upgraded last year to a terabyte of memory, it holds quite a bit. Do you want to go and see?"

"Yes I do!"

"Okay, I'll take you up there."

"Thanks for all your help!" said Miller to the customer services lady, as he followed Hazel, who had set off walking quickly, keen to sort this out and then get back to what it was that she was supposed to be doing..

"No problem," said the lady, who looked as though she wanted to get back on the microphone and announce to the shoppers that it wasn't a little girl in the canal.

Miller was led through a door that was practically hidden in the wall by the side of the noisy, bleeping check-outs which went on for as far as the eye could see. It was Saturday afternoon and the store was heaving with customers. The DCI followed the store manager up some stairs and then down a long, shiny corridor. All along the corridor were mirrors that had writing across the top. "Smile. This is what our customers see!"

Eventually, Hazel opened a door and ushered Miller through. There was a bank of CCTV monitors all along the back wall, and a happy, jolly-looking black man was sat inside there, watching the screens.

"Nathan, this man is a detective."

"I haven't done nothing!" he said, holding his hands in the air. He laughed loudly at his joke. Miller laughed too, and was instantly endeared to the security man. Hazel looked sternly at the security officer.

"We need to find CCTV footage from inside the store on Saturday the fourth of June at... what time was it again Detective?"

"Oh, er the sale took place at half past three."

Nathan started typing information into a box on his computer screen.

"Oh that might be a bit too long ago, let me see."

Miller was watching Nathan, his heart was in his mouth. If the security guard could just say "yes, I've got it here," then Miller would have the major piece of prosecution evidence.

The screen flickered and Nathan's text-box had disappeared.

"Zero Four Zero Six." Hazel was reading the digits in the top of the screen. "That's it! Good work Nathan." She tapped his shoulder tenderly.

"What, is this it?" asked Miller, he looked like an excited kid.

"This is the store footage, every camera, every angle from three o' clock in the morning on Saturday the fourth of June."

"Holy shit! That's amazing."

"Great. Well I'll leave you to it detective." Said Hazel. "Thank you Nathan."

"Thanks, cheers," said Miller, reluctantly turning his face away from the monitor screens.

Hazel closed the door behind her, setting off at a similar speed that she'd arrived at.

"What time was the sale again?" asked Nathan.

"Three thirty on the self serve tills. Can you get the DIY section on there?" asked Miller, who was sweating slightly, and desperately excited to see who would appear on the screen and buy the five rolls of duct tape.

"Sure thing, no problem just give me ten seconds." Nathan rolled the footage back to 3.20am, and activated the household goods aisle feed so that it was on full screen. "Do you know who you are looking for?" he asked.

"No. Well, I've got an idea. One of two possible suspects, but I've an open mind."

Nathan pressed the forward x8 button and the footage speeded up slightly, noticeable only because the shelf-stacker further along the aisle was suddenly working extremely quickly.

And then it happened.

"I don't believe it." Said Miller. "Can you get a better picture of them?" said Miller. He could see Rachel and Mick, looking scared, looking around, over their shoulders. They looked suspicious and panicky. Mick bent down and picked up the rolls of tape and they both headed quickly toward the camera, on their way to the tills.

"Got you!" shouted Miller, he was absolutely buzzing and it made Nathan laugh out loud again, his big booming laugh was infectious.

"Is that what you wanted?" asked Nathan, smiling widely and still laughing at Miller's reaction.

"Yes, it certainly is. Thanks a lot. Can you save that for me, the whole section, from them coming in, to paying, and leaving?"

"Sure. I'll put it on a disc. It will take me a few minutes…" said Nathan.

"That's fine, I've got all day. Thanks for this. I really

didn't think you'd have this. These two are the ones who threw the body in the canal."

"No way, you're joking me. Really?" asked Nathan. From his security office window, he could see the police vans and cars and the road closed signs further along the road. He suddenly looked more serious, and his smile had faded as the macabre nature of their crime caught up with him. "Will you be putting this on the news?" he asked.

"What for?" asked Miller.

"To catch them."

"Oh right, no, no. They're both in custody. He's saying that he did it on his own. That's his wife. She's committed the murder, and he's trying to confess for it, and get her off. This evidence is all I have to link her to it. She's going to jail mate, and it's all thanks to you!"

Nathan suddenly looked quite moved. He turned to Miller and searched the detective's face. "That's a very sad situation."

"It's more sad for the bloke they killed."

Chapter 39

"Right, don't start saying no comment, because it will make you look even worse when it comes to court. Do you understand me?" Miller was getting beyond tired now, he'd been on this mad case for over twenty four hours, and hadn't been to sleep for fifty odd hours. He just wanted this final part to be fast and painless.

"No comment."

"Rachel. If I present you with a piece of evidence that will tie you to the crime scene, will you please grow a pair of bollocks and stop saying no comment?"

There was a judder. A flicker of panic flashed across Rachel's face. But her stubbornness was unrelenting. Her poker face was strong.

"No comment."

Miller reached into his plastic file. He rummaged around, taking a long time for added dramatic effect, until he found what he was searching for. He pulled it out, and placed it on the table facing Rachel Birdsworth. The colour drained from her face. Her number was up, and this A4 laminated picture of her and Mick at the tills of Asda in Accrington, paying for five rolls of duct tape at half past three in the morning was the proof.

"I'm satisfied that I have enough evidence here to charge you both with murder. But I know that there were others involved. If not one, maybe two others who will share the same amount of guilt as you and Michael."

"No comment."

"Rachel, are you deliberately ignoring the seriousness of this situation?"

"No comment."

"Who are you protecting?"

"No comment."

"Rachel. Listen to me. I have enough here to charge you. You'll stay here over the weekend, then you'll be in court on Monday, and you'll be remanded in custody. That's a fact. So all I'm saying is, it's game over."

Rachel looked up and nodded at Miller. She was

accepting her fate.

"Saying no comment is not going to help you. But if you answer my questions, you'll start improving your chances."

"No comment." Rachel started crying. She couldn't help it, and she felt quite stupid with Miller watching her. He didn't look as though he had any sympathy for her whatsoever.

"Last chance Rachel. Who else was there?"

"No comment."

"That's such a silly thing to do. Right, well I'm not spending anymore time on this nonsense. Rachel Alice Birdsworth, of number sixteen Fir Trees Avenue, you are charged with the murder of Graham Ashworth. You do not have to say anything, but it may harm your defence if you do not mention something that you later rely on in court. Anything you do say may be given in evidence."

*****

"Hello again Michael." Miller was shattered now. He just wanted to get home and crawl into bed. But first he needed to charge Michael Crossley, and let him know that he was going to be staying in a cell for a considerable amount of time, and so would Rachel.

"Hello again," said Mick. Miller could see that his bravado had slipped. Michael Crossley was missing a bit of his confidence.

"I've got bad news." Said Miller.

"Right?" Mick looked down at the floor.

"I've got this picture." Miller pulled it out of his file. "It clearly shows you and another person, Rachel Birdsworth, your common-law wife, at Asda in Accrington, buying five rolls of the tape that was used to wrap Graham Ashworth's body. As you can see from the picture, the date is the fourth of June. The time is three thirty in the morning." Miller pointed to the date that was printed in red digitals along the top left hand side of the picture. "That's the date upon which you told me that you, and you alone killed and disposed of

Graham Ashworth."

Mick's foot had started tapping. His eyes were filled with tears. He could see how scared he and Rachel looked on the picture. How out of their depth they were. How fucking stupid. A tear broke free from Mick's eye and landed next to the damning photograph.

"It's an honourable thing you've tried to do, I guess." Said Miller.

"No comment." Mick was properly crying and his words sounded more like noises.

"It's a bit late for all that. I've just shown this to Rachel. She's given me a full confession. She told me that it was her, who killed Graham. She told me that you wanted to help her. She told me that you wanted to take the blame." Miller didn't care if he told the odd white lie in pursuit of the truth, but Mick wasn't buying it.

"That's fucking bullshit."

"It's not bullshit. She's sensible enough to see that you haven't got away with your scheme. So she's taking the blame for the murder, that she did."

"I don't believe you!" Mick was sobbing properly now, his shoulders were heaving, and his face was full of hot, stinging tears. He was confused, he had no idea what was what now.

"Well, listen. That's not my problem. But you're going to be in a load of shit for this. Murder, aiding an offender, concealing a body, perverting the course of justice, attempting to pervert the course of justice. You're snookered Michael."

"Just leave me alone!" said Mick as he wiped his face with his sleeve.

"This is your last chance to tell me who else was there. Who was the other person, or other people who helped you?"

"Fuck off."

"Okay. Well, I don't know who you're protecting, or why. But I don't think that you and Rachel managed to wrap that body up so well on your own. But that was your last chance to tell me. Michael Crossley, along with Rachel Alice

Birdsworth who I have just charged, I am charging you with the murder of Graham Ashworth."

Chapter 40

"Right, come on you." Miller was talking through the hatch on the cell door. Suzanne Ashworth was lay on her back on the mattress, staring up at the ceiling.

"I hope you're releasing me." She said, snottily as she pulled herself up off the floor.

"Depends on your answer to one question."

"Oh? Go on…"

"Not here. You need to come down to the interview room."

"Oh for God's sake," said Suzanne. "I need to get home, I want to wash my hair. Look at the state of me."

"You're nearly there. Come on. Don't be horrible to me now, I'm tired out." Miller was being nice, he put his arm around Suzanne's shoulder as he walked along the corridor with her. He could see the finishing line ahead. He just needed to get this final part of the job done, and he could finally go home and fall into bed. "Shouldn't take long," he said, as they walked through the custody suite and onto another corridor. Moments later, they were inside interview room four, and Miller had set the recording machine going.

"Okay, last question from me at this stage Suzanne. If this is all true, what you've said, why didn't you just dob them in? You could have phoned the police."

Suzanne didn't blink, she just answered the question straight off. "I saw what they did to Graham, the night he went to hospital. He was beaten up, badly. They said no police or we'll set you on fire."

"So the injuries that Graham sustained, the ones he went to hospital with, were caused by Rachel and Michael?"

"Indirectly. Yes."

"What do you mean, indirectly?"

"It wasn't them personally, but it was quite obvious. After he'd started calling them names, they had him beaten up. I didn't fancy the same treatment."

"And so, you carried on, playing friends, letting them think you had you on side?"

"What else could I do? I knew it was only a matter of

time until Graham was discovered, until they were caught."

Miller looked as though he didn't believe her. He blew out an exasperated breath and wiped his face with both hands.

"But that contradicts everything you said at the beginning." He said, concerned that Suzanne was just trying to annoy him.

"You do know what all this means for me, don't you?" she asked.

"What?"

"Well, I'm finished round here. My life is going to be made a misery. I'm going to have to move away."

"Well I'm sure that you'll have enough money. I mean, you'll be okay financially Suzanne, won't you?"

"Oh yes, I'll be fine from that point of view. But I mean, I'll be in danger living in Manchester now. I need to get away, tonight."

"Well avoid Liverpool. It's even worse there."

"Oh I know. I'm thinking Cornwall or somewhere. Maybe the Cotswolds."

"Okay, Suzanne Ashworth I am releasing you on bail. You must return to this police station at nine o'clock on Monday the tenth of September. Interview suspended at sixteen forty four hours. You're free to leave."

"And what about Mick and Rachel?" asked Suzanne as Miller turned off the recorder and wrote down the digital read out details on the paperwork.

"I've just charged them. They'll appear before magistrates on Monday morning. After that they'll be remanded in custody."

"Thank God for that."

"Eh?"

"I thought they'd kill me next. I've been waiting for it. They said that if I do anything, say anything, I'll be shot in the face. God, what a relief. Thanks Detective."

*****

After walking out of the police station with a see-through carrier bag that contained her belongings, Suzanne fished about in the bag for her mobile. She grabbed it, turned it on and checked her messages as she walked briskly towards the taxi rank by the bus station. It bleeped with one text message.

"FRIDAY 16:20 Rachel: Suzanne where are you babe? Your cappuccino is going cold! R xxx"

"Ha ha Rachel, you silly bitch!" laughed Suzanne as she looked through her contacts. When she found Tania's number, she pressed the call icon.

"Hi, how's it going?" she said into the phone. "No, I've been banged up all night. It's all sorted though. Mick and Rachel have been charged with killing him. Yeah, I know. It's perfect. Come and pick me up and we'll get something to eat. Yes, don't worry, it's all sorted. Everything's sorted. I know! Amazing. Bury bus station. I'll wait by the taxi rank. Okay, see you in fifteen. Byeeee."

EPILOGUE

The television screen showed the now infamous CCTV photograph of two pale, frightened looking people in their early thirties, buying several rolls of duct tape at the supermarket check-outs.

"Life imprisonment for the killers of the much-loved Bury council executive Graham Ashworth. The couple dubbed "The Neighbours From Hell" will serve at least eight years each. Welcome to North West Tonight, I'm Roger Thompson. And, with this news story still breaking, we can cross live now to our reporter Denise Braithwaite who is at Preston Crown Court. Denise."

"Thank you Roger. Yes, The Neighbours From Hell trial has this evening concluded with a guilty verdict against both defendants, and as you have pointed out, the judge has handed down life sentences to the killers, Rachel Birdsworth and Michael Crossley, after a trial that has lasted six weeks. The victim's widow, Suzanne Ashworth spoke to the press a few moments ago."

The screen changed from the reporter's solemn face, to a clip of Suzanne Ashworth talking to microphones and reporters amid bright lights and photographers' flashes, outside the famous red brick court house. Her eyes were hidden by large sunglasses, and her hair was obscured by a vivid white head scarf. She was dressed like a celebrity.

"My husband was a kind, supportive, selfless human-being who did so much for the community. His death has left a massive void in my life, and in the lives of all the people that he helped. The killers, people that I thought were my friends, will be able to get on with their lives again in eight years. I'll never be able to get on with mine."

The screen returned to Denise Braithwaite.

"That was the widow of Graham Ashworth, speaking a couple of minutes before we came on air. Now, to re-cap, the killers were moved from a caravan site to the high-class Haughton Park estate last summer, as part of a widely-criticised and unpopular re-housing scheme run by Bury council, which brought homeless families to the expensive development. It was here that the neighbours from hell couple first came into contact with the Ashworth's. The judge said that from the moment they had arrived, Birdsworth and Crossley viewed Graham and Suzanne Ashworth "with envious eyes" and had been turned "green with jealousy" by the lifestyle that the couple enjoyed.

On the screen, a photograph of Graham and Suzanne Ashworth appeared, showing the couple looking happy and relaxed on a cruise, clinking champagne glasses together.

"You are wicked beyond words," said the judge, as he summed up – highlighting an incident that took place just a few days after Birdsworth and Crossley moved into the luxurious property that they were renting. Graham Ashworth was severely beaten up and was taken to Accident and Emergency at Bury General Hospital. It was a beating that had been organised by Birdsworth and Crossley."

The holiday image on the screen changed to depressing video footage of police activity by the canal in Accrington.

"No charges were brought in relation to that incident, it wasn't reported, because Mr Ashworth was threatened with being set on fire if the police were called. Just one month later, Mr Ashworth was dead, his body dumped in the canal in Accrington."

Roger Thompson, in the studio asked the reporter a question.

"What about a motive Denise? What reason was given for this awful crime?"

"Well, that's the really shocking aspect that has emerged from this trial Roger. The defendants had both tried to argue that Mr Ashworth was killed by accident, after he had beaten his wife unconscious in the Ashworth home – but this explanation was dismissed as fantasy, and was vehemently denied by Mrs Ashworth, who said that that her husband was a kind, gentle, loving man who wouldn't harm a fly. Rather than being beaten by her husband, Mrs Ashworth said that she was drugged by the pair, and while she was sleeping off the cocktail of sleeping tablets, her neighbours were killing, and disposing of her husband. The judge said that "in their desperation to try to justify their despicable crime, they were prepared to tarnish the reputation of a much-loved and well respected man, a man who had over thirty years exemplary service with the council, and who had done a great deal of work for the local community in that time. In answer to your question Roger – the jury have decided that there was no motive, that there was no reason, other than the extreme jealousy that Birdsworth and Crossley had of a lifestyle that they craved so much, but knew that they would never enjoy. It was a jealousy that would turn them into cold-blooded killers. The couple's four children have now been taken into local authority care."

"And what have Bury council had to say about the matter Denise?"

"There has been no official statement from them as yet, but their website does state that "the social housing deal that had been set up with Haughton Park's developers was terminated several months ago, and the last of the social housing service users have been moved off the development, and into more suitable accommodation."

"Denise, thank you. In other news now and a thousand new jobs have been created at…"

(To be continued…)

THE END

Is Maureen about to lose her shit over the outcome of this case?

Watch out for MILLER 3 – out in Spring 2016

Thank you for reading.

ALSO BY STEVEN SUTTIE

One Man Crusade

The police face an extraordinary problem.

Somebody has started shooting unsuspecting citizens dead as they go about their daily business in the north west of England.

But it is a very specific type of person that the gun man is targeting. Paedophiles.

In order to keep the public calm, the police have no alternative but to reveal the killer's motive.

And that's when things start to get really tricky for the investigating officers. Public revulsion of child molesters is at an all time high, so when the killer is hailed as a hero vigilante by the media - DCI Andrew Miller and his team face the ultimate challenge in catching a man who is determined to continue with his executions until he is caught.

PLEASE NOTE: This book contains swearing throughout. (Including the worst one.)

ALSO BY STEVEN SUTTIE

The Clitheroe Prime Minister

A funny and politically incorrect satire novel that straight talking folk just can't get enough of.

IS GREAT BRITAIN ABOUT TO GET A WELDER IN AS PRIME MINISTER?

This is a laugh-out-loud adventure about an ordinary egg and chips eating kind of man, who finds himself accidentally becoming the most famous bloke in Britain.

Jim Arkwright is having a really weird week. After learning that a video of him messing about and talking politics in the pub has gone viral, he finds himself on the radio, wiping the floor with the experts and politicians live on the air. The British public, sick to death of the sleazy, money grabbing, out of touch political figureheads are instantly endeared by the straight-speaking Lancashire man. They love his ideas and his friendly, warm nature.

Jim hears the things that ordinary folk say, on buses, in cafes and down the launderette. Big Jim is a man who is in touch with the public, unlike the nation's politicians.

The following morning's newspapers start a campaign demanding that Big Jim should become Prime Minister. But Jim has got a really big job on at work. He doesn't have any time for all this nonsense.

Can Big Jim be tempted to join the Government? The people of Clitheroe hope so, as the picturesque little Lancashire town has become over-run with media gangs, press trucks, television channels and happy go lucky tourists.

Printed in Germany
by Amazon Distribution
GmbH, Leipzig